Productivity management
A practical handbook

PRODUCTIVITY MANAGEMENT

A practical handbook

Joseph Prokopenko

International Labour Office   Geneva

ISBN 92-2-105901-4

First published 1987

Printed in Switzerland

IRL

PREFACE

In a period of timid economic growth achieving productivity gains has acquired a new sense of urgency. This is particularly felt in developing countries where rapid population growth, reductions in export prices of raw materials, growing indebtedness and inflation cloud the future. Raising productivity can offset the impact of some of these problems and at the same time help the cause of social development.

Over the years interest in productivity has taken various forms. At the macro level, productivity measurement has been a useful guide to policy-makers in setting wage policies or in combating inflation. At the enterprise level, it has helped in ascertaining performance. More important, perhaps, has been the interest in methods and techniques for raising productivity. Recently, considerable gains in productivity have been achieved through advances in process technology. But here interest has focused more on the technology itself than on the rational management of productivity or on the social implications of the introduction of new technology.

The present book approaches productivity issues from a new and refreshing angle. Productivity is treated as an area which has to be managed, by means of various methods and techniques drawn from quantitative analysis and the field of operations management, and also the behavioural sciences. The emphasis is on practical approaches that have proved effective in certain contexts and on helping readers to select the best approach for their particular organisation. The simple and clear explanations help the reader to understand the complex issues involved.

Thus this book constitutes a valuable guide-line to practitioners: to managers, management consultants and trainers, productivity specialists and also trade unions.

The book was written by Joseph Prokopenko, a senior consultant in the ILO Management Development Branch. The author has had extensive discussions with internationally recognised specialists and writers on productivity improvement and with colleagues both at ILO headquarters and in field projects. In addition, he has examined an impressive amount of material on productivity issues in both industrialised and developing countries. Therefore, we believe that the book constitutes a valuable contribution to the literature in a field that is again regarded as a high priority.

George KANAWATY
Director
ILO Training Department

CONTENTS

FOREWORD

The role of productivity in increasing national welfare is now universally recognised. In every country, developed or developing, with a market economy or a centrally planned economy, the main source of economic growth is an increase in productivity. Inversely, slackening of growth, stagnation and decline entail or are accompanied by a slow-down in productivity improvement.

Many studies have analysed the decelerating growth of productivity, particularly in the advanced industrialised countries in the 1970s and 1980s. Despite this keen interest, no adequate single explanation for low productivity growth has yet been found.

It has been suggested that the decline in productivity in recent decades is the result of a combination of many factors. These include the discontinuation of the favourable circumstances of the 1950s and 1960s (high demand, economies of scale, extensive use of new resources), and the functional disturbances which have disrupted the national and world economies (business cycle). Increasing oil prices during the 1970s were also a crucial, if not a determining, factor. Investment cuts are often attributed to inflation and growing capital costs. Over-regulation and indiscriminate direct state intervention in the economy sometimes weaken competition and decrease the motivation and mobility of the workforce.

Despite this, *technological* development has not slowed down; it has continued and in many fields it has accelerated. Recent decades have witnessed an important shift from extensive to intensive use of human and capital resources, which means their more productive utilisation. This has increased productivity potential but the question of absorbing the resulting unemployment has become an urgent problem. Paradoxically, despite unemployment, the developed countries are increasingly faced with shortages of skilled manpower and have found it necessary to substitute capital-intensive technology in some areas. At the same time, scarcity of capital and very high unemployment in developing countries define other priorities — encouraging the development and more effective use of available human resources and creating new jobs.

However, neither of these processes is occurring in a simple form. Both the developed and the developing countries have to deal with two questions simultaneously: to try to use both human and capital resources more effectively. The real problem, in every country, is to find the optimal balance between intensive and extensive methods of economic development. The development of modern equipment and the development of human resources must go together. Therefore, it is important to note that productivity improvement or the effective use of available resources is the best, indeed the only way, for future development in any kind of society.

High and rapidly rising productivity, which seems to be an adjunct of the new technology, could become a problem in itself if some of the distribution issues associated with it are not grasped and solved. Who will benefit from high productivity? How can we ensure that enough people participate in the gains so that demand increases fast enough to absorb the increased production achieved by greater efficiency?

There is another side to this subject — the need to improve international co-operation to narrow the gap between developed and developing countries. The need to transfer physical and financial resources to developing countries through economic and technical co-operation should go without saying. However, there is a limit to the physical resources which can be transferred. Consequently, many international organisations and programmes now focus on transferring know-how, which can be regarded as the most important element in productivity improvement.

To many people, effective use of resources can mean simply development of technology and organisation, but it is often more important for total productivity improvement to contribute to human development in its broadest sense. Productivity is the point where human skills and interests, technology, management, and the social and business environment all converge.

It is necessary to recognise the importance of all the major factors which contribute to or put barriers against productivity growth at the macro level. These factors include government policy, economic and social policies and strategies, business cycles and international competition, the natural environment and demographic and structural changes. Nevertheless, the place where productivity growth is actually created is the enterprise or the company. This is the context where the whole range of available resources come together in order to produce goods and services.

The effectiveness of their combined functioning is reflected in productivity.

Thus, the main emphasis of this book is on the organisational level. We do, however, analyse the environment of the organisation from the point of view of how it could contribute to or hamper productivity improvement.

Many books and studies have been devoted to the importance of productivity, and even more to productivity measurement. However, it is not widely recognised that productivity should be managed, not only measured.

The second emphasis in this book is on shifting the balance a little from the academic to the practical world of productivity management. This concept is even more important when productivity improvement is accepted by management as a main criterion or objective of a company or enterprise. It is well known that many failures occur when a company's main objective is only to maximise sales or profit, or to minimise costs. However, only productivity, when it is a main company objective, can integrate and balance the areas of marketing, profits, production costs, return on investments, sales and output.

To improve productivity one has to pay attention to a fast-changing world and improve the organisation's capacity to adjust to change. Even highly efficient and committed managers and workers will not survive if the organisation cannot adapt to its constantly changing environment. The understanding and management of change have a vital role to play in productivity improvement. The organisation must learn how to adjust to change and how to learn during change. The active management of productivity is the subject of this book. The book has the following objectives:

- To promote understanding and improve awareness of what productivity is, its role and significance in economic and social development.
- To describe practical methods of productivity measurement and analysis.
- To analyse some existing methods and techniques of productivity management within an organisation and to advise on how to overcome various barriers to productivity growth.

The book is intended for people practising productivity improvement — managers, human resource development professionals, management consultants, experts and advisers in productivity improvement fields. The approaches described are relevant in developed and developing countries, in both public and private enterprises, in different economic sectors, and in government organisations.

Since its main emphasis is on the organisation level, management practitioners, whether in a market economy or in a centrally planned economy, will find some useful hints for practical implementation. Some details of a method may need to be adjusted according to the context, but the essentials do not depend on factors external to the organisation.

The book consists of eight chapters.

Chapter 1 presents some definitions and explains the essential role of productivity in the business expansion which is necessary for social and economic development.

Chapter 2 examines the principal external and internal factors which have an impact on productivity improvement in an organisation or production system. These factors include the labour force, capital, materials and energy, structural changes, and the role of government and its infrastructure.

Chapter 3 is devoted to methods and techniques for productivity measurement and analysis, and an evaluation of the contribution made by different productivity factors to organisation performance.

Chapter 4 deals with the range of practical methods and techniques for productivity management. It discusses productivity improvement processes, strategies and programmes together with their major variations. Such variations include performance programmes, action learning, inter-firm comparison and business clinics, etc. A number of practical examples and cases are given.

Chapter 5 describes the main productivity improvement techniques such as work study, Pareto analysis, value management, work simplification, cost-benefit analysis and just-in-time methods. It also presents some techniques for increasing human initiative and creativity such as brainstorming, force-field analysis and nominal grouping which could be used in a number of different performance improvement programmes.

Chapter 6 examines the most vital areas of productivity improvement where the application of productivity improvement programmes has a high probability of success. These areas include waste reduction and energy conservation, maintenance of equipment and facilities, and the quality of products and services.

Chapter 7 is devoted to the most important productivity improvement factor — human resource management. Here the role of management in raising productivity awareness and culture, in manpower motivation, training and development and in developing new forms of work organisation is discussed in great detail.

The last chapter is devoted to some approaches and strategies for productivity improvement at the national level and also describes international co-operation in this field. Here the reader can find useful information about national productivity promotion mechanisms and the experience of different countries in productivity campaigns and education. The trade union role in productivity improvement is also discussed. This chapter also describes the contribution made to the productivity movement by the main international associations at the regional level.

Acknowledgements

A great many people have assisted the author in writing this book by contributing their ideas, information, cases and experience. I wish to acknowledge especially George Kanawaty, John Wallace, Milan Kubr, Colin Guthrie, Bernard Wittich and Stelios Theocharides of the ILO Training Department, Management Development Branch, who provided some valuable ideas, critical comments, cases and material for this book.

I would like to extend my thanks to Alan Lawlor and George Boulden from Action Learning Associates (United Kingdom), Tony Hubert from the European Association of National Productivity Centres, Joji Arai from Japan Productivity Centre, to the Asian Productivity Organisation as well as to many experts in ILO field projects whose experience, ideas and suggestions have greatly improved the international character of the book.

A lot of hard work has also been done by Barbara Cooper and Heather Jaouani in editing the manuscript and assisting in compiling the index and bibliography. The ILO would like to thank all those who contributed to the book and who cannot be mentioned here by name.

PART I

PRODUCTIVITY: NATURE, ROLE AND SOURCES

PRODUCTIVITY: CONCEPT AND DEFINITION

1

1.1 What is productivity?

A general definition is that productivity is the relationship between the output generated by a production or service system and the input provided to create this output. Thus, productivity is defined as the efficient use of resources — labour, capital, land, materials, energy, information — in the production of various goods and services.

Higher productivity means accomplishing more with the same amount of resources or achieving higher output in terms of volume and quality for the same input. This is usually stated as:

$$\frac{\text{Output}}{\text{Input}} = \text{Productivity}$$

Productivity can also be defined as the relationship between results and the time it takes to accomplish them. Time is often a good denominator since it is a universal measurement, and it is beyond human control. The less time taken to achieve the desired result, the more productive the system.

Regardless of the type of production, economic or political system, the definition of productivity remains the same. Thus, though productivity may mean different things to different people, the basic concept is always the relationship between the quantity and quality of goods or services produced and the quantity of resources used to produce them.

Productivity is a comparative tool for managers, industrial engineers, economists and politicians. It compares production at different levels of the economic system (individual and shop-floor, organisational, sectoral and national) with resources consumed.

Sometimes productivity is viewed as a more intensive use of such resources as labour and machines which should reliably indicate performance or efficiency if measured accurately. However, it is important to separate productivity from intensity of labour, because while labour productivity reflects the beneficial results of labour, its intensity means excess effort and is no more than work "speed-up". The essence of productivity improvement is working more intelligently, not harder. Real productivity improvement is not achieved by working harder: this results in very limited increases in productivity due to man's physical limitations.

The ILO has for many years promoted an advanced view of productivity which refers to the effective and efficient utilisation of all resources, capital, land, materials, energy, information and time, in addition to labour. In promoting such views, one must combat some common misunderstandings about productivity.

First, productivity is not only labour efficiency or "labour productivity" — although labour productivity statistics are still useful policy-making data.

The false conclusions which may be drawn from analyses of single factor productivity are demonstrated by a major British productivity success story: agriculture. Because of improvements in breeding, fertilisers and sprays, land and technology, labour productivity in agriculture rose 60 per cent between 1976 and 1982, as did yield per hectare. But one unit of energy (which includes fertilisers) grew less wheat in 1983 than in 1963.[1] A more appropriate yardstick of efficiency is, then, the yield produced for each monetary unit spent. Hence the emerging importance of multi- (if not total-) factor productivity.[2] Productivity is now much more than just labour productivity and needs to take into account the increase in cost of energy and raw materials along with a growing concern for unemployment and the quality of working life.

The second misconception is that it is possible to judge performance simply by output. The latter may be rising without an increase in productivity if, for instance, input costs have risen disproportionately. Moreover, increases in output compared with previous years should take into account price increases and inflation. Such an approach is often the result of being process-oriented at the expense of paying attention to final results. This is common in any bureaucratic system.

The third problem is confusion between productivity and profitability. In real life profit can be obtained through price recovery even though productivity may have gone down. Conversely, high productivity does not always go with high profit since goods which are produced efficiently are not necessarily in demand.

Hence there is one more misunderstanding — confusing productivity with efficiency. *Efficiency* means producing high-quality goods in the shortest possible time. But we have to consider if these goods are needed.

A fifth mistake is to believe that cost-cutting always improves productivity. When done indiscriminately, it can make matters worse in the long term.

Another myth which causes damage is that productivity can only be applied to production. In reality, productivity is relevant to any kind of organisation or system, including services, notably information. With the changing structure of occupations, information specialists have become a new target for productivity drives. Information technology itself gives new dimensions to productivity concepts and productivity measurement. In these days of flexible automation, microprocessors, just-in-time manufacturing and distribution systems, and mixed-flow production systems, work-hours are less relevant as a measure of effectiveness than in the past. In fact, in industries and regions where "steel-collar" workers or robots are replacing blue-collar workers, the productivity of capital or other expensive, scarce resources such as energy or raw materials is of far more concern than labour productivity.

The concept of productivity is also increasingly linked with quality — of output, input and the process itself. An element of key importance is the quality of the workforce, its management and its working conditions, and it has been generally recognised that rising productivity and improving quality of working life do tend to go hand in hand.

In this sense productivity must be considered in both social and economic terms. Attitudes towards work and achievement may be improved through employees' participation in planning goals, implementing processes, and through sharing productivity gains.

The importance of the social side of productivity has increased considerably. A study among managers and trade unions in some American firms [3] shows that most managers (78 per cent) and union leaders (70 per cent) do not employ only quantitative definitions of productivity. They prefer a broader, more qualitative conception, related to the organisation concerned. By productivity, management and union policy-makers refer, essentially, to the overall effectiveness and performance of individual organisations. This includes less tangible features such as the absence of labour stoppages, rate of turnover, absenteeism and even customer satisfaction. Given this broad concept of productivity, it is understandable that policy-makers see a link between worker satisfaction, customer satisfaction and productivity.

It is, therefore, important to define *effectiveness* as the degree to which goals are attained. This concept, based on a systematic and comprehensive approach to social and economic development, permits us to work out productivity definitions suitable for any given enterprise, sector or nation. A complication arises, however, because the numerator and denominator for effectiveness comparisons may be quite different, reflecting specific features such as organisational structures and the political, social and economic goals of the country or sector.

Thus, the definition of productivity is complex and it is not only a technical and managerial problem. It is a matter of concern to government bodies, trade unions and other social institutions. And the more different their goals, the more different their definitions of productivity will be. But if all social groups agree on more or less common goals, the definition of productivity for the country, even for different segments of the economy, will have more common features. Hence *the main indicator of improving productivity is a decreasing ratio of input to output at constant or improved quality.* If productivity is defined for the individual worker as the relation of the volume of specific work done to the potential capacity of the worker (in numerical, cost or time terms), then for the enterprise or sector it can be expressed as the relation between value added and the cost of all input components. For example, in an enterprise or shop-floor dealing with homogeneous products, productivity can be defined as the relation of output expressed in physical terms (in tonnes or numbers of goods produced) to input expressed in work-hours. At the national level, productivity is the relationship of national income to total expenditure (or labour costs if we are interested only in labour productivity).[4]

Generally speaking, productivity could be considered as a comprehensive measure of how organisations satisfy the following criteria: [5]

- Objectives: the degree to which they are achieved.
- Efficiency: how effectively resources are used to generate useful output.
- Effectiveness: what is achieved compared with what is possible.
- Comparability: how productivity performance is recorded over time.

Though there are many different definitions of productivity, the commonest approach (not a definition) to designing a productivity model is to identify the right output and input components in accordance with the long, middle and short-term development goals of the enterprise, sector or country.

1.2 The importance and role of productivity

The significance of productivity in increasing national welfare is now universally recognised. There is no human activity that does not benefit from improved productivity. This is important because more of the increase in gross national income, or GNP, is produced by improving the effectiveness and quality of manpower than by using additional labour and capital. In other words, national income, or GNP, grows faster than the input factors when productivity is improved.

Productivity improvement, therefore, results in direct increases in the standard of living under conditions of distribution of productivity gains according to contribution. At present, it would not be wrong to state that productivity is the only important world-wide source of real economic growth, social progress and improved standard of living.

For example, the report of the Singapore National Productivity Board on a Productivity Survey in 1984 says that more than half of the contribution to the increase in per capita gross domestic product (GDP) in Singapore is attributed to labour productivity for the period 1966-83. This means that labour productivity has been the main factor in the rise in Singapore's standard of living, as attested by a fourfold increase over the past 17 years.[6]

At the same time, we can easily see the effect of low productivity in the Philippines. The vast majority of increases in the country's total output (97.7 per cent) from 1900 to 1960 are due to increases in the extensive factors of production (that is, the use of more resources) and only 2.3 per cent can be attributed to productivity. This highlights a key defect in the process of long-term economic growth in the Philippines — the fact that it has been input-intensive.[7]

Thus, changes in productivity are recognised as a major influence on many social and economic phenomena, such as rapid economic growth, higher standard of living, improvements in a nation's balance of payments, inflation control, and even the amount and quality of leisure. These changes influence wage levels, cost/price relationships, capital investment needs and employment.

Productivity also largely determines how competitive a country's products are internationally. If labour productivity in one country declines in relation to productivity in other countries producing the same goods, a competitive imbalance is created. If the higher costs of production are passed on, the country's industries will lose sales as customers turn to the lower cost suppliers. But if the higher costs are absorbed by industries, their profit will decrease. This means that they have to decrease production or keep production costs stable by lowering real wages.

Some countries that fail to keep pace with the productivity levels of competitors try to solve their problems by devaluing their national currencies. But this lowers real income in such countries by making imported goods more expensive and by increasing domestic inflation.

Thus, low productivity results in inflation, an adverse balance of trade, poor growth rate and unemployment. Figure 1.1 presents a simplified causal relationship between many variables and factors affecting productivity.[8]

Figure 1.1.   Model for a low-productivity trap

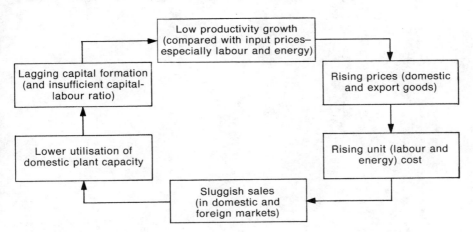

Source: D. Scott Sink, 1985, p. 8.

It is clear, then, that the vicious circle of poverty, unemployment and low productivity can be broken only by increasing productivity. Increased national productivity not only means optimal use of resources, but also helps to create a better balance between economic, social and political structures in the society. Social goals and government policy largely define the distribution and utilisation of national income. This in turn influences the social, political, cultural, educational and motivational work environment which affects the productivity of the individual and the society.

₁ "British farming's rich harvest", in *The Economist* (London), 5 Nov. 1983, pp. 88-89.

₂ Tony Hubert: "The (brave) new world of productivity", in *Europroductivity Ideas* (Brussels, EANPC), May 1984, pp. 1-3.

₃ R. A. Katzell et al.: *Work, productivity and job satisfaction: An evaluation of policy-related research* (New York, Psychological Corporation, 1975).

₄ Joseph Prokopenko: *Improving productivity in developing countries*, Management Development Working Paper No. 16 (Geneva, ILO, 1978).

₅ Alan Lawlor: *Productivity improvement manual* (Aldershot, United Kingdom, Gower, 1985), p. 36.

₆ "Productivity growth in Singapore", in *APO News* (Tokyo, Asian Productivity Organisation), Aug. 1985, p. 6.

₇ "Does productivity have a place in a sinking economy?", in *Business Day* (Manila, Business Day Corporation), 19 Mar. 1984.

₈ D. Scott Sink: *Productivity management: Planning, measurement and evaluation, control and improvement* (New York, John Wiley and Sons, 1985), p. 8.

PRODUCTIVITY IMPROVEMENT FACTORS

2

Productivity improvement is not just doing things better: more importantly, it is doing the right things better. This chapter aims to identify the major factors, or "right things", which should be the main concerns of productivity programme managers. Before discussing what to tackle in a productivity improvement programme, it is necessary to review the factors affecting productivity.

The production process is a complex, adaptive, on-going social system. The inter-relationships between labour, capital and the socio-organisational environment are important in the way they are balanced and co-ordinated into an integrated whole. Productivity improvement depends upon how successfully we identify and use the main factors of the socio-production system. It is important, in connection with this, to distinguish three main productivity factor groups:

— job-related;

— resource-related;

— environment-related.

Since our main concern here is the economic analysis of managerial factors rather than productivity factors as such, we suggest a classification which will help managers distinguish those factors which they can control. In this way, the number of factors to be analysed and influenced decreases dramatically. The classification suggested here is based on a paper by Mukherjee and Singh.[1]

There are two major categories of productivity factor:

● External (not controllable).

● Internal (controllable).

The external factors are those which are beyond the control of the individual enterprise and the internal factors are those within its control.

To deal with all these factors we require different institutions, people, techniques and methods. For example, any performance improvement drive which plans to deal with external factors affecting the management of the enterprise must take such factors into consideration during the planning phase of the programme, and try to influence them by joining forces with other interested parties.

Productivity management

Thus it can be clearly seen that the first step towards improving productivity is to identify problem areas within these factor groups. The next step is to distinguish those factors which are controllable.

Factors which are external and not controllable for one institution are often internal to another. Factors external to an enterprise, for example, could be internal to governments, national or regional institutions, associations and pressure groups. Governments can improve tax policy, develop better labour legislation, provide better access to natural resources, improve social infrastructure, price policy, and so on, but individual organisations cannot.

Factors external to an enterprise are of interest to that enterprise because an understanding of them can motivate certain actions which might change an enterprise's behaviour and its productivity in the long run. We suggest the following integrated scheme of factors constituting a major source of productivity improvement.

Figure 2.1.   An integrated model of enterprise productivity factors

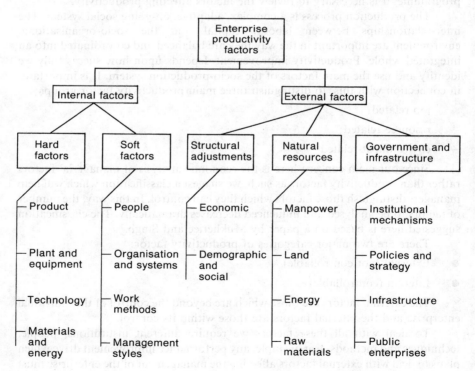

Source: Adapted from S. K. Mukherjee and D. Singh, 1975, p. 93.

10

2.1 Internal factors of enterprise productivity

Since some internal factors are more easily changed than others, it is useful to classify them into two groups: hard (not easily changed) and soft (easily changed). The hard factors include products, technology, equipment and raw materials, while the soft factors include the labour force, organisational systems and procedures, management styles and work methods. This classification helps us build priorities — which factors can easily be dealt with and which factors require stronger financial and organisational interventions. A brief description of some key aspects of each internal factor follows.

Hard factors

Product

Product factor productivity means the extent to which the product meets output requirements. "Use value" is the amount that the customer is prepared to pay for a product of given quality. "Use value" can be improved by better design and specifications. Many companies around the world fight a constant battle to incorporate technical excellence into marketable products. Breaking down the walls between research, marketing and sales has become a major productivity factor. For example, leading Japanese companies continually redesign products which are on the market. Product "place value", "time value" and "price value" refer to the availability of the product at the right place, at the right time and at a reasonable price. The "volume factor" in particular gives us a better notion of the economies of scale through increased volume of production. Finally, the cost-benefit factor can be enhanced by increasing the benefit for the same cost or by reducing the cost for the same benefit.

Plant and equipment

These play a central role in a productivity improvement programme through:
— good maintenance;
— operating the plant and equipment in optimum process conditions;
— increasing plant capacity by eliminating bottle-necks and by corrective measures;
— reducing idle time and making more effective use of available machines and plant capacities.

Plant and equipment productivity can be improved by attention to utilisation, age, modernisation, cost, investment, internally produced equipment, capacity maintenance and expansion, inventory control, production planning and control, and so on.

Technology

Technological innovation constitutes an important source of higher productivity. Increased volume of goods and services, quality improvement, new marketing methods, etc., can be achieved through increased automation and information technology. Automation can also improve materials handling, storage, communication systems and quality control.

During the past 25 years, considerable productivity increases have been realised through the use of automation and current developments in information technology suggest great improvements to come. Significant examples of the application of this technology are the development of automatic downtime recording systems and automatic lubrication systems which have reduced the idle time of men and machines, and reduced overtime expenditure. New technology is normally introduced as a result of such productivity improvement programmes as fighting obsolescence, process design, R & D and the training of scientists and engineers.

Materials and energy

Even small efforts to reduce materials and energy consumption can bring remarkable results. These vital sources of productivity include raw materials and indirect materials (process chemicals, lubricants, fuels, spare parts, engineering materials, packing materials). Important aspects of materials productivity include:

— material yield: output of useful product or energy per unit of material used. This is dependent upon selection of the right material, its quality, process control and control of rejects;
— use and control of wastage and scraping;
— upgrading of materials by initial processing to improve utilisation in the main process;
— use of lower grade and cheaper materials;
— import substitution;
— improving inventory turnover ratio to release funds tied up in inventories for more productive uses;
— improved inventory management to avoid holding excessive stock;
— developing sources of supply.

Soft factors

People

As the principal resource and the central factor in productivity improvement drives, the people in an organisation all have a role to play — as workers, engineers, managers, entrepreneurs and trade union members. Each role has two aspects: application and effectiveness.

Application is the degree to which people apply themselves to their work. People differ not only in their ability but also in their will to work. This is explained by a law of behaviour: motivation decreases if it is either satisfied or blocked from satisfaction. For example, workers may do their jobs without working hard (no motivation), but even if they did work to their full capacity they would not be satisfed (motivation is blocked from satisfaction).

In order to stimulate and maintain motivation, the following few factors should be considered:

A set of values conducive to higher productivity should be developed in order to bring about changes in the *attitude* of managers, engineers and workers.

Motivation is basic to all human behaviour and thus to efforts in productivity improvement. Material needs are still predominant, but this does not mean that non-financial incentives are not effective or have no place. Workers' success in increasing productivity should be reinforced immediately by rewards, not only in the form of money, but also by improving recognition, involvement and learning opportunities, and, finally, by the complete elimination of negative rewards.

If management can plan and execute effective incentive schemes, then the result is invariably a significant improvement in productivity. Wage incentives must always be related to the amount of change accomplished.

It is also possible to improve productivity by eliciting co-operation and participation from workers. Labour participation in goal-setting, for example, has been quite successful in many countries. Human relations can be further improved by reducing the complexity of communications procedures and by minimising conflicts. Labour productivity can be tapped only if management encourages workers to apply their creative talents by taking a special interest in their problems and by promoting a favourable social climate.

Standard of performance plays an important role in productivity. It should be set at a high but realisable level. Management expectations of high performance need to be considerably raised in many cases. However, standards should always be achievable to maintain confidence and the "will to do".

The "will to do" is affected by job satisfaction which managers can enhance by making jobs interesting, challenging and bigger, more worth while and self-contained. Job enrichment and job enlargement can influence job satisfaction and motivate higher productivity.

The second factor in the role played by the people involved in a productivity drive is effectiveness. Effectiveness is the extent to which the application of human effort brings the desired results in output and quality. It is a function of method, technique, personal skill, knowledge, attitude and aptitude — the "ability to do". The ability to do a productive job can be improved through training and development, job rotation and placements, systematic job progression (promotion), and career planning.

To summarise, the following key approaches, methods and techniques can be used to improve labour productivity: wages and salaries; training and education; social security — pensions and health plans; rewards; incentive plans; participation or co-determination; contract negotiations; attitudes to work, to supervision and to change; motivation to higher productivity; co-operation;

organisation development; improved communications; suggestion systems; career planning; attendance; turnover; job security.

Organisation and systems

The well-known principles of good organisation such as unity of command, delegation and span of control, are intended to provide for specialisation and division of work and co-ordination within the enterprise. An organisation needs to be dynamically operated and led towards objectives and must be maintained, serviced and reorganised from time to time to meet new objectives.

One reason for the low productivity of many organisations is their rigidity. They fail to anticipate and respond to market changes, ignore new capacities in the labour force, new developments in technology and other external (environmental) factors. Rigid organisations lack good horizontal communication. This slows down decision-making and inhibits delegation of authority close to the point of action, encouraging inefficiency and bureaucracy.

Compartmentation according to professional groups or functions also inhibits change. For example, the decision-making steps may have been designed for a particular existing technology, for a definite product or service mix. Things have now changed, but procedures have survived because managers want to minimise change.

No system, however well designed, is efficient in all situations. Dynamism and flexibility should be incorporated into the system design in order to maximise productivity.

Work methods

Improved work methods, especially in developing economies where capital is scarce, technology intermediate and labour-intensive methods dominant, constitute the most promising area for productivity improvement. Work method techniques aim to make manual work more productive by improving the ways in which the work is done, the human movements performed, the tools used, the workplace laid out, the materials handled and the machines employed. Work methods are improved by systematically analysing present methods, eliminating unnecessary work and performing the necessary work more effectively with less effort, time and cost. Work study, industrial engineering and training are the main tools of improving work methods.

Management styles

There is a view that in some countries management is responsible for 75 per cent of productivity gains, because management is responsible for the effective use of all resources under enterprise control. One productivity expert and consultant to many leading Japanese companies believes that as much as 85 per cent of the quality and productivity problems in United States industry are common problems of the system that lie within the province of management, not the individual worker, to correct.[2] There is no perfect management style. Effectiveness depends upon when, where, how and to whom a manager applies a style. Management styles and practices influence organisational design, personnel policies, job design, operational planning and control, maintenance and purchasing policies, capital cost (working and fixed capital), sources of capital, budgeting systems and cost control techniques.

Figure 2.2 summarises the main productivity factors internal to an enterprise.

Figure 2.2.   Model of internal productivity factors

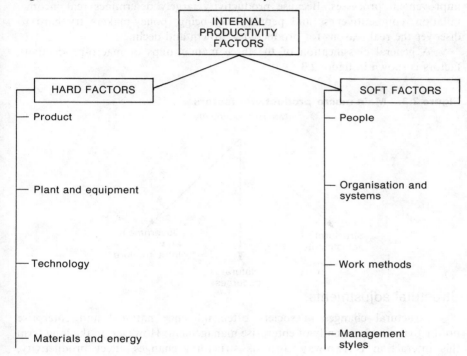

Source: Adapted from S. K. Mukherjee and D. Singh, 1975, p. 93.

This model serves as a checklist for identifying the most promising productivity areas for management analysis planning and intervention.

2.2 External factors affecting enterprise productivity

External factors include government policies and institutional mechanisms; political, social and economic conditions; the business climate; the availability of finance, power, water, transport, communications and raw materials. They affect individual enterprise productivity, but the organisations concerned cannot actively control them.

These factors should be understood and taken into consideration by management when planning and implementing productivity programmes. What is outside the control of individual enterprises in the short term might be controllable at higher levels of society's structures and institutions. Bearing in mind all the social, political, economic and organisational links between consumers, workers, managers, government, and different pressure groups, and between institutions and organisational infrastructure, it is useful to discuss here the main macro-productivity factors which speed or hinder productivity improvement processes. Because productivity largely determines real income, inflation, competitiveness and people's well-being, policy-makers try hard to discover the real reasons for productivity growth and decline.

A general classification of the three main groups of macro-productivity factors is shown in figure 2.3.

Figure 2.3.   Main macro-productivity factors

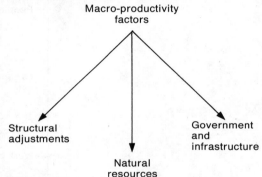

Structural adjustments

Structural changes in society often influence national and enterprise productivity independently of enterprise management. However, in the long term this interaction is two-way. Just as structural changes affect productivity, productivity changes also modify structure. Such changes are not only the result, but also a cause, of economic and social development.

Understanding these changes helps improve government policy, makes enterprise planning more realistic and purpose-oriented and helps develop the economic and social infrastructure. The most important structural changes are economic, and social and demographic.

Economic changes

The most important economic changes are in employment patterns and the composition of capital, technology, scale and competitiveness.

Employment shifts from agriculture to manufacturing industry have caused an economy-wide increase in productivity that has surpassed productivity growth within any one sector in developed countries. The number of people employed in agriculture, forestry and fisheries in these countries has now become so small that this historical source of productivity growth has very limited potential as a source of future growth. However, in many developing countries these shifts will continue to be a source of high growth of productivity in future, since more people will move from the low-productivity agricultural sector into manufacturing.

A second historical structural change is *the move from manufacturing into service industries.* These include wholesale and retail trade, finance, insurance, real estate, personal and business services, and a number of others. Even in Japan, with its heavy emphasis on manufacturing, employment and consumer spending have shifted to the service sector, which now accounts for more than one-half of each. In the United States nearly three-quarters of all non-farm employees work in services. The effect on productivity of this second major wave of structural change is controversial, since productivity in the service sector has tended to climb more slowly than productivity in general. However, it has held down the price of labour relative to the rapidly escalating price of capital and raw materials. As a result, in many countries wages declined absolutely during the late 1970s. This stimulated the shift of capital and energy away from equipment into investment in the labour force. Thus, the productivity of other production factors was enhanced at the expense of labour productivity.

Variations in the composition of capital, its relative intensity, age and kind also affect productivity. The growth of capital depends on saving and investment. The age of the capital stock also influences the diffusion of innovations to the extent that technological change is embodied in new investment goods. However, above average capital input per worker does not necessarily increase output per worker. Much of the capital investment that did take place in the 1970s, for example, did little to raise labour productivity. In Canada, Japan and the United States capital intensity differs significantly from relative productivity performance. Some manufacturing industries achieve high productivity with relatively low capital intensity, barely exceeding that of commerce.

A wide discrepancy between productivity and capital intensity often indicates large unused capacities in the economy, over the conventionally measured capacity, which could be tapped by better management.

The structural *impact of R & D and technology* is another important factor in productivity improvement at the macro-level. The management of R & D and technology and the implementation of new methods, techniques, products and processes can significantly influence productivity and at the same time change structure: examples are the introduction of assembly lines, computers and microprocessors, and modern communications equipment. Foreign investment is often an important factor in the introduction of new technology.

However, indiscriminate imports of technology can injure countries. There is a growing awareness of the need for indigenous technological competence and research within the countries and industries concerned.

Economy of scale or scale of production is also closely related to productivity and the industrial structure. Small and medium-sized enterprises can be fully competitive if they specialise and have long production runs. Some developing countries such as India, Indonesia, the Philippines and Thailand have deliberately promoted decentralised cottage, rural and other small-scale industries in order to reduce unemployment and poverty, to curb urban migration and to help traditional artisans. Japan encourages small-scale industry to introduce and adapt important technology and improve economic viability. In this sector, capital productivity can be high and innovative. Even reverse engineering- and technology-transfer from the small to the large-scale sector can be effective.

Industrial competitiveness affects the productivity of both the economy and individual enterprises. The European Management Forum defines industrial competitiveness as "the immediate and future ability of, and opportunities for, entrepreneurs to design, produce and market goods within their respective environments whose price and non-price qualities form a more attractive package than those of competitors abroad or in domestic markets".[3]

Ten major factors affect competitiveness:

- The dynamism of the economy measured by criteria such as growth rates, monetary strength, industrial production and per capita performance.
- Industrial efficacy, which involves direct and indirect employee costs, per capita output, employee motivation, turnover and absenteeism.
- The dynamics of the market, when efforts to improve competitiveness are increased and better directed to more intensive market forces.
- Financial dynamism, that is the strength and importance of the commercial banking sector, stock and bond markets and their ability to provide capital.
- Human resources, that is the dynamism of the population and the labour force, employment, unemployment, executive quality and motivation.
- The role of the State in fiscal policies and other regulations.
- Resources and infrastructure (transport and communications facilities), domestic energy and raw materials sources.
- Outward orientation, the will to promote trade actively, buying and selling goods, service-related investments or any other form of international exchange.
- Innovative forward orientation which emphasises national research and development efforts, corporate and government attitudes to exploiting new ideas, products and production processes.
- Socio-political consensus and stability, the degree to which strategies and policies reflect a society's aspirations.

Demographic and social changes

Structural changes in the labour force are both *demographic* and *social*. The high birth rates and low mortality rates of the post-war period sent world population soaring from 2.5 thousand million in 1950 to 4.4 thousand million in 1980. By the mid-1960s, the post-war baby boom was beginning to reach the job market. At the same time, the number of women entering the labour force was steadily rising. In addition to this, workers in the industrialised countries have increasingly had to compete not only with each other but also with labour from the developing countries. Productivity and wages in the developing countries tend to be lower and the total cost of production is competitive. Two different and somewhat contradictory pressures influence productivity. On the one hand, producers in more developed countries must try to increase productivity in order to hold down production costs; on the other hand, the restraining influence of competition on wages encourages producers to use more labour, rather than investing heavily in capital equipment. This tends to reduce the growth of productivity. These demographic changes have an impact on jobseekers, on worker experience and useful work skills, and on the demand for goods and services. Geographic shifts of the population will probably also affect productivity as population density varies from region to region.

Among the *social factors*, special attention should be paid to the increasing percentage of women in the labour force. Women's participation in the labour force is still well below that of men but it is increasing. A change in the ratio of working men to women affects earnings. Men currently have a higher average income than women. Much of this difference has been attributed to education, full or part-time work and length of work experience. As these facts change, so, most likely, will productivity and the income structure. The retirement age may drift upward, as health and longevity improve. Economic pressures may also persuade many older people to stay in the labour force.

All aspects of education affect productivity. Over the past few decades, educational spending has grown significantly. By the end of the 1970s educational expenses in Canada, for example, represented 8 per cent of GNP, and government spending on education accounted for 22 per cent of total government expenditure.[4]

Cultural values and attitudes can promote or hinder productivity. For example, the Chinese are known for their belief in hard work, their entrepreneurial spirit and their propensity to save. The Japanese are famous for their ability to seek, accept, assimilate and adapt to changing needs and circumstances, for their team spirit and discipline. In some countries, greater respect is traditionally given to brain power than to manual work; in others, the elderly are valued, not merely tolerated.

It is important to study and understand these beliefs, attitudes and traditions, all of which change with new technology and economic development. The countries that have become development-oriented are under increasing pressure to upgrade their development policy and institutionalise social change through education and the media.

Natural resources

The most important natural resources are *manpower, land, energy and raw materials*. A nation's ability to generate, mobilise and use these resources is crucially important to productivity improvement and is, unfortunately, often overlooked.

Manpower

People are the most precious natural resource. Several developed countries such as Japan and Switzerland, which lack land, energy and mineral resources, have found that their single most important source of growth is people, their skills, education and training, attitude and motivation, and development. Investment in these factors improves the quality of management and of the labour force. Such countries take great care to invest in educating and training their manpower. Countries with higher per capita GNP generally have a better trained and educated population. Attention to health and leisure has resulted in a tremendous saving due to less illness, longer life expectancy and increased vitality. The general quality of labour has improved with improving health.

Land

Land requires proper management, development and a national policy. For example, industrial expansion and intensive farming have become aggressive consumers of the most fundamental material input, land. Pressure to increase farm productivity per worker and per hectare can accelerate soil erosion. Such land loss can often be masked by using more fertiliser, but at increasingly high cost and at risk of environmental pollution. The rising cost of energy-intensive agricultural input, the limited availability of new land, and the urgent need for more careful husbandry to prevent serious erosion all argue for more prudent use of available land.

Energy

Energy is the next important resource. The drastic change in energy prices during the 1970s was the single most important cause of declining productivity and economic growth. Much of the capital investment that took place during that decade did little to raise labour productivity since it was directed towards retooling the economies to adjust to higher energy prices.

As the price of a barrel of oil rose from US$3 in 1973 to about US$36 in 1980, before dropping back in 1985, a considerable amount of capital stock became obsolete and urgently needed to be replaced or used less intensively. As producers cut back on energy use and capital investment, their only recourse was to use more labour. Thus, demand for labour tends to follow energy prices upwards. However, though more hours are worked, total output may not rise commensurately.

Thus, the supply of energy influences capital/labour combinations and increases or decreases productivity. This fact should be learned, understood and taken into consideration by industrial and enterprise management.

Raw materials

Raw materials are also an important productivity factor. Raw materials prices are subject to the same kind of fluctuations as oil prices, though in less extreme forms. As the richest and most accessible sources of minerals are mined out, the need to exploit lower grades of ore in more difficult locations has called for more intensive use of capital and labour. This reduces productivity growth in mines despite increasing automation in many countries. The exploitation of increasingly marginal mines decreases productivity further.

As the cost of materials rises, the economic rationale for repair, re-use and recycling becomes more compelling since, though productivity in the strictly conventional sense is lower for such work, it is much less expensive for society as a whole than buying new materials.

Government and infrastructure

Government policies, strategies and programmes greatly affect productivity through:
— practices of government agencies;
— regulations (such as price control, income and wage policies);
— transport and communications;
— power;
— fiscal measures and incentives (interest rates, tariffs, taxes).

Many structural changes that affect productivity result from laws, regulations or institutional practices. In addition, the whole area of government productivity itself is extremely important because it enables governments to render more services with the same resources or to provide the same services at lower cost.

We are not going to discuss the government's role in productivity in great detail at this stage, since it is covered in the last chapter. It is sufficient to mention the significant part it plays in economic development.

In this chapter we have considered the major internal and external productivity factors or areas for improvement and we would like to stress again that the internal factors are those under the full control of enterprise management. However, to design good policies, plans or programmes for productivity improvement, all the external factors should be analysed, understood and considered. The best way to do this is to introduce sound productivity measurement systems at all levels of society. This will be discussed in the next chapter.

---

[1] S. K. Mukherjee and Duleep Singh: *Towards high productivity*, Report of a seminar on higher productivity in public sector production enterprises (New Delhi, Bureau of Public Enterprises, 1975), pp. 91-103.

[2] Harold E. Dolenga: "Productivity: Problems, paradigms and progress", in *SAM Advanced Management Journal* (New York, Society for the Advancement of Management), Autumn 1985, pp. 39-45.

[3] Robin Pauley: "Sliding down the scale of industrial efficacy", in *Financial Times* (London), 10 Dec. 1984.

[4] Imre Bernolak: "The whole and its parts: Micro and macro productivity research", in *Dimensions of productivity research* (Houston, Texas, The American Productivity Center, 1980), Vol. II, pp. 755-764.

PRODUCTIVITY ANALYSIS 3

Productivity analysis is important for productivity improvement. Even as a separate element, it is a very effective tool for decision-making at all economic levels.

The success of productivity measurement and analysis depends largely upon a clear understanding by all parties concerned (enterprise managers, workers, employers, trade union organisations and government institutions) of *why* productivity measurement is important for the effectiveness of the organisation. The answer is that it indicates where to look for opportunities to improve and also shows how well improvement efforts are faring.

At the national and sectoral levels, productivity indices help us evaluate economic performance and the quality of social and economic policies. These policies influence such diverse matters as the level of technological development, the maturity of management and the labour force, planning, incomes, wages and price policies and taxation. Productivity measurement helps identify factors affecting income and investment distribution within different economic sectors, and helps to determine priorities in decision-making. Productivity indices are also used by local and central authorities to detect problem areas and to evaluate the impact of national development programmes. They provide valuable, objective information for directing public resources.

In enterprises productivity is measured to help analyse effectiveness and efficiency. Its measurement can stimulate operational improvement: the very announcement, installation and operation of a measurement system can improve labour productivity, sometimes by 5 to 10 per cent, with no other organisational change or investment.

Productivity indices also help to establish realistic targets and check-points for diagnostic activities during an organisation development process, pointing to bottle-necks and barriers to performance. Furthermore, there can be no improvement in industrial relations or proper correspondence between productivity, wage levels and gains-sharing policies without a sound measurement system.

Productivity indices are also useful in inter-country and inter-firm comparisons designed to detect factors accounting for economic growth. That is why productivity measurement should be among the first priorities for any productivity improvement project manager, both at the national and enterprise level. To achieve a balance between productivity, profits and prices, a sound productivity measurement system must be an integral part of the management information system.

3.1 An approach to productivity appraisal

Productivity appraisal at the macro-level means measurement of the absolute level of productivity and its historical trends expressed through a series of indices. Without such a measurement Gross Domestic Product (GDP), Gross National Product (GNP), National Income (NI) or value added (VA) may not reflect a true picture of the nation's or sector's economic health. For example, GDP may increase year after year, but productivity may actually be on the decline when cost of input has increased faster than output.

Two types of productivity ratio can be used to measure productivity at all economic levels.

$$\text{Total productivity} = \frac{\text{Total output}}{\text{Total input}}$$

$$\text{Partial productivity} = \frac{\text{Total output}}{\text{Partial input}}$$

Total productivity

Total productivity can be measured by the formula:

$$Pt = \frac{Ot}{L + C + R + Q}$$

where Pt = total productivity
  Ot = total output
  L = labour input factor
  C = capital input factor
  R = raw material and purchased parts input
  Q = other miscellaneous goods and services input factor

Total productivity is the average of labour and capital productivity weighted and adjusted to price fluctuations. It can be calculated either by a labour-time or by a financial method.

Labour-time methods

All materials, depreciation, services and final products can be converted into manpower equivalents by dividing the output by input in financial terms, this being divided again by the national (or sectoral) average annual income per employee, i.e.:

$$\frac{\text{Sales output}}{\text{Total number of employees} + \dfrac{\text{Capital} + \text{external expenses}}{\text{Average earnings per annum}}}$$

The indices used above are complex and not very precisely defined. To overcome this problem net output, or value added per worker, can be used as a measure for productivity where VA represents the value added to materials by the production process.

$$\text{Net output per employee} = \frac{\text{Added value per annum}}{\text{Total number of employees}} = \frac{VA}{Ly}$$

Value added is obtained by subtracting input from output, or total sales (S) minus external expenses (X):

$$VA = S - X$$

In some cases "work-hours completed" might be a better unit to use than "number employed" since we are measuring the effectiveness of all the workers.

Financial methods

Where productivity indices cannot be obtained directly, financial ratios can be used:

Figure 3.1. Elements of output used in calculating total productivity

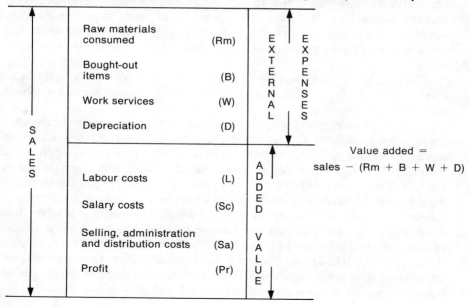

Total productivity is:

$$Pt = \frac{\text{Added value}}{\text{Conversion costs}} = \frac{\text{Sales} - (Rm + B + W + D)}{L + Sc + Rm + B + W + D + Sa}$$

Labour productivity

At the national level, labour productivity is computed by taking the entire economically active population as the input and the total value of goods and services produced as the output.

$$\text{National productivity} = \frac{\text{GNP}}{\text{Population}}$$

Also at the national level, or at the sectoral level, labour productivity is often measured in terms of physical output per work-hour. However, this measure is generally unsatisfactory because the amount of work required to produce a unit of output varies for different products. For this reason, labour-time methods of measurement (hour, day or year) are better. Here, output is converted into "units of work", which are commonly defined as the amount of work that can be performed in one hour by a qualified worker working at standard performance.

However, labour is only one input and comparing the value of output only to the value of labour obscures the relative efficiency with which other factors of production are used. For example, the results of a poor investment policy in capital equipment could, in productivity figures, appear as a deterioration in the quality of labour. Using the number of paid work-hours to measure labour input at the national level masks the economy-wide inefficiency caused by unemployment, because unemployed workers simply drop out of sight in the productivity equation. Also, unused resources in enterprises reduce productivity but the decline would not be apparent in calculations that divided output by paid hours of work only.

Thus, a more useful way of measuring national labour productivity is to divide output by "hours potentially workable" in order to take account of labour wasted by unemployment.[1]

Total productivity and the profit/total investment index seem to be the most appropriate approaches to measuring the productivity of the manufacturing sector. Using the total productivity approach, two measures of output are normally adopted: total production and gross value added. The first is defined as the sum of producers' shipments and net inventory stock changes; the second is the difference between total production and intermediate input. Capital input is measured in terms of gross capital stock for which no adjustment is made. For labour input, the number of workers is taken as basic information. Average annual cash earnings and hours worked are taken from the sectoral statistics. The relative share of labour can be derived from the ratio of annual cash earnings to gross value added at constant prices and capital. To calculate total factor productivity, labour input is measured in two ways: number of employed persons and work-hours.

The total factor productivity index is defined as:

$$Pt = \frac{Vt}{It}$$

where Vt and It are total output and total input indices respectively.

It is very important in manufacturing industries to measure the productivity of indirect labour. For example, the productivity of materials handlers or maintenance men may be measured by the equation:

$$\text{Productivity index} = \frac{\text{Number of indirect labour hours to serve direct labour}}{\text{Number of direct labours hours}}$$

The basic difficulty of productivity measurement for services and office work lies in measuring output, and in reducing various types of output to one common denominator. Revenue generated per work-day may be a more suitable and goal-oriented measure for any service industry. In financial terms, this might be the volume of services sold and input costs; in time terms it might be work measurement time standards. The financial method of calculating can be introduced using a common costing system; the labour-time method through applying clerical work measurement. This includes:

● *Clerical time standards.* These systems assume that the time required to perform certain basic activities will be constant. All basic activities or motions are measured using stopwatches or filmed records of work.

● *Time study.* This is a form of the above process using measurement techniques for simple operations.

● *Random sampling (activity sampling).* This method is used to reduce the data collection costs of a study. Jobs are randomly selected and checked to build an overall picture of reasonable assumptions.

The daily output of an administrative office can be counted in terms of letters answered, persons interviewed, pages typed, forms filed, and so on. The time spent on each activity can be measured with work-sampling techniques. The most appropriate measure may be the percentage of time spent by each person on useful and desirable activities.

A large bank, for example, may have a productivity measurement system based on time per function (for example, the time taken to process a letter of credit). The time spent on a particular function is recorded in a work measurement-performance report. A separate entry is made for the average hours allowed per day to produce the volume of work.

The bank's data on output per unit are compared with the number of workers in the unit to show trends in output per employee (for example, the number of cheques processed in an operations unit and the number of transactions per teller). The number of hours allowed is divided by the number of hours available to arrive at a percentage effectiveness (per month). The trend in this ratio is a measure of productivity change, a rising ratio indicating improvement.

One insurance company measures the percentage of the norm obtained in each pay period for each operation and for each employee. For example, for the operation in which workers screen applications for insurance, the norm could be 12 minutes to examine a file and process the application. The actual time per unit is measured and the utilisation rate (the actual rate divided by the norm) is calculated. Change in the utilisation rate is an indicator of change in productivity.

For supermarkets or department stores, the use of space, the turnover of capital and/or the sales per square metre of space per day could be used as productivity indices, in addition to revenue per work-hour.

Government and public sector productivity appraisal

With the increased importance of the government role in economic development, the number of government workers (in the United States it accounts for one out of seven employed people), and growing concern over rising costs, the need to develop measurements for public agencies has become increasingly important.

There is a significant difference in the appraisal of public (government) sector productivity and that of private industry. The output of the latter can be counted at the point of sale and directly related to the relevant labour or other input. In the public sector there is a difference between an agency's output and the achievement of the agency's mission. An agency's final output compared with its input is its "efficiency". The impact made by the agency's programme is its "effectiveness".

For example, when a government trains unemployed persons to help them find employment, the number of people trained per teacher is an efficiency measure; the proportion of trained people who obtain jobs is an effectiveness measure. So an internal government agency productivity measure (efficiency) should be supplemented by an evaluation of the validity of the causal relationship between the agency's output and the achievement of its objectives.

To determine effectiveness indicators, agencies must identify specific units of service which are countable, fairly homogeneous over time, adjustable for quality changes, and which reflect a significant proportion of the agencies' workload. In addition, since historical trends are of interest, it is important that the measures be derived from readily available records.

The nature of the output indicators varies substantially. They include such diverse items as trademarks registered, weather observations made, square metres of buildings cleaned, electric power generated, staff trained, etc. The output volumes range from several hundred units completed per year to millions (e.g. mail delivery).

Worker-year indices are based on paid worker-years derived from agency data and are often treated as homogeneous and additive. For example, in the United States, federal government productivity indices are prepared for 28 major functional activities for relatively homogeneous groups such as library services, procurement, finance and accounting, electric power production and postal services.[2] Though these measures are crude, they make a good start. Government productivity must fundamentally focus on increasing services at a given cost.

The greatest potential payoff in using productivity statistics is in internal agency operations, and not only for national policy decisions. They can also be used for:

— goal setting tailored to the specific agency;

— resource estimation;

— budget justification;

— evaluation of change in the way the agency is organised and of management initiatives;

— operational control.

The United States social security administration is responsible for establishing eligibility and paying social security benefits. With 82,000 employee-years and an administrative budget of about US$3,500 million, productivity change can have a major impact on the agency budget and personnel requirements. This agency has measured its productivity for several decades. In the 1983 fiscal year it was estimated that productivity increased by 6.6 per cent which meant a reduction of about 5,700 jobs.

About 90 per cent of social security positions are covered by productivity measurements of 68 different types of output.

Regular evaluation is an integral part of social security management. Estimates of future staff needs and workloads for each agency are made in accordance with estimated changes in productivity. Budget justifications also reflect projected productivity changes. Productivity is analysed as part of the budget execution process, and resources are reprogrammed if projected productivity improvements are not achieved. Work measurement and productivity data are used to monitor field office operations and to compare the productivity of different field offices.

Summary

The different approaches to productivity measurement in different sectors can be summarised as follows:

● In capital-intensive sectors and operations an increase in productivity often reduces work-hour requirements and may be generated by additional fixed capital and not by labour. Here productivity can be measured in terms of productivity of capital only.

● In labour-intensive sectors and operations an increase in labour productivity does not decrease the fixed capital requirements, but indicates an increase in the productivity of capital. For such situations it is sufficient to measure the productivity of direct labour alone.

Output per person or output per work-hour is a good measure of productivity in most industries, except the few very capital-intensive ones, because the cost of labour input usually far outweighs capital input. In most industrialised countries the labour share of net national income is about 80 per cent.

Comparing and analysing productivity

International and intersectoral productivity comparisons help nations or sectors learn from each other. Central governments, for example, are interested in the level and rate of change of per capita income compared with that of other countries. In designing a national economic plan it is important to consider the background of such comparisons (i.e. the structural situation of industrial productivity for each industry).

In this connection it is useful to point out some of the main sources of productivity variations in comparisons. The most obvious elements to analyse are the volume and composition of the output, the variety of products and the degree of vertical integration in processing; the availability and nature of raw materials and components and their sources; the availability and use of energy; the volume and composition of labour input; the state of technology; the volume and composition of capital output; the impact of scale of production; the nature and location of markets, impact of tariffs, taxation, ownership, standards and government regulations.

The most significant characteristics of labour input are the number of white-collar and production workers, production work-hours, basic average hourly earnings and salaries, total compensation including overtime and the composition of the labour force, i.e. skilled, semi-skilled and professional workers, their age and turnover. The education and training of the workforce, both blue- and white-collar, is of obvious importance as well.

Price ratio for the individual types of product

To apply this method it is necessary to evaluate all expenditure data (Gross National Expenditure) in one country by another country's price index and to make the overall quality comparison by using a price ratio corresponding to each category of expenditure:

$$\frac{\Sigma \text{ Ipxy Py Qy}}{\Sigma \text{ Px Qx}} = \frac{\Sigma \text{ Px Qy}}{\Sigma \text{ Px Qx}} = \text{Iqxy}$$

where Px,Py = price of country x and y

      Qx,Qy = quality of expenditure of country x and y

      Ipxy = Px/Py is the price ratio

      Iqxy = index number of overall quantity of country x compared with country y

Quantity ratio for the individual types of product

$$\frac{\text{I xy.Px Qx}}{\text{Px Qx}} = \text{Iqxy}$$

where Iqxy = Qx/Qy

      Iqxy = weighted arithmetic average of the index of quantity for the value of each product of the base country.

We have only touched on the basic principles of productivity measurement here. It is not our intention to go into the econometrics and statistical details of the many formulae; these can be found in the relevant literature (see, for example, Westwick, 1973; Gold, 1976; Kurosawa, 1980; Clark and Clark, 1983; Dogramaci, 1983; Nakazawa, 1985; and Sink, 1986). Our intention is to concentrate more on the organisational level.

3.2 Productivity analysis in the enterprise

There are many approaches to productivity measurement and analysis in enterprises. This is because different groups of people are concerned with the enterprise (managers, workers, investors, customers, trade unions) and these groups have different goals. Some simple and practical approaches to productivity analysis are:

— measurement of workers' productivity;
— measurement systems for planning and analysing unit labour requirements;
— measurement systems of labour productivity aimed at the structure of labour resource use;
— value added productivity at the enterprise level.

Normally the method of measurement is determined by the purpose of the productivity analysis. Three of the most common purposes are:

— comparing an enterprise with its competitors;
— determining the relative performance of departments and workers;
— comparing relative benefits of various types of input for collective bargaining and gains sharing.

For example, if an organisation's goal at a particular time is to maximise the return on invested capital and to expand its operations, the company should measure its cost and profit structures.

Let us discuss a few of the most practical approaches in productivity measurement.

The Kurosawa structural approach [3]

Dr. Kazukiyo Kurosawa, Professor of Management Science at the Tokyo Institute of Technology, is well known for his research and publications on productivity measurement. He has undertaken a number of assignments as an expert on productivity improvement, both with the ILO (International Labour Office) and with the APO (Asian Productivity Organisation). He focuses on the structure of the enterprise. We are grateful for permission to reproduce the elements of his approach.

In accordance with his concept, productivity measurement in the enterprise helps to analyse the past and to plan new activities. It can be used to set up an information system for monitoring operational activities. For this reason it is

31

important that productivity measurement systems be built according to the decision-making hierarchy. A very general system could be as shown in figure 3.2.

Figure 3.2. Fundamental framework of productivity measurement in management

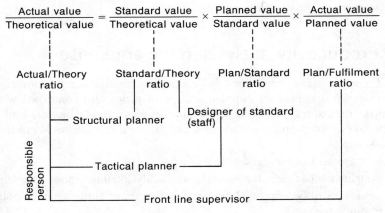

Source: K. Kurosawa, 1980, p. 97.

Applying this equation over time, we can use this system as a sort of inter-linked index system.

Individual productivity

A worker's productivity (Pw) is defined as follows:

$$Pw = \frac{Output}{Input\ of\ worker's\ effort}$$

Productivity measurement ratios (PMR) are based on the structure of work-hours given in figure 3.3 (opposite).

Thus, the ratio system is devised as follows:

$$\tau'r = Ew \times le(1) \times le(2)$$

$$\frac{Ls}{Lr} = \frac{Ls}{Le} \times \frac{Le}{Lr'} \times \frac{Lr'}{Lr}$$

$$\tau''r = \frac{Ls}{Lr'}$$

where Ls = standard work-hours (quantity produced × standard time)

Lr = total input work-hours (number of workers on payroll × duty hours)

Figure 3.3.   Structure of work-hours

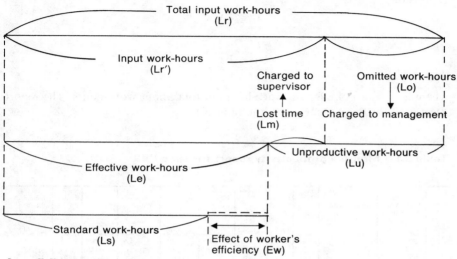

Source: K. Kurosawa, 1980, p. 99.

Le = effective work-hours

Lr = Lr′ + Lo

$\qquad$ Lr′ = Le + Lm

Lr′ = input work-hours

Lo = work-hours omitted from this account such as work-breaks, mealtimes, cleaning and maintenance time, transport time

Lm = lost time due to supervisor or management such as breakdown and repair, shortage or defects of materials or parts, last-minute assignment to another task

le(1) = ratio of effective work-hours to input work-hours

le(2) = ratio of input work-hours to total input work-hours

$\tau''r \quad = \dfrac{Ls}{Lr'}$: process efficiency

$\tau'r$ = overall efficiency of labour

Ew = worker efficiency.

Then the meaning of the above equation is as follows:

> Overall efficiency of labour = worker's efficiency × ratio of effective work-hours × ratio of input work-hours = process efficiency × ratio of input work-hours.

A simpler and more practical system could be reduced from the following expression:

$$\tau'r = Ew \times le$$

$$\frac{Ls}{Lr} = \frac{Ls}{Le} \times \frac{Le}{Lr}$$

where le = ratio of effective work-hours to total input work-hours. The report sheet used for this system is given in table 3.1.

Table 3.1.   Monthly productivity report for shop "X"

Crew	Standard Work-Hours	Total Input Work-Hours	Input Work-Hours	Omitted Work-Hours	Lost Time	Effective Work-Hours	Worker's Efficiency	Ratio of Effective Work-Hours	Process Efficiency	Ratio of Input Work-Hours	Overall Efficiency of Labour	Standard Productivity	Overall Labour Productivity
	Ls	Lr	Lr'	Lo	Lm	Le	$Ew=\dfrac{Ls}{Le}$	$le^{(1)}=\dfrac{Le}{Lr'}$	$\tau''R=\dfrac{Ls}{Lr'}$	$le^{(2)}=\dfrac{Lr'}{Lr}$	$\tau'R=\dfrac{Ls}{Lr}$	$\tau F=\dfrac{Q}{Ls}$	$\tau R=\dfrac{Q}{Lr}$
	(1)	(2)	(3)	(4)	(5)	(6)	(1)/(6) (7)	(6)/(3) (8)	(7)×(8) (9)	(3)/(2) (10)	(9)×(10) (11)	(12)	(11)×(12) (13)
1													
2													
3													
⋮													

Source: K. Kurosawa, 1980, p. 100.

A weekly report should be prepared analysing productivity problems in order to decide on actions for the following week.

The application of the approach to enterprise productivity

Value added can be used meaningfully in productivity management in combination with various physical parameters as well as other related variables.

As can be seen in figure 3.4, value added at the enterprise can have several forms. Selection of each form depends upon management objectives.

In routine business activities, value added is usually evaluated at current prices. Value added evaluated at constant prices is estimated more for analytical purposes. The essence of value added labour productivity is in the differentiation between industries and enterprises. A commonly used method to eliminate the price effect on value added is the double deflation method.

Figure 3.4.   Structure of production value and value added variants

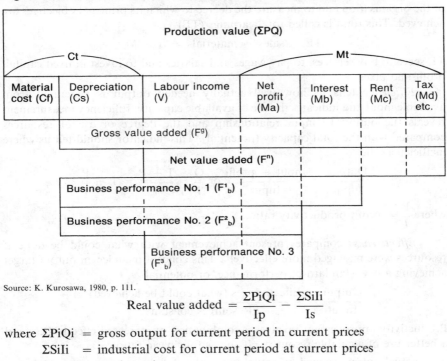

Production value (ΣPQ)						
— Ct —			— Mt —			
Material cost (Cf)	Depreciation (Cs)	Labour income (V)	Net profit (Ma)	Interest (Mb)	Rent (Mc)	Tax (Md) etc.
	Gross value added (F^g)					
		Net value added (F^n)				
	Business performance No. 1 (F^1_b)					
	Business performance No. 2 (F^2_b)					
		Business performance No. 3 (F^3_b)				

Source: K. Kurosawa, 1980, p. 111.

$$\text{Real value added} = \frac{\Sigma PiQi}{Ip} - \frac{\Sigma SiIi}{Is}$$

where ΣPiQi = gross output for current period in current prices
  ΣSiIi = industrial cost for current period at current prices
  Pi   = market prices
  Qi   = quantity of items sold
  Si   = price of the "i" item of intermediate input factor
  Ii   = quantity consumed of the "i" item of intermediate input factor
  Ip   = price index number of products
  Is   = price index number of intermediate input

Lawlor's approach [4]

Alan Lawlor is a director of Action Learning Associates, in the United Kingdom, and a director of Productivity Audits. He has worked in management for over 35 years, both in senior positions in industry and as a principal lecturer in a college of higher education. In recent years he has worked extensively with the Manpower Services Commission on a number of new developments in productivity improvement.

Productivity concept and appraisal

Alan Lawlor considers productivity as a comprehensive measure of how efficiently and effectively organisations satisfy the following five aims: objectives, efficiency, effectiveness, comparability and progressive trends.

35

Productivity management

Objectives can be met when the total fund is adequate to meet the demands of the organisation and to measure the degree to which its principal objectives are achieved. This fund is called total earnings (TE)

$$TE = sales - materials = S - M$$

TE serve to buy services, to pay wages and salaries and to invest in fixed capital, profit and taxes.

Efficiency tells us how well actually needed output is generated from available input and indicates the use of available capacity. Efficiency measurement reveals the output to input relationship and the degree of use of resources compared with the total capacity (potential). This indicator should tell us where inefficiencies lie.

$$\frac{Output}{Input} = \frac{Input + profit}{Input} \text{ or } \frac{O}{I} = \frac{I + P}{I} = 1 + \frac{P}{I}$$

where $\frac{P}{I}$ = profit productivity ratio.

Effectiveness compares present achievement with what could be done if resources were managed more effectively. This concept includes an output target achieving a new standard of performance, or potential.

$$\frac{Output}{Input} = \frac{Effectiveness \text{ (what could be achieved)}}{Resources \text{ consumed}}$$

Productivity improvement involves a combination of increased effectiveness and a better use of available resources. It shows four basic ratios:

— actual output divided by actual input, the status quo;
— higher output divided by current actual input;
— actual current output divided by lower input;
— the higher level of effectiveness; maximum output divided by minimum input.

Comparability is a guide to organisational performance, since productivity ratios alone tells us little without some form of comparison. Generally speaking, productivity measurement means comparisons at three levels:

● Comparison of present performance with a historical base performance. This does not indicate whether current performance is satisfactory — only whether it is improving or deteriorating and to what extent.

● Comparison of performance between one unit — an individual, a job, a section, a process — and another. Such a measure indicates relative achievement.

● Comparison of actual performance with a target. This is best, because it concentrates attention on objectives.

Trends, that is the aim of achieving progressive trends, must be associated with a comparison between current performance and a historical base in order to identify whether enterprise performance is moving up or down and how fast.

This approach calls for at least two levels of productivity measurement within the enterprise: primary and secondary. The primary level deals with total earning productivity (E) which is:

$$E = \frac{\text{Total earnings}}{\text{Conversion cost}} = \frac{T}{C}$$

where conversion cost (C) = total wages and salaries (W) + total purchased services (Ps) + depreciation (K). Thus, obtaining a high level of total earnings ensures a healthy organisation.

An example of the secondary level is profit productivity (Ep) which is:

$$Ep = \frac{P}{C} = \frac{T - C}{C} = \frac{T}{C} - 1 \text{ or } Ep = E - 1$$

An example

Total earnings in a particular month are US$100,000. Conversion costs = US$75,000

$$E = \frac{100,000}{75,000} = 1.33 \qquad EP = \frac{100,000 - 75,000}{75,000} = 0.33$$

$$\text{or } 1.33 - 1 = 0.33$$

This means that for every dollar of conversion costs US$1.33 of total earnings and US$0.33 of profit have been generated.

Total earnings productivity (E) reveals a primary or overall measurement of efficiency for any kind of organisation. It also shows three more aspects of conversion efficiency:

— the rate at which input generates output;
— the quantity of input used to generate a given output;
— the potential output which could be obtained from a given input, i.e. the measurement of effectiveness.

Secondary productivity measurement provides the ratio of used resources to the total cost of all available resources. The total conversion costs include two main divisions:

● The costs incurred when resources are used productively (Cd). These costs can be subdivided into productive work costs (Ce) and ancillary work costs (Ca).

● Unused or idle resources costs (Ci), when people and equipment are wholly idle.

The relationship between these costs is shown below:

Productive work costs (Ce)	Ancillary work costs (Ca)	Idle resources costs (Ci)
←——— Processing costs (Cd) ———→		
←——————— Total conversion costs (C) ———————→		

37

Thus it is possible to state resource or conversion utilisation productivity as follows:

$$\frac{\text{Time or costs incurred on productive and ancillary work}}{\text{(Total time (or conversion costs) available (including idle time))}} = \frac{Cd}{C}$$

The basic resource productivity indicator is used to relate pure productive work (Ce) to total conversion costs (C).

Thus,

$$\frac{\text{Time or costs incurred on purely productive work}}{\text{(Total time or conversion costs available)}} = \frac{Ce}{C}$$

Truly productive work, as distinguished from ancillary work, is what directly adds value to materials. The concept of productive work forms an important part of productivity measurement.

There are two other secondary productivity measurements: working capital and inventory productivity.

$$\frac{\text{Productivity of}}{\text{working capital}} = \frac{\text{Total earnings}}{\text{Throughput materials + conversion costs}} = \frac{T}{M + C}$$

This equation gives total earnings per unit of working capital employed or the rate of turnover of working capital. Similar ratios could be employed using sales (S) or profit (P) output, i.e.

$$\frac{S}{M + C} \text{ and } \frac{P}{M + C}$$

The productivity of inventory (total materials, work in progress and finished stocks) is similar to working capital, but should include a carrying charge (Cinv) to cover the time the inventory has been in the system:

$$\frac{\text{Total earnings}}{\text{Throughput materials + carrying charge}} = \frac{T}{M + Cinv}$$

A more conventional way of measuring the productivity of inventory is the rate of stock turnover which is:

$$\frac{\text{Sales}}{\text{Average stock carried}}$$

Productivity potential

The potential total earnings of an organisation are the earnings that would be gained if all input were fully used — with no idle capacity costs.

In other words, Cd = C

$$\text{Tpot} = \frac{T}{\text{Total Cd}} - \times C$$

For example, if total earnings are US\$100,000, total conversion costs US\$75,000, processing costs US\$48,000 and productive work costs US\$30,000, we can make the following calculation:

$$\frac{\text{Utilisation}}{\text{Productivity}} = \frac{Cd}{C} = \frac{48,000}{75,000} = 0.64$$

Just under two-thirds of resources are occupied productively and about one-third are idle. The existing and potential total earnings are:

$$\text{Existing total earnings} = \text{US\$100,000}$$

$$\frac{\text{Potential total}}{\text{earnings}} = \frac{I}{Cd} \times C = \frac{100,000}{48,000} \times 75,000 = \text{US\$156,250}$$

It can be seen that productive work has a big lever effect on total organisational productivity, with a similar effect on profit. Comparisons made between overall total earnings productivity and total earnings productivity with idle costs reveal large differences.

Summarising his approach, Alan Lawlor gives a hierarchical structure of productivity indices and a table for comparison of the degree of usefulness of the different productivity measurement indices from the points of view of organisational levels, complexity and basic aims of measurement. These are reproduced on the following pages.

Figure 3.5. Framework of productivity analysis

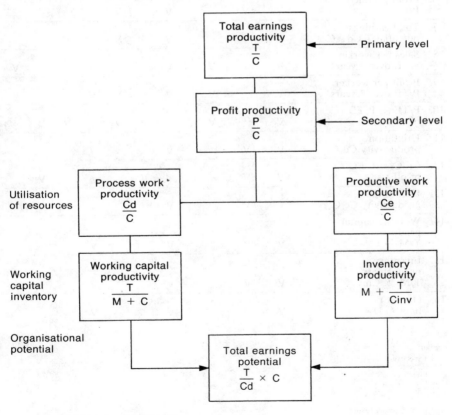

Source: Adapted from A. Lawlor, 1985, p. 86.

Table 3.2. Comparison of productivity measures

No.	Measures	Level		Complexity		Order		Five basic aims				
		Macro	Micro	Simple	Complex	1st	2nd	O	Ef	E	C	T
1.	GNP per capita — GNP/PC	V			V	V		V	V			
2.	GNP/PC ÷ GNP/PC of others	V			V		V	V	V	V	V	
3.	Added value per worker AV/Pw	V			V	V		V	V			
4.	Total earnings productivity T/C		V	V		V		V	V			
5.	T/C ÷ T/C of others		V	V			V	V	V		V	
6.	Profit productivity P/C		V	V		V		V	V			
7.	Total earnings potential T/Cd × C		V	V		V		V		V		
8.	Sales per worker S/TE over 3 years		V		V	V			V			V
9.	Profit per worker P/TE over 3 years		V		V	V		V	V			V
10.	P/TE ÷ P/TE of others		V		V		V	V		V	V	
11.	Utilisation productivity Cd/C		V	V		V			V			
12.	Cd/C ÷ Cd/C of others		V	V			V			V	V	
13.	Utilisation productivity Ce/C		V	V		V				V		
14.	Working capital productivity T/M + C		V	V		V			V			
15.	Inventory productivity T/M + Cinv		V	V		V			V			
16.	Output per hour O/H	V				V			V			

Legend:
O = Objective
Ef = Efficiency
E = Effectiveness
C = Comparison
T = Trend

Source: A. Lawlor, 1980, p. 88.

Gold's approach [5]

Professor Gold has been concerned with productivity studies in the United States for many years and his research programme in industrial economics has covered a variety of industries, ranging from steel to agriculture. Gold's measure focuses on the rate of return on investment, and attributes profit to five specific elements of performance:

— product prices;

— unit costs;

— use of facilities;

— productivity of facilities;

— allocation of capital resources between fixed and working capital.

The five elements can be integrated into one equation:

$$\frac{\text{Profit}}{\text{Investment}} = \left\{ \frac{\text{Product revenue}}{\text{Output}} - \frac{\text{Total costs}}{\text{Output}} \right\} \times$$

$$\frac{\text{Output}}{\text{Capacity}} \times \frac{\text{Capacity}}{\text{Fixed investment}} \times \frac{\text{Fixed investment}}{\text{Total investment}}$$

In this equation, the first three ratios after the equals sign stand for short-term changes and the last two ratios represent long-term changes. This expression also illustrates how changes in profitability from one period to the next depend upon interactions between product contribution, capacity utilisation, and the proportion of total investment allocated to production capacity.

Quick productivity appraisal approach (QPA)

Essence and structure

This simple, practical method for small and medium enterprises was developed and tested in the Productivity Development Centre of the Development Academy of the Philippines.[6] It is relevant to such enterprises in any part of the world and deserves to be widely known.

QPA, an integrated audit approach, includes both diagnosis and monitoring of a productivity improvement programme covering a whole organisation (see figure 3.6). It is a systematic assessment of the company's profitability and productivity performance, its inherent strengths and weaknesses.

The purpose of QPA is twofold:

— to isolate problem areas and identify priority areas for improvement;

— to establish productivity indicators for the whole organisation.

QPA consists of three components (see figure 3.7):

— company performance appraisal (CPA);

— qualitative assessment;

— industry performance appraisal.

Figure 3.6. Productivity audit cycle

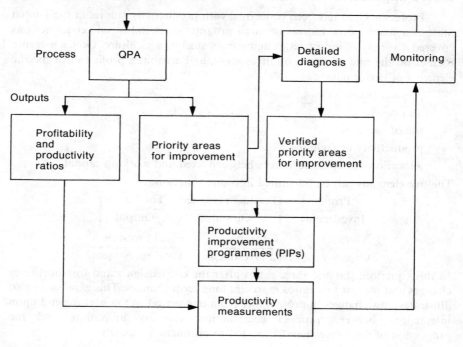

Source: E. Avedillo-Cruz, 1984, p. 3.

Figure 3.7. Components of QPA

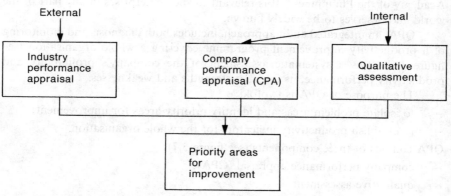

Source: E. Avedillo-Cruz, 1984, p. 4.

Company performance appraisal (CPA)

CPA studies the trends of specific profitability and productivity ratios derived from financial statements for the past four (at least three) periods (year, quarter or month). Its main purpose is to diagnose problem areas through establishing productivity indicators for continuous monitoring and control of the whole enterprise, in order to set up an appropriate productivity improvement programme (PIP).

In conducting CPA, two basic comparisons have to be made:

— between current performance and a historical base performance;

— between actual performance and the target.

The former indicates whether performance is improving or declining and at what rate. The latter requires that performance or productivity targets be set and matched against actual performance.

Using profitability alone as the basis for evaluating the overall performance of an organisation makes it difficult to identify the cause of profitability changes. Are they due to productivity or price-cost movement? The following demonstrates this relationship:

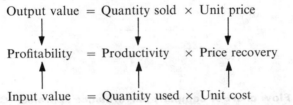

Considering the relationships over time, profitability is defined as change in output value compared with change in input value; productivity as the change between quantity of output and/or quantity in unit price, and change in unit cost.

In effect, what is computed are performance ratios classified into:

— change in profitability;

— change in productivity;

— change in price recovery.

These performance ratios are then evaluated in relation to their effect on profits. In general, a drop in profitability, in productivity or in price recovery reduces profits. Lower productivity signals a need for further analysis and for corrective action. However, increased productivity does not necessarily lead to profitability on a short-term basis. The effect of increased productivity will be realised only in terms of long-term profitability (see table 3.3).

These four relationships between profitability and productivity provide insights on the approaches to be used in improving performance.

How to conduct CPA

Collect the financial statements (i.e. balance sheet and income statement) for the past few periods, and undertake the steps in figure 3.8.

Table 3.3. Profitability/productivity relationships

Case	IF		THEN	
	Profitability	Productivity	What will happen	What should be done
1	HIGH	HIGH	Financial condition will be sound and stable	Maintain or increase productivity further
2	HIGH	LOW	High profitability may not be sustained on a long-term basis. In the long run, low productivity will eat up profits	Improve productivity
3	LOW	HIGH	The company may soon be operating at a loss and may be on the brink of a shut-down	Improve profitability, strengthen market strategy, market research, market promotion/advertising, and pricing policy
4	LOW	LOW	Shut-down/bankruptcy	Improve productivity and strengthen market

Source: E. Avedillo-Cruz, 1984, p. 9.

Figure 3.8. Flow chart of company performance appraisal (CPA)

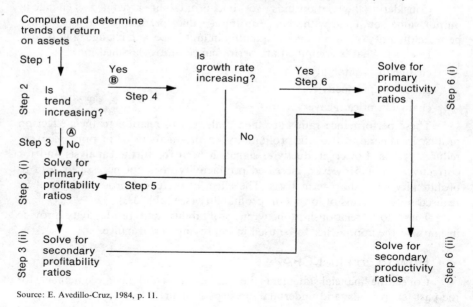

Source: E. Avedillo-Cruz, 1984, p. 11.

Step 1: Compute return on assets (ROA) for the past periods (a year, a quarter, a month) as net profit over total assets.

Step 2: Determine the trend of return on assets.

Step 3: (Branch A)

If ROA trend is decreasing or constant:

(i) Compute primary profitability ratios

$$(a) \quad \frac{\text{Net profit}}{\text{Net sales}}$$

$$(b) \quad \frac{\text{Cost of goods sold}}{\text{Net sales}}$$

$$(c) \quad \frac{\text{Operating expenses}}{\text{Net sales}}$$

$$(d) \quad \frac{\text{Interest expense}}{\text{Net sales}}$$

Determine trends (increasing, decreasing or constant)

(ii) Compute secondary profitability ratios

$$(a) \quad \text{Total assets turnover} = \frac{\text{Net sales}}{\text{Total assets}}$$

$$(b) \quad \text{Accounts receivable turnover} = \frac{\text{Net sales}}{\text{Total inventory}}$$

$$(c) \quad \text{Fixed assets turnover} = \frac{\text{Net sales}}{\text{Fixed assets}}$$

$$(d) \quad \text{Inventory turnover} = \frac{\text{Net sales}}{\text{Total inventory}}$$

Determine trends

Perform Step 6

Step 4: (Branch B)

If ROA trend is increasing, compute growth rate (GR) of return on assets (ROA)

$$GR = \frac{\text{ROA present} - \text{ROA preceeding}}{\text{ROA preceeding}} \times 100\%$$

Step 5: If GR of ROA is decreasing or constant, perform Step 3.

Step 6:

(i) Compute primary productivity ratios:

$$\text{Total productivity} = \frac{\text{Value added}}{\text{Labour} + \text{capital inputs}}$$

$$\text{Labour productivity} \quad (a) \quad \frac{\text{Value added}}{\text{Total work-hours worked}}$$

$$(b) \quad \frac{\text{Value added}}{\text{Number of workers}}$$

$$(c) \quad \frac{\text{Value added}}{\text{Salaries and wages}}$$

Capital productivity

$$(a) \quad \frac{\text{Value added}}{\text{Tangible and intangible assets}}$$

$$(b) \quad \frac{\text{Value added}}{\text{Tangible and financial capital}}$$

$$(c) \quad \frac{\text{Value added}}{\text{Tangible assets}}$$

$$(d) \quad \frac{\text{Value added}}{\text{Fixed assets}}$$

$$(e) \quad \frac{\text{Value added}}{\text{Machinery and equipment}}$$

Determine trends

(ii) Compute secondary productivity ratios:

Labour productivity

(a) By type of worker: $\dfrac{\text{Value added}}{\text{Number of direct workers}}$

Example: $\dfrac{\text{Value added}}{\text{Number of indirect workers}}$

(b) By shift: $\dfrac{\text{Value added}}{\text{Number of hours worked on first shift}}$

Example: $\dfrac{\text{Value added}}{\text{Number of hours worked on second shift}}$

(c) By functional area: $\dfrac{\text{Value added}}{\text{Salaries and wages of production department}}$

Example: $\dfrac{\text{Value added}}{\text{Salaries and wages of finance department}}$

Capital productivity

(a) Tangible and intangible assets (i.e. marketable securities, cash, accounts receivable, notes receivable, land, building and structures, etc.).

Example: $\dfrac{\text{Value added}}{\text{Marketable securities}}$

(b) Tangible and financial capital (i.e. cash, accounts receivable, notes receivable, land, building and structures, etc.).

Example: $\dfrac{\text{Value added}}{\text{Accounts receivable}}$

(c) Tangible assets (i.e. inventories, land, building and structures, etc.).

Example: $\dfrac{\text{Value added}}{\text{Inventories}}$

(d) Fixed assets (i.e. land, building and structures, machinery and equipment, furniture and office equipment, transport equipment, etc.).

Example: $\dfrac{\text{Value added}}{\text{Machinery and equipment}}$

(e) Machinery and equipment (i.e. hydraulic press, lathe, drill press, etc.).

Example: $\dfrac{\text{Value added}}{\text{Drill press}}$

Determine trends.

Qualitative assessment

How to evaluate profitability

The following example represents financial data for the past five years. Return on assets has increased. It is necessary to compute the growth rate in order to determine which type of ratios to calculate first — profitability or productivity.

	1	2	3	4	5	TREND
ROA	0.018	0.026	0.028	0.035	0.043	
GR		44%	8%	25%	23%	

The growth rate (GR) is decreasing which means that profitability ratios should be considered first.

Whenever the basic ratio, ROA or its growth rate is decreasing or constant, profitability ratios must be computed and their trends determined prior to a productivity analysis. A deterioration in ROA may be attributed to the performance of its two component ratios:

— net profit to net sales;

— total assets turnover (see figure 3.9).

For analysis, net profit to net sales is broken down into cost of goods sold ratio, operating expenses to sales, and interest expenses to sales. Total assets turnover is broken down into accounts receivable, inventory, and fixed assets.

An increasing trend towards any of the above indicates the priority areas to be improved. Further investigation must be done at the detailed diagnosis phase.

47

Figure 3.9. Evaluation of profitability trends

Priority area for improvement (by functional area)

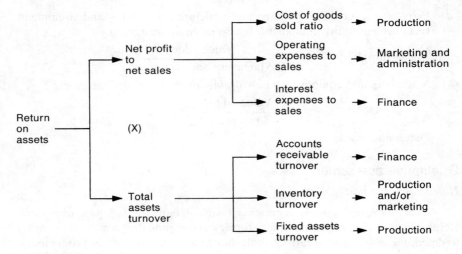

Source: E. Avedillo-Cruz, 1984, p. 15.

For example, if the priority is cost of goods sold, then at the next diagnosis phase the following costs are investigated:

— raw materials used;

— subcontracting expenses, if any;

— direct labour;

— manufacturing overheads;

— work-in-progress inventory;

— finished goods inventory.

Priorities can also be identified through the different functional areas of the organisation (cost of goods sold falling under the production function). If the ratio of operating expenses to sales is increasing, it may be advisable to look into the cost items under operating expenses. In terms of functional areas, the priority areas would be marketing and administration.

If the ratio of interest expenses to sales is increasing, the priority area will be finance. It would be advisable to look into financial management (in securing and investing loans, or in tending to borrow too much).

A decreasing trend in total assets turnover is likely to decrease the ROA trend. When this happens, a breakdown must be made of the different assets comprising total assets turnover:

— accounts receivable;

— inventory;

— fixed assets.

A decreasing trend in accounts receivable turnover requires an investigation into the credit and collection system of the organisation. The priority area here, therefore, is finance again.

In the case of a decreasing trend in inventory turnover it may be necessary to look into:

— raw materials;

— work-in-progress;

— finished goods.

Depending on which inventory in particular is exhibiting a decreasing turnover trend, the priority area may be either production or marketing or both. A decreasing trend in fixed assets turnover indicates low sales per value of fixed assets used. The priority area here is production.

Thus, from the analysis of profitability trends it can be inferred that a decline in the ROA trend may be due to either costs or assets turnover or both. The priority areas for improvement could be any one or a combination of the following specific functions:

— production;

— marketing;

— finance;

— administration.

These priority areas will become the starting-point for the detailed diagnosis.

How to evaluate productivity trends

The trend exhibited by total productivity indicates the overall performance of an organisation. Whether the trend is improving or deteriorating, it is necessary to discover the reason (see figure 3.10).

Labour productivity shows how well the labour force has been used. If the trend is decreasing, then this becomes a priority area for improvement. To understand this deterioration in behaviour, it is important to look into the secondary labour productivity ratios. For example, pin-pointing the specific type of worker who is contributing to an unprogressive labour productivity trend will greatly help in identifying problems and analysing causes.

Dividing the organisation into functional areas (production, marketing, finance) can be helpful in locating the source of the problem.

Capital productivity evaluation shows how well available capital is allocated and managed. Whenever capital productivity shows a decreasing trend, the secondary capital productivity ratios must be scrutinised. A decreasing capital productivity trend may be traced to any or a combination of the components of fixed capital.

However, increasing labour productivity may not necessarily mean that workers are more productive; it may be due to new equipment. Studying the relationship of capital to labour by evaluating the trend of capital/labour (C/L) ratios may explain the behaviour of labour productivity and capital productivity.

Figure 3.10. Evaluation of productivity trends

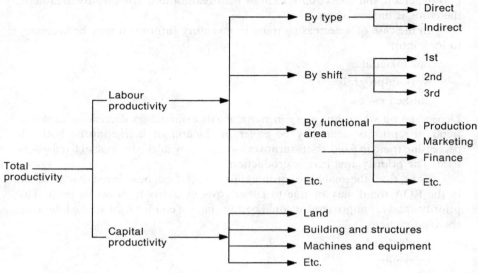

Source: E. Avedillo-Cruz, 1984, p. 24.

An increasing trend in C/L ratios indicates the use of more and more capital goods per labour unit. A decreasing trend indicates the use of more and more manpower resources per capital good.

Table 3.4 will help to evaluate what is happening within an organisation and indicates what should be done to correct the situation.

Thus, the internal components of Quick Productivity Appraisal provide management with a step-by-step approach to productivity measurement that will yield the necessary information for decision-making.

Industry performance appraisal

An external, industry performance appraisal can be made by analysing the same indices in the same way as for an individual enterprise, if there are enough statistical data. Or the sum of individual enterprise assessments can also be used for an industry performance appraisal.

Inter-firm comparison (IFC)

IFC is organised by an external organisation or consultant. It is an exchange of information regarding costs, performance, efficiency and other relevant data between firms engaged in similar activities. Firms in the same industry make their data available on a voluntary and confidential basis to other organisations (industrial departments, national productivity centres, consultants, etc.). Firms engage in IFC in order to improve their productivity and profitability.

Table 3.4.   Capital/labour relationships

Case	IF			THEN	
	Labour productivity	Capital productivity	C/L ratios	What happens	What should be done
1	↗	↗	↗	Good productivity performance	Maintain or increase productivity further
2	↗	↗	↘	Good productivity performance	Maintain or increase productivity further
3	↗	↘	↗	Unfavourable productivity performance	Increase capital productivity
4	↘	↗	↗	Satisfactory productivity performance	Increase labour productivity by: *(a)* developing/ identifying other jobs for displaced labour; *(b)* retraining displaced labour for other jobs
5	↘	↘	↗	Poor productivity performance	First, increase capital productivity, then increase labour productivity. Adapt available manpower to machines
6	↗	↘	↘	Satisfactory productivity performance	Increase capital productivity
7	↘	↗	↘	Unfavourable productivity performance	Increase labour productivity
8	↘	↘	↘	Poor productivity performance	First, increase labour productivity, then increase capital productivity

Source: E. Avedillo-Cruz, 1984, p. 26.

Among the main objectives of IFC the following are the most important:

— to show management how its firm's performance compares with that of similar enterprises;

— to draw management's attention to areas of comparative weakness and strength within the business;

— to give management an objective basis for judging progress and effectiveness.

IFC is a very powerful tool for comparative performance analysis and normally uses the same basic statistics and ratios as conventional productivity measurement.

Table 3.5. Performance indices in the companies in the Federal Republic of Germany

	Company A	Company B	Company C
Turnover (DM'000)	987	1 766	3 800
Materials plus subcontracted work (DM'000)	130	133	554
Wages plus salaries (DM'000)	570	950	1 884
Overheads (DM'000)	106	460	322
Depreciation (DM'000)	41	128	240
Profit (DM'000)	140	95	800
Average hourly rate of skilled worker (DM)	13.40	10.40	13.70
Additional per cent on total costs including 6 per cent for overtime premium	55	55	55
Total hourly costs (DM)	20.77	22.32	21.24
Ratio:			
$\dfrac{\text{Added value}}{\text{Total employment cost}}$	1.32	1.24	1.55
Index:			
Performance ratio after adjusting for worker cost differences. Lowest company in whole study (not just mould sector) = 100	141	142	169

Source: NEDO, 1981, p. 10. Reproduced by permission of the Controller of Her Majesty's Stationery Office.

An example follows of IFC for three companies in the Federal Republic of Germany and four in the United Kingdom. The companies are in the tool-making sector, making moulds.[7]

Case study: IFC in the mould-making sector

The performance indices collected from these companies and the productivity ratio calculations are given in tables 3.5 and 3.6.

Analyses showed that on average the firms in the Federal Republic of Germany achieved approximately 20 per cent more output than their United Kingdom counterparts. The best British company had an output level similar to the least effective company in the Federal Republic of Germany. Four separate elements are considered to contribute equally to this difference: *(a)* management and non-productive overheads; *(b)* balance of work between machinery and fitting; *(c)* general organisation of workload; *(d)* technology, equipment and attitude to investment.

(a) *Management and non-productive overheads*

The firms in the Federal Republic of Germany in general operated with fewer managers, administrative staff and other non-productive workers in relation to the size of the business (see table 3.7).

Table 3.6. Performance indices in the companies in the United Kingdom

	Company E	Company F	Company G	Company H
Turnover (£'000)	277	600	866	1 116
Materials plus subcontracted work (£'000)	44	85	181	198
Wages plus salaries (£'000)	133	255	415	605
Overheads (£'000)	52	120	80	135
Depreciation (£'000)	5	24	26	58
Profit (£'000)	43	116	164	120
Average hourly rate of skilled worker (£)	3	3	3.30	3.10
Additional per cent on total costs including 6 per cent for overtime premium	35	35	35	35
Total hourly costs (£)	4.05	4.05	4.45	4.19
(DM)	17.00	17.00	18.70	17.60
Ratio:				
$\dfrac{\text{Added value}}{\text{Total employment cost}}$	1.36	1.55	1.46	1.29
Index:				
Performance ratio after adjusting for worker cost differences. Lowest company in whole study (not just mould sector) = 100	119	135	140	117

Source: See table 3.5.

Despite this fact, the managers had more financial and statistical information available to them. The top managers were deeply involved in the running of the firm on a day-to-day basis.

One reason why these firms require less management is the expanded role of their supervisors.

Table 3.7. Breakdown of total workers in mould-making companies

	Federal Republic of Germany			United Kingdom			
	A	B	C	E	F	G	H
Total "blue collar"	14	20	42	16	21.5	38	41
Office personnel	1	4	4	1	2.5	9	13
Design	1	3	5	1	3.0	1	5
Apprentices	2	—	16	1	3.0	6	11
Total	18	27	67	19	30.0	54	70

Source: See table 3.5.

(b) *Balance of work between machinery and fitting*

Employees in the firms in the Federal Republic of Germany can do more work on the machines than those in the United Kingdom. This is because less time is spent on fitting, which means that working methods are better developed in the Federal Republic of Germany.

(c) *General organisation of workload*

In the Federal Republic of Germany firms achieve up to 10 per cent more output from a team because of the way that individual members interact and communicate with each other under the general co-ordination of the supervisor. In the United Kingdom the tendency is for a manager to issue a series of instructions instead of deciding, co-ordinating and correcting mistakes. Many mistakes are only identified when assembly starts, which means a loss of production time.

In the Federal Republic of Germany managers do not receive a series of separate instructions from above. Rather, supervisors and their key staff discuss the job and divide it between themselves, remaining in very close communication with each other as the job proceeds so as to anticipate problems whenever possible.

(d) *Technology, equipment and attitude to investment*

In the Federal Republic of Germany there was evidence of greater investment in machine tools, electronic devices, etc. A skilled worker deals with a series of associated parts, and is expected to fit, drill, tap and screw the parts together. The greater selection of machines in relation to the number of workers makes it easier to shut down a particular machine for a time and allows the worker to move elsewhere to complete the sub-assembly. This results in more accurate machinery, gives workers a greater sense of involvement in the finished product and simplifies the shop-floor manager's responsibilities.

Some problems of productivity analysis

The problems and difficulties in productivity analysis fall into two main groups: those concerned with the techniques of productivity measurement, and those concerned with the organisation.

Technical productivity measurement problems

There is no single universal measure of productivity because various groups (such as materials suppliers, buyers, users, product sellers, etc.) have different goals and therefore use different sets of productivity measurements.

The most common problems which the designers of particular productivity measurement systems should take into consideration are:

—   how to combine different types of input into one acceptable denominator;

—   how to deal with qualitative changes in input or output over time;

—   how to keep input and output measurements independent of each other.

An example of incorrect measurement would be if hospital managers considered productivity to be bed-days used per patient-year; the correct measure should be the weighted number of patients treated, where the weighting represents the seriousness of the illness.

Some organisations focus all their attention on the productivity of one particular section. Another mistake, especially in public offices, is when managers confuse activities, output and results. For example, in training programmes an incorrect measure would be the number of people trained; the correct one would be the number of trainees who were placed in jobs or who improved their performance.

It should be remembered that some significant changes over time complicate measurement. Among these are:

— major changes in plant facilities, wage rates, materials costs, product prices, or even in accounting practices;

— purchase of more fabricated components;

— addition of more automated equipment;

— increase in machine speeds without additional labour;

— expansion of capacity through technological innovation;

— change in output which cannot be quantified by the old measure.

Another complication arises because production input-output relationships are not always linear; so it is essential that productivity in such cases be measured over a long period of time.

Confusion about indirect costs and avoidable costs is another frequent mistake. Indirect input or costs (such as planning and control, product development, training, supervision, maintenance personnel) must never be ignored.

At the same time such avoidable costs as ill-designed accounting procedures, cost-allocation and overtime cannot be considered as input.

Significant errors may also be introduced when the analysts count unfinished products, or when the output has no bearing on the desired goals of the organisation, or when they measure output which does not result from the input. Analyses based on such errors are worthless.

Here are a few important characteristics of a sound productivity measurement system which would help to avoid the above-mentioned problems and mistakes:

— provide simple and unambiguous signals to improve performance (productivity, profit, quality);

— break down change in profit to reflect the contribution from each resource used in production (labour, capital, materials, energy);

— break down the contribution to profit change from each resource into productivity terms and a price recovery term. This will isolate the effect of disparate change in product vis-à-vis resource price;

- use the price recovery term to evaluate whether productivity loss or gain for a given resource is appropriate;
- transform the above measures of change in profit into corresponding measures of change in profitability, change in cost per unit of output, and change in performance index numbers (e.g. productivity index numbers);
- provide consistent signals for profit improvement regardless of the units in which the measure is expressed.

Implementing a measurement technique

The implementation of a productivity measurement technique involves several steps:

- making the decision to measure productivity;
- defining the target organisational system and the required level for intervention;
- defining the measurement time period;
- selecting the measurement technique;
- using the measurement technique.

To choose a specific measurement technique a number of variables should be considered:

- *purpose and audience*: what the measure is supposed to do and who will use it;
- *commitment to measurement*: the extent to which an organisation sees productivity measurement as a critical part of its effort to remain competitive;
- *awareness/understanding of management*: the extent of management understanding/awareness of productivity measurement systems;
- *centralisation/decentralisation*: the extent to which measurement is a decentralised/centralised function;
- *maturity of control system*: the extent to which measurement control systems are part of the organisational culture;
- *management style*: measurement techniques should complement and extend the existing management style;
- *output variability*: the extent to which the physical characteristics of the output change over time;
- *type of technology*: ranges in manufacturing technology where input and output may vary considerably over time;
- *process cycle time*: length of time for one unit of output to be produced;
- *controllability*: the extent to which management can "manage" or control input levels;

— *resources as a percentage of costs*: amount of costs associated with each of the component resources as a proportion of total cost. In selecting a method of productivity measurement, feasibility and costs are major concerns.

Organisational productivity measurement problems

As is the case with any organisational change, the introduction of a productivity measurement system will encounter resistance. There are a number of potential sources of concern about and sometimes even fear of productivity measurement both for managers and for workers. These include:

Potential misunderstanding and misuse of measurement: The fear of many workers that managers who are not intimately involved with the work process will exaggerate or otherwise misinterpret the changes or trends in measurement data.

Exposure of inadequate performance: Since many workers (especially white-collar) are not sure where they stand with their boss, a measurement system that would clarify the situation may pose a threat.

Additional time and reporting demands: A frequently stated fear of productivity measurement is that it will increase the paperwork and take too much time.

Reduction in staff: There are obvious relationships between productivity and the staffing level, since one of the important benefits of productivity measurement is to maintain more rational staffing. Therefore, fears will be raised that the productivity data will be used as an excuse to cut staff. In this case there will be little co-operation from workers in productivity measurement.

Reduction of autonomy: Individual staff members differ in terms of their desire for autonomy. Introduction of tighter management controls as a result of productivity measurement may be seen as a constraint.

Many of the perceived threats described above are the result of problems in the organisation that need to be understood and resolved. Implementing a productivity measurement system is an organisational change. Changes meet resistance that seeks to maintain the status quo. Therefore, managing the introduction of a productivity measurement process involves managing resistance to change.

A useful technique for helping managers understand the change process is force-field analysis.[8] This is a process of analysing the forces for and against a change in behaviour by an individual or a group. The forces are illustrated in figure 3.11.

The analysis is a four-step process:

Step 1: Define the desired outcome of a productivity measurement system.

Step 2: Identify the "pressure" items working for and against achieving the desired outcome. For example, figure 3.11 shows a force-field analysis from the point of view of a division manager and from the viewpoint of a department manager or a worker. It is easy to see that there is a wide

57

Figure 3.11. A model of force-field analysis

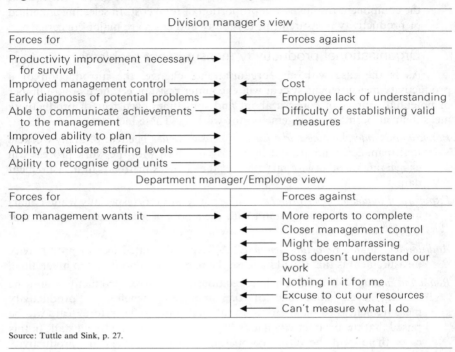

Division manager's view	
Forces for	Forces against
Productivity improvement necessary ⟶ for survival	
Improved management control ⟶	◀— Cost
Early diagnosis of potential problems ⟶	◀— Employee lack of understanding
Able to communicate achievements ⟶ to the management	◀— Difficulty of establishing valid measures
Improved ability to plan ⟶	
Ability to validate staffing levels ⟶	
Ability to recognise good units ⟶	
Department manager/Employee view	
Forces for	Forces against
Top management wants it ⟶	◀— More reports to complete
	◀— Closer management control
	◀— Might be embarrassing
	◀— Boss doesn't understand our work
	◀— Nothing in it for me
	◀— Excuse to cut our resources
	◀— Can't measure what I do

Source: Tuttle and Sink, p. 27.

gap between the perceptions of the division manager and the lower level managers and workers. While the measurement system appears positive to the former, it will be strongly resisted by the latter.

Step 3: Select the most important items from the forces for and against.

Step 4: Develop a plan for increasing the forces for and decreasing the forces against.

The success of the productivity measurement will depend to a great degree on how effectively the division manager can decrease the forces against the change and increase the forces for it.

Decreasing the forces against measurement

The strategy for intervention should concentrate first of all on minimising the opposing forces since any increase in the driving-force would provoke strong counter pressures from negative forces. One of the effective methods of decreasing negative forces is to involve managers and workers in designing and implementing the measurement process. This can build a sense of ownership and help change perceptions. This process should be coupled with a participatory planning process, shared information and accountability.

Increasing the forces for measurement

One implementation strategy to increase positive forces is to share previously undisclosed business information. This will create a sense of trust, educate subordinates to economic realities, and suggest that survival of the organisation and job security depends on maintaining effectiveness.

Another strategy is to develop and communicate a collective vision of the organisation's objectives and values. A shared organisational philosophy plays an important role in directing the diverse values of members towards a common purpose. One such approach is a strategic productivity planning process that involves organisation members at all levels in defining future organisation goals. A logical part of this process is the development of a measurement system.

Positive forces can be developed through top management leadership. By means of their behaviour, top managers should communicate that productivity is important and explain why. They should require lower-level managers to prepare productivity measurement plans, which would make them responsible for this process.

When a sound productivity measurement system is built into an organisation as an integral part of the whole management system, productivity improvement efforts should have a very positive effect on the organisation's performance.

---

[1] Kathleen Newland: *Productivity: The new economic context*, Worldwatch Paper 49 (Washington, DC, Worldwatch Institute, 1982), pp. 1-47.

[2] Jerome A. Mark: *Public sector productivity measurement: The US federal experience*, Paper submitted to the EANPC Meetings, Reykjavic, Iceland, September 1985 (EANPC, Brussels).

[3] Kazukiyo Kurosawa: "Structural approach to the concept and measurement of productivity (2)", in *Keizai Shushi (Economic Journal of Nihon University)*, Vol. 50, No. 2, 1980, pp. 96-135.

[4] Alan Lawlor: *Productivity improvement manual* (Aldershot, United Kingdom, Gower, 1985), Ch. 4.

[5] Bela Gold. Reprinted with permission from "A framework for productivity analysis", Ch. 2 in Samuel Eilon et al.: *Applied productivity analysis for industry* (Oxford, Pergamon Press, Copyright 1976), pp. 22-23.

[6] Elena Avedillo-Cruz: *A manual on quick productivity appraisal (QPA)* (Manila, Development Academy of the Philippines, 1984).

[7] NEDO: *Toolmaking. A comparison of UK and West German companies* (London, National Economic Development Office, 1981).

[8] Thomas C. Tuttle and D. Scott Sink. Reprinted with permission from "Taking the threat out of productivity measurement", in *National Productivity Review* (New York, Copyright Executive Enterprises Publications) Vol. 4, No. 1, p. 27.

PART II

IMPROVING PRODUCTIVITY

MANAGING ORGANISATION EFFECTIVENESS 4

4.1 General considerations

Productivity improvement in an enterprise is a function and a result of management efficiency, synonymous with good management. It is a prime management objective and responsibility to increase productivity and maintain its growth. In fact, creating the conditions for higher performance is the essence of productivity management.

At the same time, productivity improvement is a process of change. To improve productivity it is therefore necessary to manage change; this means motivating, inducing and generating change. It is important to plan and co-ordinate the scale and speed of change in all major organisational elements, including people and manpower structure, attitudes and values, skills and education, technology and equipment, products and markets. These changes develop positive attitudes and an organisational culture which will be favourable towards productivity improvement as well as technological change.

There are situations where change has to be brought about in spite of resistance or reluctance. Programme managers should not hesitate to order change in such cases, using their executive authority. Such use of authority as a calculated risk is desirable even in the most democratic management styles and organisational cultures; the manager must of course be ready to face the consequences. We are far from recommending either a democratic or an autocratic style, because neither exists in its pure form. In reality, different management styles simply represent points on a continuum. Any particular style depends upon many specific circumstances, such as the character of the technology, the skill level of the workers, management education and training, economy of scale, the type of industry and the structure of the society.

A method of organising production which completely rejected human values in favour of organisational ones would not be effective: neither would the reverse. It is unrealistic to expect organisational objectives to be perfectly compatible with human values. A certain level of contradiction is normal and it is the task of management to strike the best balance between them in particular circumstances, for a specific task, and to change the balance as the need arises.

A systems approach to productivity management is based on two fundamental concepts: focus on output (the results of the system); and the integration of all the subsystems of the organisation into a whole. Introducing these two concepts into management practice helps to replace managers' orientation towards input or towards process by orientation towards results. Managers oriented towards input or process think mostly about documents, data, rules and instructions, but results-oriented managers are more concerned with adding new value to resources and achieving better final results. They are more flexible and are more ready for organisational changes which improve output. The ways in which they communicate with people and reward them are based on results and not procedures or directives. They encourage innovation and initiative in their subordinates.

Results-orientation is more appropriate for creating and running a productivity management system.

In a productivity improvement process there is a significant need to gain full human commitment to the changes. That is why managers of good productivity programmes use two main inter-related and mutually supportive groups of activities: motivational and technical.

Motivational activities create and sustain people's desire to improve; they educate and encourage people to find and use better ways of producing goods and services. Technical activities provide the analytical, behavioural, organisational and technical tools that people need when they are searching for and implementing solutions. A good productivity programme manager keeps these two groups of activities balanced and in constant use.

However, managers are often preoccupied with designing new products, buying new technology, running expensive marketing campaigns, etc. Most managers do not work at improving the performance of the human resource. There seems to be a fundamental preoccupation with the technical fix as the solution to all ills without the realisation that it is the way the technical fix is applied which determines the success or failure of a particular action.

Though everyone recognises that there are real gains to be made from more effective management of human resources, few organisations actually concentrate on this. Indeed, it is much more difficult to deal with people than with a simple process such as buying a new piece of plant. Improving human resources requires an ongoing commitment.

The most important strategy for productivity improvement is based on the fact that human productivity, both positive and negative, is determined by the attitudes of all those who work in the enterprise. Thus, to improve labour performance it is necessary to change attitudes. That is the theory — but the practice is much more difficult. The human resource, unlike other resources, has a will of its own; a will based on individual and cultural values, historical prejudice and perception of roles. In fact, a whole set of behavioural norms determines the individual's response.

In a management-subordinate relationship this is not so much based on what the manager actually does but on the subordinate's perception — what he *thinks* the manager is doing, which is conditioned by his experience. Managers themselves have natural in-built barriers to the major steps involved in setting up the performance improvement process. The necessary measurement and control are in direct conflict with the traditional needs, styles and attitudes of people in organisations. These barriers need to be overcome before the process of change can even begin.

All these considerations, especially technical fix and human behaviour and attitudes, call for a sound long-term productivity improvement strategy.

Productivity improvement strategy

A sound productivity improvement strategy calls for a systems approach to productivity improvement which recognises the inter-relationships between the elements of the system and their environment. It defines the performance of the system and maintains equilibrium while effecting change.

Guide-lines for a good strategic approach were given by Stephen Moss as follows: [1]

Translate competitive requirements into specific goals for operations in the light of the present and potential operating strengths and weaknesses of the company and its competitors.

Review and rethink the entire operating system from product design through service after sale. Consider the full range of inputs, and do not be constrained by conventional wisdom, always keep in mind the interdependencies within the system.

Assume ongoing change is both inevitable and desirable. New technologies become available, market requirements and resources change, and competitors act and react. Therefore, the system must be innovative and flexible so it can improve and adapt continually.

Thus, productivity strategy is the pattern of decisions in the enterprise that determine its objectives, procedures and principal policies and plans for achieving long-term productivity improvement goals. A good productivity improvement strategy should, as a minimum:

—   develop a clear and easily communicated definition of the productivity improvement concept;

—   explain why organisational improvement is important;

—   evaluate current operating status and the reasons for the current status;

—   develop models of excellence;

—   develop improvement policies and plans.

Organisations with clear productivity concepts should identify clear goals and objectives.

The objective of productivity improvement should always be expressed in terms of organisational "improvement" in recognition of the past and current success of the divisions and subsidiaries within an organisation. Some of the objectives could be broad; for example, to improve the organisation's productivity by 8 per cent in two years, with detailed objectives for individual units in the organisation.

The overall goals and objectives should be supplemented by detailed action plans on how to improve productivity. In this connection it is useful to set the objectives for identifiable smaller groups so that performance can be assessed.

A productivity improvement plan is most effective if it is integrated into the organisation's strategy planning. It should assign priorities and must be written in order to ensure that it is on the record for follow up.

Below are some examples of questions which can indicate the state of this planning and which draw attention to potential areas of productivity improvement:

- Does the enterprise have written productivity objectives, goals and a productivity plan which covers the whole organisation?
- Are the objectives set for small, identifiable groups so that their performance can be assessed?
- Does the plan include the methods by which productivity improvement objectives can be reached?
- Are target dates set for the achievement of objectives?
- Are the objectives and actions set against labour costs and other costs?

Normally, productivity improvement plans should involve such management responsibilities as:

— promoting creativity and innovation, creating an environment which encourages new ideas;
— introducing a suggestion scheme and inviting suggestions on specific problems;
— setting up a permanent or temporary task force or study groups where necessary for multi-disciplinary study of problems;
— identifying research and development activities.

Another key aspect of productivity improvement plans covering an entire company is their integration into the long-term strategy and planning of the organisation as a whole. Managers should fully understand that concentrated efforts to improve productivity may lead to a chain of reactions among many of the operating and output variables. For example, if management intensifies efforts to control rising costs in one specific area of operations, it may hurt other cost areas badly.

Further, labour-saving innovations do result in cost reduction, but this may be offset by rising labour costs in the form of rewards for productivity gains. Another example of a chain reaction concerns reductions in costs. The dissemination of innovations bringing about savings in materials causes demand to fall, and falling demand results in falling prices.

To summarise briefly, a productivity improvement strategy should include:

— setting objectives, planning, co-ordinating and using industrial engineeering techniques;
— getting staff involvement and commitment to productivity improvement;
— developing new skills among the staff and providing opportunities to use the skills;
— providing proper leadership and rewards;
— starting long-term productivity improvement programmes.

Obviously, it is necessary to make sure that the financial and social benefits of the productivity improvement strategy selected are greater than the implementation costs, in the long term.

The basic structure of productivity improvement

Alan Lawlor suggests four general stages of any productivity improvement process.[2]

(a) Recognition: We have to recognise the need for change and improvement.

(b) Decision: After convincing ourselves that we should improve, a decision must be made to act.

(c) Permission: There must be opportunities to implement decisions.

(d) Action: Actually implementing plans for productivity improvement, which should be the ultimate objective.

These general stages can be broken down and rewritten into the practical steps normally used in a successful productivity improvement process. They are:

Step 1: Identify and put into order of priority the objectives of the enterprise.

Agree on three or more most important goals to be achieved through productivity efforts. Decide on priorities.

Step 2: Identify criteria for output within organisational limitations.

Quantify each of the goals. Study all limitations with regard to capital, personnel, technology, or market, etc.

Step 3: Prepare an action plan.

Work out details of action items. Design organisational changes. Make assignments to individuals. Finalise detailed activity lists showing implementation procedures.

Step 4: Eliminate known barriers to productivity.

Correct visible defects in the operations such as:
— capacity bottle-necks;
— wasteful repetitive work-elements and cost expenditure.

67

Productivity management

Step 5: Develop productivity measurement methods and systems.

Choose productivity measures for the set of goals.
Use them to calculate the base-period productivity indices.
Use them for comparisons in the future.

Step 6: Execute action plan.

Introduce changes which promise a substantial increase in productivity in the existing projects.
Focus attention on priority action items with quick potential results.
Concentrate on short, visible, urgent, and easily achieveable activities and goals (the level of effort should be in proportion to anticipated returns).
Start step-by-step periodic measurement and reporting.

Step 7: Motivate workers and managers to achieve higher productivity.

Train workers in identifying constraints and in problem-solving.
Reduce fear of change through planning, advance training and education.
Give appropriate recognition to workers and supervisors for the best group results.
Keep full workload for workers during the day.
Encourage workers' participation in the productivity drive (productivity and quality circles, consultative committees, etc.).

Step 8: Maintain the momentum of productivity efforts.

Never allow relaxation after completing a project.
Be ready to start new productivity projects one after the other.

Step 9: Keep monitoring the organisational climate.

Provide for mutual trust between workers and their supervisors.
Maintain high quality of measurement procedures.
Generate regular reports on costs and quality of production.
Provide continued interest and support to operating managers and staff specialists in productivity efforts.

> Never attempt to accomplish several
> major productivity projects
> simultaneously.
> Do not ignore the perpetual need for
> training of workers and supervisors.

These steps are to be considered only as a kind of check-list, which could and should be expanded or reduced depending upon specific tasks and circumstances.

All productivity programmes operate in organisations, and to run them a productivity programme manager must be able to suggest processes that managers and workers can use to identify problems, to work out and implement solutions. The in-enterprise productivity processes include suggestion systems, quality circles, task forces, action teams, productivity committees and steering committees. These should all be fully understood and used by the productivity programme manager.

Major management responsibilities

The main management responsibilities in a productivity drive are to identify the objectives, to set up a productivity improvement programme and to establish a productivity measurement system.

(a) Identifying the objectives

To start any productivity improvement programme, management has to identify the area where improvement is necessary and achieveable, and also identify the specific elements of productivity that are critical to the enterprise's operation — quantity, quality, customer satisfaction, or other elements.

(b) Setting up a productivity improvement programme

The structure of the organisation must be carefully examined in order to identify the changes to be aimed at by the productivity improvement programme. In spite of the differences in enterprise goals and approaches, a general check-list for establishing a productivity improvement programme can be suggested:

1. Top management has a key role in determining the need for a programme and initiating it, in the development and adoption of a productivity improvement policy.

2. A team which includes all parties concerned has to be formed. Outside consultants may be called in.

3. Depending on the size of the enterprise, a small unit can be established to carry on a productivity programme. A special co-ordinator can be named from functional or top management staff.

4. Educating management and supervisors in productivity improvement is crucial. The key people involved in implementing the programme will need training sessions covering the concept of productivity, how to measure it, and the tools and techniques for improving it.

5. Personnel at all levels should be involved through group meetings and informal discussions at the plant, departmental or office level. Joint labour-management committees can be established. Continuous communication through existing information channels is essential.

6. The programme should provide for periodic review and evaluation of results. This requires the establishment of measures and goals for each organisational unit. Immediate visible goals can be set, such as improving quality, reducing scrap, saving energy, increasing output, increasing safety, reducing tardiness, turnover and absenteeism, and giving rewards. Periodic reports must be provided to identify units with below-standard performance so as to serve as a basis for rewarding improved achievement.

7. It is vital to raise the awareness level within the organisation of all the factors that will influence productivity and of the system for improving it.

(c) Establishing a productivity measurement system

One of the important steps in productivity improvement is establishing a productivity measurement system within the enterprise. This in itself brings some improvement in performance by making people more aware of the meaning of productivity. The following advice could be useful in setting up the measurement system:

● Determine the elements of the enterprise that most need to be monitored.

● Determine the types of measure to be used.

● Select preferred concepts and units of measurement for the output and input of the company as a whole, and for the critical sub-activities.

● Ascertain the availability of data and make necessary compromises.

● Select a pilot activity, section or group within the organisation, and test the measurement system to obtain periodic feedback on the results.

● Assess the system's value, make any modifications and conduct a new pilot activity if the modifications completely change the original system design.

A measurement system must consider cost effectiveness, the limitations of productivity measurement and whether total factor measurement is necessary; in other words, it must determine the range and terms of the measurement system tasks. It must be easy to use and serve to identify the reasons for the organisational changes.

These general considerations on productivity management help us to identify the so-called organisational meta-structure of a productivity improvement process. Every given method of productivity improvement covers:

— organisational forms of productivity improvement;

— productivity improvement areas;

— productivity improvement techniques.

The rest of this chapter is devoted to a consideration of the forms, areas and techniques of these three most important structural elements of the productivity improvement process.

4.2 Productivity Improvement Programmes (PIP): Concept and key elements

Definition

Since improving productivity has become a major objective of many organisations, an increased number of them all over the world have already started or are initiating productivity improvement programmes. The programmes have many different dimensions, scales, targets and even names. Some of them are called "planning for improved performance", or "performance improvement planning", others are called "performance improvement programming", etc.

Based on practical experience in many countries and organisations, these programmes represent a consulting and training methodology, or a planned systematic approach to introducing positive changes. Abramson and Halset give the following definition: [3]

Performance improvement planning is a total system effort, involving top management, with the goals of increasing general organisation effectiveness and health and helping in the accomplishment of specific organisation objectives and targets by means of planned interventions in the organisation's structure and processes using the behavioural and management sciences and any other relevant knowledge.

Within the framework of a PIP approach, the organisation and its management team are encouraged to engage in self-identification of objectives and problems and in designing action plans and programmes for improvement.

Programme objectives

The most general objective of productivity improvement programmes is to provide a link between the establishment of an effective productivity measurement system and the human task of improving organisational performance by means of changes in all or several elements of the organisation — the people, structure, culture and technology.

Some more specific objectives of the programme could be:
— to improve managerial, planning and problem-solving skills;
— to improve teamwork and human relations;
— to set up an effective productivity information system;
— to trigger a breakthrough to a higher level of organisational performance;
— to help revitalise the organisation and its climate.

Among the benefits of such an approach are the following:
— increased awareness of the factors affecting productivity among workers and management;
— the creation of a link between existing accounting procedures, productivity measurement and regular performance monitoring;
— the establishment of new competitive standards;

- gaining commitment to the need for continuing attention to productivity improvement;
- more extensive and conscious use by the participants of productivity improvement techniques.

When to use productivity improvement programmes

To use PIPs effectively, certain favourable conditions should exist. Among them are the following: [4]

(a) *Pressure for change:* There must be significant pressure for change both internally within the organisation and also in its external environment.

(b) *Intervention at the top:* There must be managers or consultants at or near the top who are committed and who provide leadership in programme design and implementation.

(c) *Diagnosis and participation:* There must be active participation at several management levels in diagnosis of problem areas and improvement planning.

(d) *Invention of new solutions:* The invention and development of new ideas, methods and solutions to problems must be encouraged.

(e) *Experimentation with new solutions:* There must be willingness and permission from the top to take risks and experiment with new solutions in a search for results.

(f) *Reinforcement from positive results:* There must be monitoring, review and positive reinforcement over a long-term period in order to make short-term improvements permanent, and to ensure the spread of the change effort.

With these points in mind, it is necessary, both for the top manager and for any consultants involved, to be cautious and not to rush into large-scale change until they are sure that there are enough positive factors to give a reasonable chance of success, that the time is right and that conditions are generally favourable.

The main elements of productivity improvement programmes

Briefly, the main elements of a successful productivity improvement programme are the following:

- Top management must be wholly committed to the programme.
- An effective organisational arrangement headed by someone responsible to top management for the programme is essential.
- Full awareness and understanding of the programme objectives must exist at all organisational levels. Good labour-management relations are vital.
- There should be free-flow communication between different structural elements of the organisation.
- Recognition of the key role played by workers is crucial and must be demonstrated through a sound productivity gains-sharing system.

- The programme should be linked with measurement processes that are practical and easily understood. Goals should be set on the basis of feasibility as well as desirability.

- The productivity improvement techniques (technical, behavioural and managerial) chosen for the programme have to fit the situation and needs.

- Monitoring, evaluation and feedback processes to identify results and barriers provide a basis for design improvements.

4.3 Organisational approaches to productivity improvement programmes

The discussion of programme concepts, objectives, basic elements and conditions in the previous section gives a lot of information on how to organise a productivity improvement programme. However, the most reliable knowledge is that which has already been tested and applied. That is why the best way to answer questions on how to organise a programme is to describe a few successfully applied examples. For this purpose we have chosen the following approaches and cases:

Approach 1: The ILO Organisation Development/Performance Improvement Planning (OD/PIP) approach.

Approach 2: The ALA Performance Improvement Programme approach.

Case 1: The Meralco Productivity Improvement Programme.

Case 2: Blue Circle Industries PLC.

Approach 1: The ILO OD/PIP approach

The ILO OD/PIP approach represents the collective experience of ILO management trainers and consultants, gained on field assignments for a number of ILO management development projects. It is described in detail by Robert Abramson and Walter Halset,[3] so we will just briefly outline it here.

The Organisation Development/Performance Improvement Planning approach is a cyclical process. The OD/PIP cycle normally has five components or phases:

1. Preliminary diagnosis.
2. Orientation to OD/PIP.
3. Organisation diagnosis and action planning.
4. Implementation.
5. Review and revision.

During the preliminary diagnosis phase management and consultants (whether internal or external) assess the health of the organisation and jointly explore possible approaches for improving organisational performance and results. A brief management audit or survey may form part of this phase.

The next phase is the orientation of top management to OD/PIP. This is intended to give top managers a chance to test the applicability of the approach, assuming that preliminary diagnosis has shown that OD/PIP holds promise of being helpful to the organisation. This testing takes place through a two- or three-day orientation programme.

This phase is also designed to give the parties involved a direct exposure to and a feel for the philosophy, methodology and possibilities of the OD/PIP process as well as an introduction to the performance improvement (planning) instrument and its various stages and steps. In an abbreviated fashion the participants actually go through the OD/PIP process of determining the objectives of the organisation, the problems and the action programmes for improvement.

The organisation diagnosis and action planning stage requires the running of as many one- or two-day management workshops as may be necessary. Workshop participants are managers of all levels. The duration of this phase may be anywhere from one or two weeks to several months, depending upon the organisation's commitments and work pressures.

These workshops have to ensure the identification of organisational objectives, performance indicators and problems, the factors associated with these problems and the impeding/impelling forces. They also help to develop strategies and action programmes for performance improvement and to make arrangements for their implementation.

Implementation of the action programme can actually begin, in part, during the preceding phase of diagnosis and action planning workshops especially if that phase is prolonged. During the implementation phase the performance improvement plan, and its objectives and action programmes, are translated into specific operational objectives and targets for organisational units and individuals.

During the last phase of review of results and revision of plans, the entire performance improvement plan and implementation effort are reviewed, including assessment of performance indicators and the rate of attainment of objectives and action programmes. This review of progress should take place at least twice yearly and preferably on a quarterly basis during the first year of the OD/PIP effort.

Data from these performance reviews are then used to revise or establish new objectives, performance indicators and action programmes. This ensures that the organisation will be sufficiently flexible to meet new demands.

Actually this phase becomes part of a second round of diagnosis and action planning, which was the third phase of the original process. The idea is to establish a continuous recycling process for performance improvement and organisational renewal, a process which ensures that the three key phases of diagnosis and action planning, implementation, and review and revision are repeated indefinitely.

The OD/PIP approach and methodology have been tried in a number of United Nations and ILO technical co-operation projects. They have been used most extensively in East Africa and Nigeria, but also in Ecuador, the Islamic Republic of Iran, Jordan, Somalia, Sri Lanka, the Syrian Arab Republic, Venezuela, Zambia and other developing countries. They have also been employed by international project teams to enhance their own performance effectiveness.

Experience has shown that the OD/PIP approach is applicable to any organisation, whether in the public or private sector. However, the specific OD/PIP model that is considered valid for use in any particular organisation should be carefully designed to take into account the requirements and special features of the local situation. The testimony of the vast majority of OD/PIP participants has been that this process is a very stimulating and rewarding experience.

Generally, the OD/PIP improved or facilitated: the building of more effective teams; increased commitment to the decisions and actions agreed upon; the measurement of enterprise performance; the definition and articulation of performance problems; the derivation of practical solutions; better qualitative and quantitative performance results; the introduction of positive changes; increased flexibility of organisation.

Approach 2: The ALA performance improvement programme [5]

Action Learning Associates (ALA), in the United Kingdom, has accumulated good experience in the design and practical application of productivity improvement programmes. The basic concept and philosophy of the ALA performance improvement programme (PIP) does not differ very much from the ILO OD/PIP just described. Therefore, we shall concentrate here only on the practical side of the ALA process.

The four main stages of the ALA approach and their instruments are presented below:

Stage	Productivity audits
1. Identify where you are now and how you compare with others.	Measure and analyse productivity. Make inter-firm comparisons.
2. Identify the main productivity problems.	Analyse audit results.
3. Decide where you want to be.	Identify action areas and agree on action plans.
4. Introduce action for improvement.	Implement programme through internal and external action learning groups.

Let us briefly consider this process.

Productivity audits are an important part of PIP measurement. They quantify the performance position, help to reveal problems and potential areas for intervention and increase awareness of the need for productivity information.

The following few conditions of audit are important:

— a quick appraisal of current performance is used;
— agreement must be reached on the information required and how it is to be obtained;
— the audit system must be simple and low-cost;

Productivity management

— it should increase productivity awareness and provide information for management quickly;

— it should highlight the areas for improvement.

After a routine system for measurement has been established it is important to ensure its proper maintenance. This means that:

— the agreed productivity information must be available on a routine basis and within an agreed time;

— it should reach the people who can use it to improve upon the current position.

The quality and general success of the productivity audit depend upon the degree of involvement and participation of those workers and managers in the audit who are concerned with productivity improvement. An existing accounting-type system should be integrated into the audit process, which should, in turn, be a natural part of day-to-day management. Inter-firm comparisons (IFC) (see the subsection on IFC in section 3.2) could be an important part of the audit process, used to evaluate the enterprise performance position compared with other companies and to spot the major problem areas or productivity improvement barriers. They are powerful stimulants to improving awareness and recognition of the need for productivity improvement.

The following are the main steps of productivity audits:

— gain commitment;

— complete and process the Basic Information Sheet (table 4.1);

— complete the Period Analysis Sheet (table 4.2) if IFC is to be a part of the audit, and return it to each company;

— interpret the results of analysis;

— maintain procedures;

— take part in external action learning meetings (see the subsection on action learning programmes in section 4.4).

After this primary audit a more detailed study of the productivity of the organisation should be made, using the following steps (secondary audits):

● Discuss the results of the primary audits with managers representing a cross-section of the organisation.

● Agree upon the area, function, department, process, and product which constitute the subsystem to be investigated. This investigation should be agreed with senior management. It is necessary to agree on the basic objectives of the subsystem, to identify its productive work and to define its maximum capacity; to agree upon the key factors which influence overall productivity and to collect information on the structure, attitudes, equipment and work layout in the subsystem.

As a result of these steps an agreement should be worked out on the action plan to improve productivity. This will form the basis of the in-plant action

Table 4.1.   Basic Information Sheet

Company Code No.

Item No.	Item definition	Period No. From: To:	%	Period No. From: To:	%	Period No. From: To:	%	One-quarter totals	%
1	Sales value — less VAT and credits		%		%		%		%
2	Materials and bought-out parts		%		%		%		%
3	Total earnings — item 1 less item 2		%		%		%		%
4	Total workers — adjust for part-timers		%		%		%		%
5	Total wages and salaries		%		%		%		%
6	Total purchased services		%		%		%		%
7	Depreciation		%		%		%		%
8	Total cost — items 5 + 6 + 7		%		%		%		%
9	Average inventory		%		%		%		%
10	Net profit — item 3 less item 8		%		%		%		%

Note: Ensure all information is included for period reported and that it agrees with "definitions of information". Use form for three periods (i.e. three months — one-quarter). % columns are percentage of sales.

Source: A. Lawlor, 1985, p. 105.

learning and the inter-firm comparison programmes (see the subsections on in-plant action learning and inter-firm comparison in section 4.4).

Case 1: The Meralco productivity improvement programme [6]

The Meralco Foundation, Inc., a non-stock, non-profit corporation, was organised in order to design and implement a programme to create a broad-based customer ownership of the Manila Electric Company. Meralco's mission as a public utility company is to provide a reliable electricity supply at reasonable cost. In order to improve productivity, it launched a programme which has achieved worth-while results and which could easily be adapted for use by any type of business. We reproduce here an abridged description of the Meralco programme.

The corporate strategy. Meralco management believes that in the energy-producing field the future lies in the productive use of limited resources through effective management and decision-making at the lower organisational levels. Towards this end, participatory management was proposed as a way to

Table 4.2. Period Analysis Sheet (An example)

		MANUFACTURERS			
Company Code No.		From	To	Year	Period No. ....
Index No.	Productivity index	Your company	Company comparisons		
			Average	Lowest	Highest
1.	Total earnings productivity $\dfrac{\text{Item 3}}{\text{Item 8}}$	1.21	1.14	1.06	1.21
2.	Profit productivity $\dfrac{\text{Item 10}}{\text{Item 8}}$	0.12	0.07	0.03	0.12
3.	Profit to sales as % $\dfrac{\text{Item 10} \times 100}{\text{Item 1}}$	5.8	3.9	2.1	5.8
4.	Sales per worker $\dfrac{\text{Item 1}}{\text{Item 4}}$	£1 921	£1 437	£953	£1 921
5.	Total earnings per worker $\dfrac{\text{Item 3}}{\text{Item 4}}$	£1 073	£916	£799	£1 073
6.	Wages + salaries to sales as % $\dfrac{\text{Item 5} \times 100}{\text{Item 1}}$	31.6	37.5	31.6	43.4
7.	Purchased services to total earnings $\dfrac{\text{Item 6}}{\text{Item 3}}$	0.18	0.32	0.18	0.48
8.	Rate of stock turnover $\dfrac{\text{Item 1}}{\text{Item 9}}$	0.2	0.18	0.1	0.4

Note: Refers to items on Basic Information Sheet (table 4.1).
Source: A. Lawlor, 1985, p. 107.

promote decentralised decision-making. This emphasises that opportunities and rewards do exist for those who strive for maximum productivity. To motivate participation, well-defined tasks for key individuals and organisational units were instituted. The tasks were defined in both qualitative and quantitative terms.

The management programme. In preparing for the implementation of this corporate strategy, a reorganisation of the whole company was undertaken.

Related functions were aligned and balanced and a comprehensive job-evaluation study was implemented. Following this strategy, four major areas of activity were identified as complete programmes.

Programme No. 1: Corporate planning. The structure of the system and the activities involved were designed to allow the effective participation of managers at different levels in the planning and decision-making process. The annual planning cycle covers three phases. The first — the business or strategy planning phase — involves the president and the vice-president who head the corporate functional groups. Corporate decisions at this level are communicated to the department heads. Next, the heads of each department, together with section heads, carry out the second or departmental programming phase in line with the defined corporate tasks. Lastly, the divisions and sections work out their units' operational plans and the detailed budget for their operations in the next one or two years.

Programme No. 2: Management information system. Planning itself, and the effective implementation of plans, call for timely information. A programme to develop and enhance a formal management information system was instituted. This system was to provide managers with information for monitoring their corrective actions.

Programme No. 3: Productivity improvement. The efficient use of limited resources in carrying out these plans is of critical importance. It was in this light that Meralco embarked on further improving its productivity by launching the Meralco productivity improvement programme.

Programme No. 4: Management development. These programmes require a change of attitude on the part of managers, who have to be armed with new techniques and management skills if they are to perform effectively in the new environment. This concept also involves actual on-the-job participation by managers in the programmes mentioned. Therefore, each programme is complemented by formal training courses and workshops. This is the background of the Meralco productivity improvement programme.

The premises behind the programme. The key element of the successful Meralco productivity improvement programme is the support and concern of management, which implies careful and effective communication of the programme down to each organisational level. Given the key element, the following premises were defined as the basis of long-term success:

1. Top management must be seriously concerned with productivity as a key corporate area.

2. The productive use of human and other resources is fundamental to the success of any productivity programme.

3. Higher productivity can be attained through a conscious effort on the part of the whole organisation staff.

4. Top management support and concern must be demonstrated in a comprehensive, formal, systematic and organised productivity improvement programme.

5.   Top management is responsible for providing the structure and environment that will motivate every worker to aspire to higher productivity.

The objectives of the programme are as follows:

1.   To create a corporate climate for cost consciousness.
2.   To enhance the productive contribution of the company's human resources.
3.   To offset the pressure of rising costs and tariff regulations which are becoming more and more stringent.
4.   To enhance the efficient and effective use of resources.

The strategies of the programme. The Meralco productivity improvement programme uses the following strategies:

1.   Concentrate on the company's human resources. The productive use of non-human resources will also be attained through the improvement of labour productivity.
2.   Adopt a top-down approach in planning support for the programme. Communication starts from top management, moving down to the line managers, and, finally, to the rest of the staff.
3.   Use a behavioural approach to motivate line supervisors and managers to seek productivity improvement. This entails the following:
   (a)   positive communication, on a systematic basis, of top management commitment and support for the programme;
   (b)   the equipment of line and functional managers with various productivity improvement tools and techniques through training and development;
   (c)   the granting of freedom to line managers to choose specific productivity or cost containment programmes in order to instil a sense of achievement and fulfilment.

The phases of the programme. The Meralco productivity improvement programme is divided into three phases, namely:

—   programme support and organisation;
—   training and application;
—   decentralisation and recognition.

The initial phase is designed to set the stage and prepare the organisation for the launching of the programme. The importance of management and staff support is strongly emphasised at this stage.

The second phase is directed towards educating and training managers and supervisors in productivity concepts, tools, techniques and evaluation. The trainees participate as key figures in the implementation of productivity improvement and are encouraged to apply their acquired knowledge in establishing a productivity measurement system, setting productivity goals and developing productivity improvement or cost containment programmes in their areas of responsibility.

The last phase is aimed at sustaining the Meralco productivity improvement programme in its activities and objectives. Efforts centre on resolving problems and bottle-necks, strengthening action programmes, expanding and improving the quality of evaluation and communicating the results of the programme down the line. For further support, recognition in the form of rewards is granted to the deserving organisational units.

The organisation of the programme. A central monitoring body called the Corporate Productivity Steering Administration was formed to act as the behind-the-scenes policy-making body and overall guiding force during the implementation of the first and second stages of the programme. The committee had the company president himself as chairman and key officials as members. Still at the corporate level, a Corporate Productivity Administrator (CPA) was appointed to give full attention to the implementation of the programme throughout the company. The CPA's primary function is to manage and co-ordinate the day-to-day implementation of the various programme activities in accordance with the overall objectives and policies.

Departmental productivity councils were organised to plan and guide the implementation of the programme at the departmental level. Department productivity co-ordinators, trained to provide effective staff support in their respective departments, were likewise appointed.

Implementation. At the programme's formal initiation, a general meeting of all top and middle managers was convened where the president reiterated his full support of, and commitment to, the programme and appealed for a similar response from the entire management. Line managers, being immediately responsible for implementation, subsequently underwent a rigorous training programme consisting of a series of workshops. They studied motivation, effective supervision, systems approach to problem solving, industrial engineering tools and techniques, managerial economics, capital budgeting, economic analysis of cost, and productivity concepts and measures. Line managers were required to design their respective measurement systems and formulate their productivity improvement plans, applying the knowledge gained to actual work situations. The departments' initial activities centred on designing output measures that accurately reflected the product of their collective efforts both in quantity and quality.

All the departmental managers were urged to be economically conscious in allocating the company's limited productive resources during the annual planning of their operations. The target was for 4,900 workers or 92 per cent of the company's total workforce of 5,300 to be covered by the programme. After a year, 84 per cent of the target force had been provided with efficiency as well as effectiveness measures. To further strengthen the programme, methods and procedures were revitalised and the formal maintenance, planning, and selection process for a computer system development was established. More efforts were concentrated on refining methods of planning and scheduling work at operating levels, and on developing more precise methods for the determination of manpower requirements, the periodic assessment of functional productivity indicators and for specific productivity improvement plans. Emphasis was placed on maintaining the incentive awards system to intensify continuous improvement in productivity.

Case 2: Blue Circle Industries PLC [7]

Blue Circle Industries PLC is a large cement manufacturer operating on all five continents. In the United Kingdom it has 70 factories employing approximately 12,000 people. The company introduced a productivity improvement programme which was carefully planned and included a number of excellent innovations. However, it has been only partially successful, for reasons which will be discussed after the presentation of the programme.

In 1977/78 the company carried out studies to find the most appropriate ways of measuring true performance in order to introduce a *self-financing productivity scheme for its workers*. A number of alternative concepts were evaluated against critical factors which had to be satisfied. A wide range of criteria for operational, political and cost aspects were ranked to obtain a weighting for each scheme.

A value added scheme was chosen for in-depth analysis and evaluation. An integral part of the study was the establishment of a working party of senior managers to contribute to the design of the scheme in order to ensure management commitment and feasibility. The scheme covered two main areas:
— productivity payments for true increases in productivity — wealth gains;
— participation and worker involvement.

The main objectives were to:
— improve productivity;
— strengthen and encourage genuine staff involvement;
— improve communication;
— increase understanding of the business;
— stabilise industrial relations;
— create an environment for introducing change.

Productivity payments

The formula chosen to measure actual productivity performance was based on the value added concept and the total costs of running the business were reflected in this formula.

The formula was basically:

	Base month	Current month
Sales value	100	106.6
Less purchase of materials, fuel, power, services and fixed costs of running the company	66.5	67.3
= Value added	33.5	39.3

	Base month	Current month
Divided by:		
Wages, salaries, employment costs and benefits plus depreciation of fixed assets at replacement value	26.7	27.7
Gives productivity factor	1.25	1.42
% improvement		13.6
75% workers' share of improvement		10.2

In measuring business performance, the formula took into account the total costs of running the business. It produced a value added which was divided by the total resources of the business, the total resources being the plant, buildings and machines depreciated at replacement value, together with total labour costs.

By dividing the value added created by the total resources consumed in that period a productivity factor was arrived at for the current period. Productivity factors were calculated for each month of a 12-month base period.

The productivity factor for the appropriate base period was compared with the productivity factor in the period under review. Any increase in the productivity factor was applied to a payment formula, viz.:

$$\text{Average of all basic wages/salaries} \times \text{75\% of the \% improvement in the productivity factor} \times \frac{\text{No. of shifts/days worked}}{\text{No. of shifts/days required to be worked}} = \text{Productivity payment}$$

This system, then, directly benefited the workers. The company, of course, also benefited since the scheme was designed to protect profit margins. Payment was made for genuine productivity improvements and not for increased value added.

Participation and worker involvement

A national agreement was devised around the productivity payment formula. It was negotiated over 12 months with the unions concerned. This agreement included a structure for participation and staff involvement throughout the United Kingdom, covering more than 70 locations and 12,000 workers. Having achieved agreement with the national unions, managers had to communicate details of the scheme to the many factories in the United Kingdom. For this they devised an introductory package for workers, consisting of 16 mm colour films, slide/tape presentations, a management guide and a workers' handbook.

Teams of professionals introduced this to all the company plants and a visual aids package was given to every major unit. One hundred and nine individual professional presentations were given by the teams in the first 12 months of operation of the scheme.

Factory managers, having been involved in the first presentation, were then involved in conveying the message to every worker at their plant.

The national unions nominated participants, not representatives, to join with management participants in their local productivity groups. This was a major breakthrough — the first time that all trade unions, both blue- and white-collar, agreed to sit around the same table and discuss problems together as a group. Each productivity group consisted of a mixture of management and union nominees, who were trained to act as a group and as thinking, creative individuals, rather than as representatives of individual interest groups.

The productivity group

The size of the local productivity group was determined by the number of recognised trade unions in the factory. Each union nominated a participant to the local group. As each union basically represented a separate skill, the group then had up to seven participants with varying backgrounds. Management then nominated one participant for every union participant and used a vertical slice of the management hierarchy to ensure involvement at all levels. Disciplines were also taken into account.

The general manager of the factory was the chairman and counted as one of the management participants. No vote was taken. Consensus was the aim. The training courses had already covered the new "role of the participant" and "consensus seeking".

The functions of the local productivity groups were to:
— prepare, monitor and review the unit's productivity plans;
— consider the monthly productivity scheme information;
— encourage managers, supervisors and workers to develop productivity ideas together;
— make recommendations for possible improvements or cost savings;
— examine areas of the operation to identify opportunities to increase efficiency;
— investigate inefficient and wasteful practices to effect savings;
— provide information to workers at the unit on the operation of the scheme and productivity matters.

Attitudes and training

In devising the productivity agreement considerable thought was given to the various attitudes of workers, and judgements were made as to the expected reaction from different groups. These judgements were tabulated and used when devising the necessary training and education programme. Here is an example:

Question: What will management's reaction be to involving workers in local decision-making at the factories?

Answer: — Resistance — we are paid to manage — they have little to offer.
— It will reduce my status and authority.

— It will mean telling them more about the business, finance and production figures. We have never done that before — it's not on.

— They will know as much as I do.

Question: What will the union representatives' reaction be to becoming involved in local decision-making?

Answer: — Good — we will demand to see all the costs of the business.

— We will show them how to manage.

— We will demand full disclosure of all information on future plans and investment.

Many of the projected responses were in fact correct. The prior analysis enabled an approach to be developed which responded to these attitudes in a constructive way.

A substantial education/training programme was undertaken for 44 local groups. This consisted of two one-week residential courses for each productivity group, management and union participants together. The first such one-week workshops were entitled "How a business works" and were computer-based. At the conclusion of a workshop, participants were expected to be able to:

— explain what social role is fulfilled by business and how the individual contributes to that role;

— describe and discuss the various functions which make up an enterprise;

— explain how an enterprise fits into the local community and the economy as a whole;

— list the important areas of policy which a company must plan in order to provide for its workers, its shareholders and its customers in the future;

— read a company balance sheet and profit and loss account, identify salient features, and discuss the performance of the business;

— decide, given basic financial and economic information, on possible strategies to be adopted by an enterprise to meet its objectives.

A second one-week course was undertaken some two months later at which the same groups went through an interactive skills workshop. On completion of this participants should have:

— recognised the potential range of benefits of the scheme and fully discussed any concerns;

— examined the implications of their membership of the productivity group for their own managerial/representative role and started to resolve any conflicts;

— become more knowledgeable and practised in those skills which they require to play their part effectively in the productivity group, e.g. problem-solving skills, communication skills, consensus seeking, opportunity thinking.

During training several core modules were provided. They covered: role analysis; principles of communication; problem-solving techniques; opportunity thinking; management of meetings; inter-personal communication skills; and programme planning.

A unique feature of this training and education programme, which used closed-circuit colour television, trainee syndicates, etc., was that the trainer involved in conducting the workshops then became the counsellor for that productivity group once they were back in their factories. This was to help the members sustain the skills in the new role that they had learnt.

Disclosure of information

A further important feature of ensuring commitment to improved productivity by the local groups was to obtain a policy from the highest level on disclosure of information. This can be difficult in certain circumstances, particularly the disclosure of price-sensitive information. Nevertheless, a policy was agreed and a system was designed which was complementary to the productivity scheme's value added formula.

The system devised was Data Analysis by Ratio and Trend (DART). This system took the 14 most critical ratios which had been identified in running the business. These ratios were produced on a monthly basis for each unit, each area, and for the company as a whole. Each of the 14 ratios showed the actual performance for the month and a trend graph for the previous months, and compared them with the base periods. By scanning these ratios it was possible to identify very quickly the areas likely to improve the efficient running of the factory. In effect, the productivity groups, who had been trained to focus their attention and their skills on problem solving and creative thinking, were provided with an opportunity to become involved and to participate in improved plant effectiveness.

Management failings and pitfalls

The Blue Circle Industries productivity scheme was well planned and executed, but it failed to realise its full potential. It is interesting and instructive to consider the reasons why a good programme may not achieve the results expected, and it is for this reason that this case is presented.

Some of the main problem areas experienced in this major programme were due to managers' ingrained resistance to change. The general success of the programme would have been much greater if this had been taken fully into account at the planning and initiation stage.

Over the past two decades many new schemes which have been tried in industry have failed through lack of middle management support. Each individual scheme, often imposed from the top, is viewed with suspicion and generally expected to disappear within one to two years of introduction.

Productivity and workers' involvement often meet this fate and, as they are seen by management as a threat to status and because it is difficult to quantify the benefits, management resistance to change can be guaranteed. Although the Blue Circle Industries scheme was prepared for this resistance, the *time* taken to change attitudes and management style was underestimated. The average middle-aged British manager has been trained to expect and deal with conflict, not to deal with change. A change in these attitudes cannot be achieved in one or two years and may take ten years of sustained effort emanating from the top and reflected in all manner of policies, procedures and performance criteria.

Possibly the biggest mistakes made in introducing this productivity scheme were in underestimating the time required to gain the commitment of all managers, and the fact that the approach, having obtained Board approval, was to start at the factory level and work upwards through the organisation. Some two years into the scheme it was necessary to go back to the senior executives, who had lost touch with lower level managers, as a consequence of which the lower levels were losing impetus.

4.4 Major variations of productivity improvement programmes

In this chapter the concepts, key elements, organisational approaches, structures and full cycle of productivity improvement programmes have now been analysed.

In the next section we would like to introduce some examples of using certain parts or blocks of a programme as relatively autonomous methods for performance improvement when a specific enterprise problem has to be solved. Such methods include Action Learning, Productivity Improvement Circles, Performance Action Team Process, Productivity Campaigns, Business Clinics, and Quality Circles.

Since quality can also be considered as an important area of productivity improvement in itself, we prefer to consider Quality Circles in the section which deals with the quality of products and services (see subsection 6.3).

Action Learning Programmes (ALP) [8]

In conditions of rapid change it is more important for managers to learn how to learn than to acquire knowledge from the past. This can be done most effectively when managers work with other managers to solve real problems.

The main component of any action learning programme is the problem, which is the vehicle for development and change in the learning process. The problem must be a real one, having a blend of human and technical aspects. It should be open-ended and the answers should not be known in advance. There must also be ownership of the problem and commitment to solving it. The problem could be determined or selected by a manager, by the members of action learning groups or by the productivity audits team.

The roles in an action learning programme are as follows:

"Nominator": This is the person (manager or owner) who authorises and pays for the programme.

Client: This is the individual (or group) who actually owns the problem, knows and cares about it and has the authority to implement solutions.

Productivity management

In the early stages of a programme the senior client's role is to specify the problem and to help as required with clarification. The client can give overall direction but should not interfere. After solutions are suggested, the client decides and agrees with the group which of the proposed solutions to act on. The client's role moves from supportive encouragement to supportive direction. The client operates at this stage as a project manager, budgeting and measuring performances.

"Fellow": This is the individual, or participant, or group actually working on the programme. The groups need to be representative of all sections of the organisation which are or could be affected by the problem and its solution.

Group or set: The set is a forum in which the participants meet to learn with and from each other. All the group members report on their own projects and help the others by listening to and questioning their reports. Typically, the groups have four to six members — up to ten for in-plant programmes — and meet once every two weeks for half a day.

Once the actual position on a particular project has been agreed, the fellow defines what action is to be taken before the next meeting. With in-plant programmes the actual tasks are usually subdivided, with members working in small groups of two or three on particular aspects of the problem. These subgroups report back to the set in exactly the same manner as the fellow on the individual project. The action learning groups are concerned with *action* and therefore work in between meetings is essential.

Group adviser: The group adviser is a challenger of beliefs, a problem solver, a catalyst, an opportunity promoter, and a developer of skills. The adviser listens, questions, gives and receives critical feedback, suggests resources, and in the early stages of the programme acts as a kind of project manager. Some in-plant programmes are experimentally using two advisers in a group, one responsible for the traditional process role, and the other as a technical adviser, assisting the group in developing specific technical skills.

For in-plant programmes involving several groups it is useful to have an external adviser to help in the group process, in addition to the group advisers.

The core of any action learning programme consists of six stages and normally lasts six months. The stages are as follows:

Stage 1: Programme introduction: Form groups, choose projects, choose advisers. The length of this stage will depend on the introductory workshop and could range from a minimum of one day up to three weeks.

Stage 2: Investigation: Get information, develop solutions, choose and test. Three months.

Stage 3: Presentation of findings to clients: Fellows present their findings and recommendations formally backed by written project documentation. The length of this stage is usually less than a day.

Stage 4: Response of clients to recommendations and agreement on formal action plans for implementation, time-scales, budgets, with individuals/groups: This normally takes about one day and is done in plenary session. It should take place within two or three weeks of Stage 3.

Stage 5: Implementation: This stage normally lasts three months. Obviously, the time necessary to implement different solutions will be different for different projects.

Stage 6: Final review: This is an opportunity for all those who have been involved in the programme to meet and share their experience. This session normally lasts about half a day.

In-plant action learning

In-plant action learning, developed by G. Boulden,[8] focuses primarily on organisation development. It normally involves calling in an external consultant or adviser. The characteristics of this approach are as follows:

- It focuses on one organisation.

- It involves the total management team, with senior managers as clients, middle managers as advisers and the first line group as fellows. There could also be shop-floor groups but this has normally occurred after the first programme when the approach has already been adopted.

- It uses cross-functional groups working on common problems.

- It is concerned with solving specific, complex, cross-functional problems, particularly in the area of productivity.

- It has a strong nominator, usually the managing director, who has a strong vested interest in the success of the programme.

- There is an in-plant co-ordinator who monitors the programme and provides feedback to the organisers. This is usually the person who takes over the programme once it is established.

It is useful to start with a short two- or three-day introductory programme, mainly for first and middle line managers. The objectives of this programme are threefold:

1. Team building — as the fellows will be working together on common projects it is important that they have common ground to work from.

2. Introducing the programme. As the whole process of joint open-ended problem solving is new, participants need a little time to get used to the idea.

3. Ascertaining what the people directly concerned see as the major problems facing the organisation. It is important to get commitment from the people who will be working on the problems and to identify the problem owners.

An in-plant action learning programme follows the stages of the cycle below:

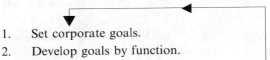

1. Set corporate goals.
2. Develop goals by function.
3. Analyse the problems.
4. Make recommendations for action.
5. Set up the action programme.

Stage 1: Set corporate goals

If corporate goals do not exist, the programme should start with their establishment. This can be done most effectively through a short (one- or two-day) workshop involving the board and senior management of the enterprise. An alternative approach could be developing corporate goals through a series of meetings between the consultant, the board and senior management.

The procedure begins with an agreed mission statement from which long-term goals and performance indicators are developed. The resulting package provides the basic guide-lines for management and lays down the goals. There are seven major steps in this process:

Step 1: Agreeing the mission statement.

Step 2: Developing corporate goals.

Step 3: Defining performance indicators.

Step 4: Agreeing on desired levels of performance.

Step 5: Identifying actual levels of performance.

Step 6: Quantifying the performance gap.

Step 7: Setting performance targets.

A detailed description of the content of these steps can be found in the manual by G. Boulden.[8]

Stage 2: Develop goals by function

The objective of this stage is to develop practical business goals by function for the achievement of the long-term objectives set out in the corporate strategy. The first step in this process is to set short-term objectives by function. The corporate goals in the total performance requirement for the enterprise are too general and at too high a level to be applied directly to its day-to-day management. For practical application it is necessary to allocate the goals to the various departments. For example, a corporate goal of a 50 per cent increase in staff training may be allocated across departments on a per capita basis so that the goal for the engineering department would be to train 20 extra people.

From the corporate goals we have to identify the most important short-term objectives as they relate to the separate business functions — those things which each function needs to achieve during the next one to three years.

It is then necessary to implement the same steps as when setting corporate goals, i.e. defining performance indicators, identifying actual and desired performance, quantifying the performance gap and setting targets.

Stage 3: Analyse the problems

The objectives of this stage are to identify the problems which stand in the way of the desired performance goals and to develop an understanding of them through analysis.

There are five steps in the process:

Step 1: Identification and ranking of problems.

Step 2: Description of problems.

Step 3: Examples.

Step 4: Classification.

Step 5: Analysis of potential for solution.

The work sheet below can be used for this stage.

Problem analysis			Date:				
Problems	Description	Examples	Category			Probability of success	Remarks
			Open		Closed		
			Int.	Ext.	Int.	Ext.	

Source: G. Boulden, 1985, p. 33.

Stage 4: Make recommendations for action

Follow the steps listed below in order to arrive at specific recommendations for solutions to the problems which have been identified.

Step 1: Choose the problems.

Step 2: Consider the recommendations for solutions.

Step 3: Decide what results you expect.

Step 4: Set target dates.

Step 5: Nominate the individual(s) responsible.

Step 6: Present the findings.

Stage 5: Set up the action programme

This is the start of the phase for solving the open-ended problems. Senior managers should by now have taken direct action on the closed-ended problems that they can solve and have agreed among themselves on which problems should be classed as open ended.

Such a discussion provides an extremely effective vehicle for the introduction of change. The objectives of this stage of the programme are:

1. To solve real business problems.
2. To improve the performance of the organisation.
3. To develop individuals and change attitudes.
4. To create an integrated organisation which can ensure its own survival in the future.
5. To enable creative talent to be used.

This stage normally runs over six months and has seven phases as follows:

Phase 1: Initiation

This phase normally involves a meeting or series of meetings with senior management. The aim is to discuss the measures to be taken on the recommendations produced by the management team. It will cover action to be taken on the closed-ended problems, together with time scales. Participants in the meetings should also identify the open-ended problems from the recommendations and decide who owns them. The owner becomes the client for that specific project. All senior managers should be involved as clients so it is important that the consultant should try to identify specific open problems prior to the meeting.

Another objective of these meetings is to ensure senior managers' understanding of, and commitment to, in-plant action learning at their own plants. Once agreement has been reached, each client should produce, with the help of the consultant, a project statement which reflects both the issues raised in the action recommendations and the client's own views of the problem. These statements should be agreed on and presented as projects to the management team in the next phase.

Phase 2: Programme launch (half a day)

This is the start of the main action learning phase and involves all participants. The managing director normally opens the session, talks about senior management's response to the action recommendations and outlines the proposed projects. The consultant then talks about how the programme will run, including target dates. Following this, the clients present their own particular projects, which are then displayed on flip chart paper around the main room. If the consultant is the adviser to all groups, it is only necessary to tell participants of this; if, however, there will be different advisers on individual projects their names should be shown against each project. Once this is over, the session breaks up and participants are given the opportunity to choose the project that they wish to work on. Once individuals have chosen the problem, an initial meeting takes place, usually involving the client at some stage. The output is an agreement on the date, time and venue for the first formal meeting of the project team.

Phase 3: Investigation and solutions

Groups normally meet once every two weeks at the start of the process, probably more often towards the end of the phase. The opportunity to do some effective work on real problems is welcomed by most people. The adviser should endeavour to attend all the meetings. The adviser's role at this stage is to help the group to function as a team and to use its resources to tackle the problem, not to try to solve it for them. The client will be involved in the early stages with any redefinition of the project and later in a questioning and supporting role.

Phase 4: Presentations

In a plenary session before all clients the groups present their recommendations for solving the particular problem they have been working on. Each client can question the group, as can other members of the audience. The groups should be encouraged to present a written report showing the data they have used to reach their findings and outlining their recommendations. This is handed over to the client, normally with copies to other senior managers.

Phase 5: Client feedback

This usually takes place informally between the client and the group. The basic objective is for the client to agree with the group on which solutions to implement and on who will do what. There may be some instant solutions which will be implemented directly by the client. Others will be more complex and will lend themselves to implementation by the group. Clients should give each group at least one meaningful solution to implement, as this is fundamental to gaining the commitment to and ownership of the proposed solutions.

Phase 6: Implementation (three months)

Here the groups actually implement specific solutions on behalf of the client. The client's role now changes from the more laissez-faire approach of the investigation and solution phases to the role of project manager. The client designates specific objectives, allocates resources, lays down time-scales, control points, etc. The group works directly for the client, still on a part-time basis.

Phase 7: Programme review (half a day)

This session is normally run by the participants themselves and involves all clients and the adviser(s). The primary objective is to evaluate the benefits of the programme; which objectives were achieved and which were not. It is an opportunity for all those involved to share their views about the experience. It is usually a very open session where success and failure can be discussed with equal candour and both are seen as the beginning of a new opportunity and commitment. to further performance improvement.

Action learning programmes are an effective problem-oriented method of productivity improvement. Their primary objective, however, is the long-term one of raising managerial competence and potential. Since action learning is based on the premise that the best results in management development can be obtained through learning by doing, the method places strong emphasis on learning how to learn, through identifying, analysing and solving organisation problems.

Productivity Improvement Circles (PIC)

The concept of Productivity Improvement Circles (PIC) was developed in 1980 by the National Productivity and Development Centre (NPDC) of the Philippines as an adaptation of the Japanese Quality Control Circles (QCC).[9] The term "Productivity Improvement Circles" was considered more appropriate than QCC since it covers the whole area of productivity improvement, not only quality.

Since 1980 the NPDC has successful installed PIC programmes in a number of organisations and has been joined by several associations in promoting the programmes within the different sectors. In the same year the Productivity Improvement Circles Association of the Philippines (PICAP) was organised to promote productivity through small group activities.

The results of a survey of PIC activity made by NPDC showed that in more than 50 per cent of cases it was the chief executive officers and company presidents who took the lead in initiating a circles programme; in about 30 per cent of cases the lead came from the quality control department and in 4 per cent of cases it came from the training groups. This means that many of the moves made for improvement still come from the highest levels of organisations.

In about 60 per cent of cases the methodology for PIC activities was acquired through consultancy and training. In installing the programme, 74 per cent of organisations used consultancy services. As to industrial areas of PIC application, almost 57 per cent of the pilot circles of the respondent companies were from manufacturing and maintenance areas, others were from services, finance and commerce.

The main themes of the PIC projects are varied. Human relations, quality improvement, work simplification, methods improvement, working conditions, and preventive maintenance account for about 95 per cent of project themes.

Out of 664 projects surveyed 94 per cent have been implemented and more than 60 per cent have been standardised.

What are productivity improvement circles?

We will now present the basic approach used by the NPDC in the Philippines, as described by Vasquez et al.[10]

A PIC is a small group of workers from the same workshop who are interested in self- and mutual development and in problem-solving activities. The aim is to enhance enterprise productivity. PICs have seven basic features:

● *Voluntary nature:* Every member has chosen to participate in PIC activities because they provide opportunities for further growth.

- *Small size:* A circle has somewhere between three and ten members.
- *Homogeneous membership:* Members come from the same workshop, perform similar or related functions, and confront similar or related problems.
- *Specific task and objectives:* PIC projects are usually within the control of the circle and in line with enterprise objectives.
- *Systematic and scientific approach:* In studying workshop problems the circles follow a step-by-step sequence and use scientific tools and techniques in the process.
- *Continuing activity:* Circle activities progress from one project or activity to another.
- *Universal application:* The concept can be applied in diverse sectors, organisations and their units (manufacturing, banking, transport, etc.).

PIC objectives

The general objectives of PICs are:
— to contribute to the productivity, stability and growth of the enterprise;
— to make the workshop a better place to work in;
— to develop human potential to the fullest.

The specific objectives of PICs are to:
— increase the competitiveness of the enterprise through product improvement and lower production costs;
— improve leadership, first line supervisors' skills and technical competence through mutual education and practice;
— give the workers opportunities for job enrichment and enlargement, more responsibility, a greater sense of independence and some participation in decision-making;
— develop in both management and workers productivity consciousness, discipline and skills through better communication.

Types of problem for PICs

The general problem areas appropriate for PICs to deal with are:
— reducing waste and costs;
— improving quality;
— improving methods;
— simplifying work;
— improving preventive maintenance;
— morale boosting (manpower turnover, discipline, complaints, etc.).

Benefits from PIC programmes

The benefits from PIC programmes are varied. However, generally, experience shows that they include:

- improved quality;
- increased output;
- reduced costs;
- improved communication, co-operation, worker morale;
- well-defined and clearly understood supervisory roles;
- improved skill of workers in solving problems;
- improved productivity and quality consciousness, improved attitude to job and workshop problems;
- higher morale of PIC members.

Organisational structure of PIC programmes

The PIC programme is an informal group process within a formal organisation. Figure 4.1 shows the recommended PIC structure within the organisation.

At the head of the PIC programme is the productivity improvement committee (PRODICOM) which acts as the policy-making body. The whole programme structure consists of top management, PRODICOM, middle management, circle leaders and members.

Figure 4.2 illustrates the interaction between the elements of the PIC structure.

The main roles in the PIC programme

Top managers: They play an important role in the PIC programe as initiators and decision-makers, by virtue of their membership in the PRODICOM.

The PRODICOM: The members of the PRODICOM are from top management with the president (or vice-president) as chairman; they act as *policy-makers* for the programmes. Particularly they must:

- define the ultimate goals of the PIC programme;
- formulate long-range plans for the programme (the number of circles to be organised, the time period, their distribution over the organisation, strategies and policies for promotion, evaluation, incentives and training, budget, qualifications and functions of the co-ordinator.

As *decision-makers*, the PRODICOM members have to:

- select the co-ordinator, who automatically becomes a committee member;
- allocate budget resources;
- act on project proposals within two weeks of the presentation.

As *evaluators*, the committee members assess the overall status of the PIC programme activities, including:

- training;

Figure 4.1. Organisational structure of the PIC within the company

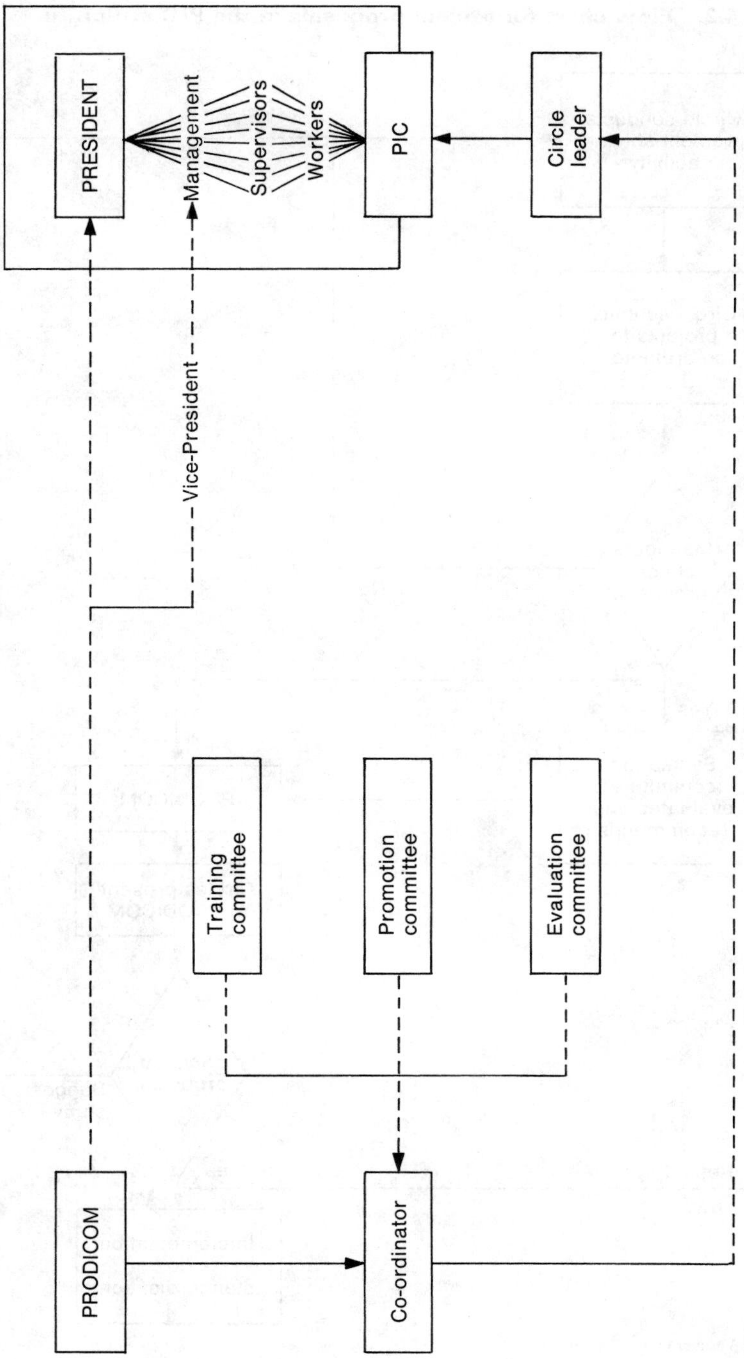

Source: Adapted from R. Vasquez et al., 1983, p. 18.

Figure 4.2. Flow chart for project proposals in the PIC structure

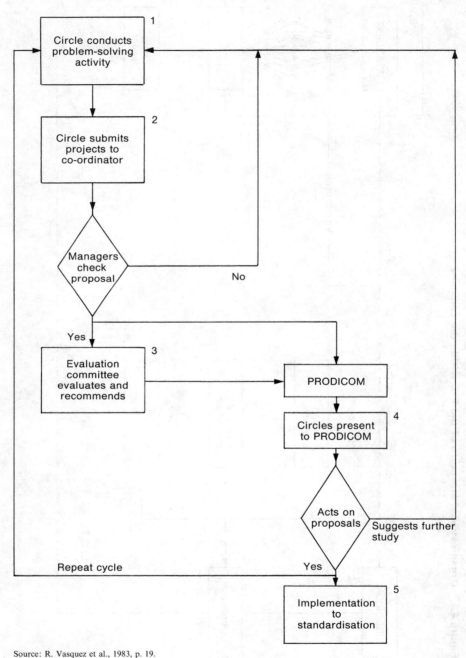

Source: R. Vasquez et al., 1983, p. 19.

— promotional activities;
— evaluation;
— incentive scheme.

Middle managers: They are asked to prepare a departmental work programme, decide on the number of circles within their department and suggest a strategy for implementation. They must also act within two weeks on projects presented to them, give necessary guidance and technical assistance to the circles under them, attend circle activities and make resources available to the circles.

Co-ordinators: They serve as the link between top management, PRODICOM, middle management, circle leaders and members. They have to:

— co-ordinate training courses, help in planning and check on participants and schedules;
— solicit support from top management, PRODICOM, middle management, circle leaders and members;
— assist circle leaders in conducting activities;
— make necessary facilities available for circle activities.

As trainers, the co-ordinators' role is to orient top and middle managers and raise their awareness of the benefits of PIC; plan, design and run training courses, and also teach circle leaders the concept, methodology, tools and techniques of PIC.

The co-ordinators also plan the PIC programmes, recommend people as members of different committees, supervise their work and evaluate their performance, and provide guidance and technical assistance to circles.

Programme committees: Three committees support the co-ordinator. They are the promotion, training and evaluation committees and their activities are self-explanatory.

The circle leader: Each circle is headed by a leader who is either a supervisor or an experienced worker. Leadership must be rotated so that each member has a chance to be both a group-member and a leader. The leader teaches the members the concepts, methodology and techniques used in problem solving, motivates them to study, analyses and recommends solutions, links up with the co-ordinator on matters of circle activities, and monitors circle meetings and projects. The leader also formulates a programme together with members.

Circle members: They are workers and supervisors and participate in all circle activities.

Basic PIC activities

Five major steps are involved in planning PIC activities:

— top management orientation;

— middle management workshop;

— training of circle leaders;

— the pilot stage;

— implementation of the programme throughout the company.

Figure 4.3 shows the flow of activities for the implementation of the PIC programme, the people and groups involved, and the output expected from these activities.

This chart should be used only as a guide-line for programme implementation, which will vary according to the type, size and objectives of the organisation and of the PIC.

A strong promotion programme is necessary in order to gain the support and recognition of every company worker and to guarantee the continuity of the programme. This promotion programme could be based on the circle programme's objectives and use activities such as meetings, group discussions, skill-competitions, training and other means of publicity.

PIC activities at the workshop level

At the workshop level the principal scheme of the flow of activities could be as shown in figure 4.4.

It is important to go through the following PIC steps at the shop-floor level:

— orientation for the rank and file;

— study meetings on tools and techniques;

— data gathering;

— problem-solving activities; identifying problems, putting them into priority order and analysing them; formulating solutions;

— project presentation;

— project implementation;

— evaluation;

— standardisation.

In summary, Productivity Improvement Circles can be effective for small groups of workers on condition that top management gives assistance and encouragement. The resulting co-operation in identifying and solving problems makes a valuable contribution to general productivity growth.

Performance Action Team process (PAT)

Performance Action Team process (PAT) is an effective variation on many team-building techniques aiming at productivity improvement. It is a

Figure 4.3. Flow of PIC activities

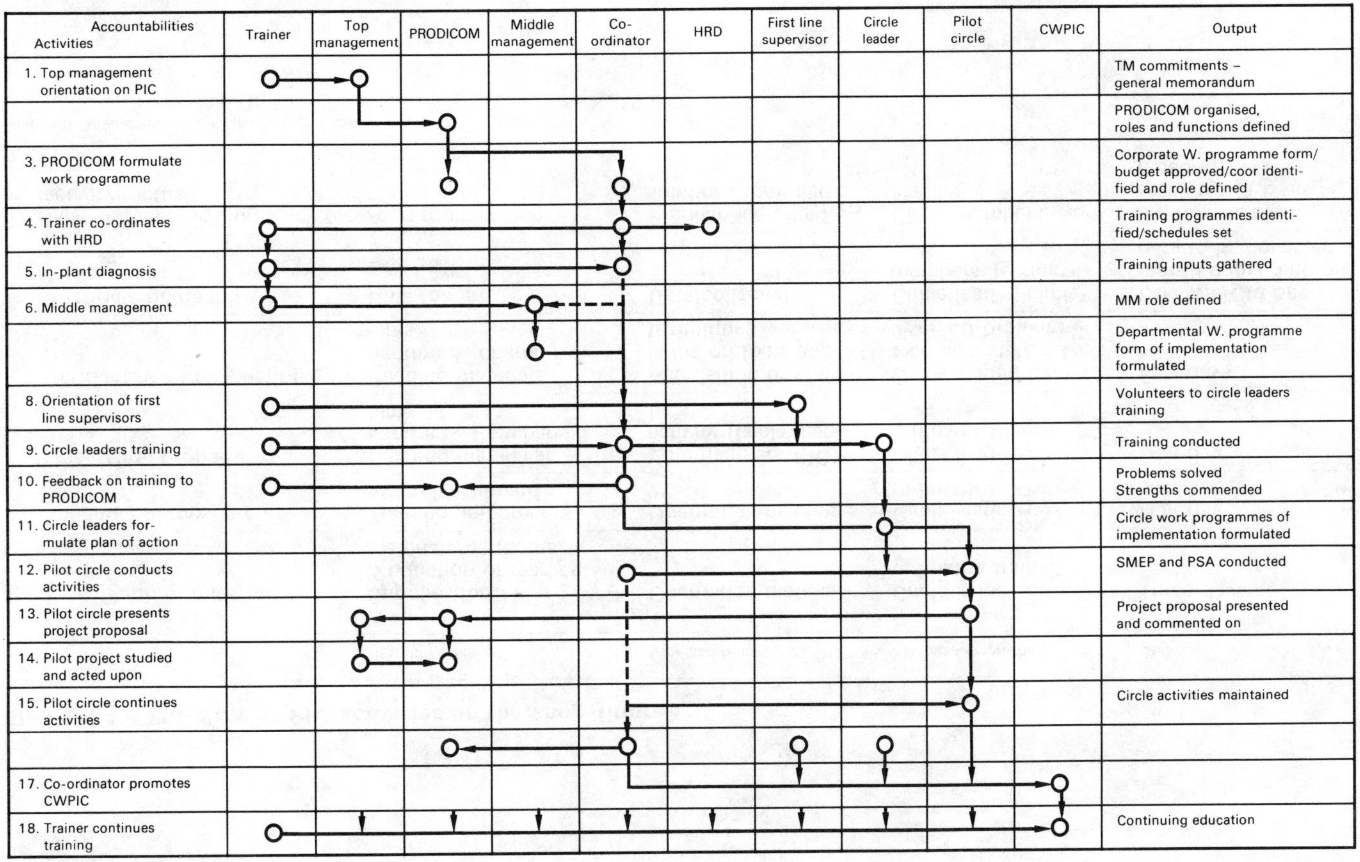

Accountabilities / Activities	Trainer	Top management	PRODICOM	Middle management	Co-ordinator	HRD	First line supervisor	Circle leader	Pilot circle	CWPIC	Output
1. Top management orientation on PIC											TM commitments – general memorandum
											PRODICOM organised, roles and functions defined
3. PRODICOM formulate work programme											Corporate W. programme form/budget approved/coordinator identified and role defined
4. Trainer co-ordinates with HRD											Training programmes identified/schedules set
5. In-plant diagnosis											Training inputs gathered
6. Middle management											MM role defined
											Departmental W. programme form of implementation formulated
8. Orientation of first line supervisors											Volunteers to circle leaders training
9. Circle leaders training											Training conducted
10. Feedback on training to PRODICOM											Problems solved Strengths commended
11. Circle leaders formulate plan of action											Circle work programmes of implementation formulated
12. Pilot circle conducts activities											SMEP and PSA conducted
13. Pilot circle presents project proposal											Project proposal presented and commented on
14. Pilot project studied and acted upon											
15. Pilot circle continues activities											Circle activities maintained
17. Co-ordinator promotes CWPIC											
18. Trainer continues training											Continuing education

Source: R. Vasquez et al., 1983, p. 25.

Figure 4.4. The flow of PIC activities on the shop-floor

Activity	Resources needed	Expected output	Persons responsible	Duration
1. Preparation of materials	Supplies for the re-production of reading materials/handouts	Orientation materials	Circle leader, co-ordinator, trainer	Three days
2. Schedule of meeting	Training equipment, room, blackboard	Orientation meeting	Circle leader, co-ordinator	Half day
3. Orientation proper	Reading materials/handouts, flip charts, films	Volunteers for PIC activity (circle members)	Circle leader, co-ordinator	One day
4. Conduct of study meeting	Reading materials, handbook, charts, films	Acquisition of know-ledge on tools and techniques	Circle leader, trainer, technical staff, ad-viser, co-ordinator	Five days
5. Start data gathering	Data forms	Data collected	Circle leader, circle members, technical staff	One week to one month depending on data to be collected
6. Start problem-solving activity (actual)	All resources men-tioned above	Problem identified, solutions formulated	Circle members, cir-cle leader	Average of eight meetings (1.5 hrs./meeting)

Source: R. Vasquez et al., 1983, p. 40.

comprehensive, participatory management process implemented from the top down. It has two major components: [11]

— a strategic planning process that focuses on developing a consensus on two- to five-year developmental goals, objectives and action programmes at all levels of management;

— a structural, participatory problem-solving process at the primary group/work level.

The two components integrated into PAT have the potential to:

— encourage "proactivity", i.e. anticipatory action rather than mere reaction to a given situation;

— facilitate, initiate and develop change and innovation;

— improve goal congruity between levels of management, functions, individuals and groups at different levels of the hierarchy;

— ensure that planning drives the budget and not vice-versa;

— improve effectiveness, efficiency, quality, productivity, quality of working life and innovation.

The PAT process was first designed and developed in 1977 and later on developed and described in detail by D. Scott Sink.[11] It has been applied and field tested in over 25 settings. This process is continually developing in an action research sense, gaining from the continued acquisition of knowledge from research and practice. The areas studied include complex organisation, motivation, participatory management, quality circles, change and innovation, organisational culture, planning and effective implementation.

The basics of the PAT process

The concept of the PAT process includes:

— management basics;

— change basics;

— behavioural and leadership control theory;

— motivational basics.

The management process (planning, organising, controlling and adapting) is directed at such organisational components as strategy, strategic planning, structure, process and behaviour. An effective performance measurement system is critical to the success of the comprehensive management process.

PAT practitioners believe that there are three critical problems that pervade most organisations:

● When policy formulation and strategic planning are non-participatory, they are inefficient. If participatory management is to achieve its full potential as a performance management technique, it must be involved in the strategic planning process.

● Many organisations and managerial processes stifle change, innovation, and "proactive" problem solving. Most organisations have measurement systems that tell us when we do something wrong and ignore us when we do something right. This encourages "reacting", "fixing it only when it's broken". The PAT process is an example of a change in such an approach to evaluation, making it a "proactive" system.

● All productivity improvements require changed behaviour. People must be willing and able to tolerate the change necessary for performance and productivity improvement. Change in most forms is normally resisted because it is often viewed as threatening, painful, difficult or unnecessary. The PAT process aims at creating support for change, and reducing resistance.

The main components of the PAT process are illustrated in figure 4.5.

Figure 4.5. The components of the PAT process

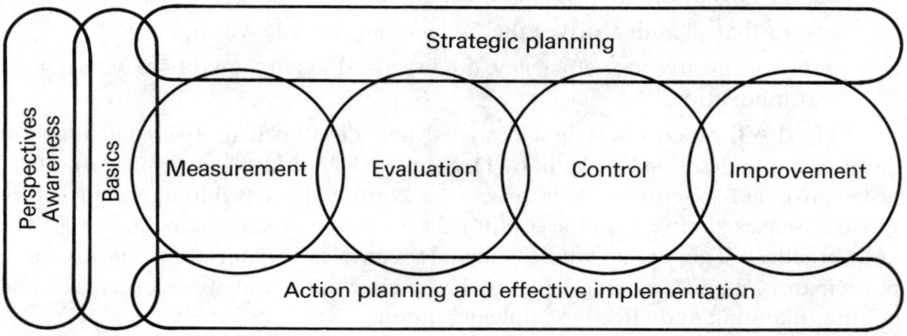

Source: D. Scott Sink, 1985, p. 1.

Implementation of the PAT process

The PAT top-down implementation process for a one-year cycle involves three groups before the problem-solving steps are started:

Stage 1: Upper management group.

Stage 2: Middle management.

Stage 3: First level management groups.

Some of the important features of the PAT process are that it:

— leads the budget process;

— overlaps strategy and policy formulation;

— feeds data and results from each stage downwards (but with some delay);

— holds action teams at all levels accountable for execution;

— makes the whole process transparent;

Two conditions of the PAT process are that it:

— should be effectively tied in to a gains-sharing system;

— should be preceded by strategic planning for productivity efforts.

104

Figure 4.6. PAT flow process chart

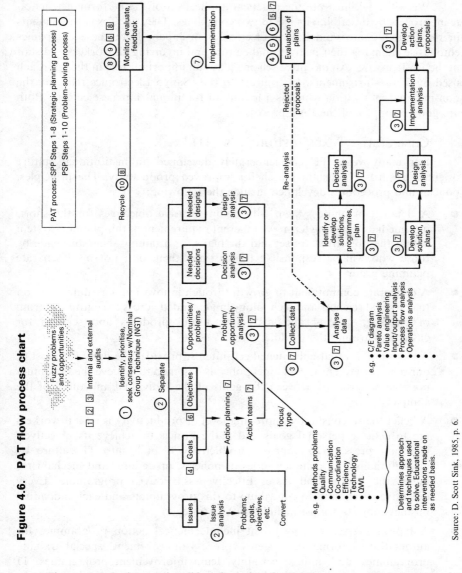

Source: D. Scott Sink, 1985, p. 6.

Figure 4.6 depicts a simplified flow for the PAT process. Various steps in both the strategic planning process component for management and the participatory problem-solving process component for workers are indicated on this diagram.

It should be mentioned that this diagram indicates only rough order sequencing and a generalised flow of events that have been observed in implementing the process.

We will now illustrate the practical application of the performance action team process by describing its use in two companies. They are Texas Instruments in the United States and Sanyo Electronics in Japan. Both these companies emphasise changing their institutional culture and involving all workers and staff in the PAT process. An incentive scheme plays an important role in the approach used by Texas Instruments. In contrast to this, Sanyo Electronics relies on the non-material motivation which is a feature of traditional Japanese culture. Both are good examples of the PAT process.

Case study: Texas Instruments (TI) [12]

For many years TI has deliberately developed an institutional culture oriented towards a constant search for improved productivity. The principles, policies and procedures developed include the following:

- A detailed planning system with comprehensive objectives for the short, intermediate and long term. An inherent requirement of this planning system is that the objectives are set and the plans for attaining them are made by those who will be responsible for carrying them out, not by a separate planning group.

- A deliberate commitment to growth through innovation, based not only on the physical sciences and technology but extended across the entire spectrum of creating, making and marketing useful products and services for customers around the world.

- An assumption that enlightened self-interest provides the drive for most of our daily work. Thus, personnel policy is designed to achieve the maximum possible congruence between the goals of the individual and those of the company.

- A belief that a constantly improving level of productivity is vital if workers are to achieve personal goals and if the firm is to achieve its objectives. Constant pressure to improve productivity is built into TI culture by institutionalising a complex series of policies, procedures and mechanisms under the People and Asset Effectiveness (P&AE) programme. Every executive is required to contribute to this programme, and each individual business objective must include P&AE strategies.

- A typical P&AE strategy might include tactical action programmes for automation, information systems, process improvement, special training programmes, and, almost certainly, team improvement programmes. TI attempts to design the job and work environment to maximise the degree to which workers plan and control their own work.

Team improvement programmes

In the team improvement programmes, which are invariably a part of each people and asset effectiveness strategy, groups of work-related individuals seek in a deliberate, organised way to improve the productivity of their particular areas.

More than 80 per cent of TI staff all over the world are participating in these programmes, and in many cases the results have been noteworthy.

For example, five managers with entrepreneurial skills led a team of operators, engineers and tool makers which designed and installed an automated production line for assembling calculator keyboards. This production line increased output by 85 per cent, from about 10,000 to 18,500 per day, and generated annual savings of more than US$1.2 million. As a result of efforts such as these, productivity has been increasing at approximately 15 per cent per year.

In the indirect areas, organisations find it both harder to measure and to achieve productivity improvement. Nevertheless, in these overhead areas, expressed in terms of net sales billed per person, an average productivity gain of 9.5 per cent per year has been achieved at TI.

The IDEA programme

The process of institutionalisation involves bureaucracy and the discipline demanded can swallow up good ideas. The sheer effort of fighting through the system can prevent many creative individuals, particularly the young and inexperienced, from pushing ideas to the point where they receive a suitable hearing.

In such cases, workers may turn to TI's IDEA programme, whose purpose is to provide an opportunity for an initial demonstration of the feasibility of concepts that do not fit within the immediate plans. This programme particularly appeals to those who want to be entrepreneurs and innovators because it provides an environment in which their ideas can flourish.

Every effort is made to keep the IDEA system simple. There are no approval cycles, delays, reviews or reports. Fifty key persons around the company are available to listen to new ideas, and each can fund, without any further discussion or approval, up to US$25,000.

The very successful "Speak and spell" learning aid started with an engineer's concept for electronically synthesising human speech using a large-scale integrated circuit. He sold his concept to one of the IDEA representatives and got the first US$25,000.

Rewards

Another vital principle involves the manner in which the individual's compensation, financial and otherwise, is related to the attempt to make individual and corporate goals coincide. A few aspects of TI compensation practices which seek to couple individual and corporate goals are described below.

Key Personnel Analysis: For the salaried TI office worker there is a comprehensive evaluation system. The essential feature of Key Personnel Analysis (KPA) is a rank ordering each year of all staff on negotiated salaries and all normally salaried people throughout the entire world-wide organisation on the basis of their present and potential contribution to TI. As individuals move up in the ranking, they are judged by supervisors and managers who rank higher and higher, and the ranking of the top few hundred reflects the personal judgements of the chairman and president.

Out of these rankings come the opportunities for significant promotions, the incentive awards which go to the top few thousand, and the stock options and performance unit awards for which those in the top few hundred are considered.

For those near the bottom of the list, the value of the award can be as little as US$500 or US$1,000; for those near the top, it can, in a good year, approach or exceed the individual's annual salary. Incentive awards, except those of US$1,000 or less, are made so that the recipients receive half in TI stock and half in cash. While they are free to sell the stock if and when they choose, a good percentage is in fact retained, and the eventual total value of the award to the individual is coupled with the future performance of TI and so helps focus each individual's efforts on the attainment of TI's goals.

Profit sharing: TI also has a profit-sharing plan through which a percentage of TI's profits go into a trust for all eligible workers. Nearly 90 per cent of TI staff around the world are covered by profit sharing.

The profit-sharing plan contribution is dependent upon the performance of the company as expressed in terms of two key indicators: Return on Assets (ROA) and the People Effectiveness Index (PEI). Two separate formulas are used to calculate the contribution based on ROA: one formula produces relatively more profit sharing when ROA is 10 per cent or more, and one when it is below 10 per cent. No contribution is necessary when ROA is less than 3 per cent of the eligible payroll.

The PEI is used to measure how effectively the talents of the staff are being used and is calculated by dividing net sales billed by the total of payroll and payroll-related benefits.

Case study: Sanyo Electronics 3 Ps productivity campaign [13]

Awareness building

Awareness building is one of the important components not only of the PAT process but of any productivity improvement campaign. Enterprises which realise the need to continuously promote awareness and understanding of the benefits of productivity growth and performance improvement have adopted various publicity campaign techniques to suit their different needs.

Many of them conduct regular intra-departmental and company-wide competitions between different kinds of productivity improvement team, either quarterly or annually. Other enterprises use slogan-, jingle- or logo-making contests, launch a poster design contest, etc.

Commonly used approaches in productivity campaigns are newsletters, magazines, posters, bulletin boards and distribution of small items such as stickers and bookmarks, together with meetings, workshops and conferences.

Exchange visits are also used to widen experience in productivity improvement. Other awareness-raising strategies are productivity circles, reunions, outside-company presentations, awards and suggestion-boxes.

The 3 Ps productivity campaign

An example of a systematic approach to organising an awareness-building campaign is the 3 Ps productivity campaign at Sanyo Electronics (Singapore). This programme was launched to raise productivity in the company. The 3 Ps mean Productivity Promotion through Participation. An important aim of this programme is to create staff awareness and understanding of their role in productivity improvement.

Since the implementation of the 3 Ps programme the staff have been striving to improve the quality of production as well as productivity.

The 3 Ps programme concentrates mainly on spreading the message of productivity through campaigns and "special days". A "Quality Awareness Day" is held once a month to increase workers' awareness of quality. They are continually encouraged to achieve zero defect in their products. On "High Efficiency Day" workers are encouraged to achieve their productivity targets. In addition to these special days, the company also organises a "Quality Campaign Month" annually in November. The aim is to inculcate quality consciousness, team spirit, good work attitudes and greater productivity.

Besides organising productivity improvement games and productivity exhibitions, each department also makes presentations on the projects they have come up with.

Other 3 Ps activities include:
— promoting good housekeeping and cost saving measures;
— organising productivity competitions for slogans, posters and suggestions;
— screening short films on productivity produced by the company.

As part of its productivity programme Sanyo has also promoted a programme for creating a productive work environment. The company organises safety competitions and in-house training, encourages effective communication and greater staff involvement in the productivity movement through quality circles. Morning gatherings are held daily for a better flow of information within the organisation.

The Inter-Firm Comparison and Business Clinic Approach (IFC/BCA)

The Inter-Firm Comparison and Business Clinic Approach (IFC/BCA) requires the services of an outside consultant. It uses inter-firm comparison techniques to help participating managers identify problems in their own organisations. It complements these techniques with group discussions where the accumulated experience and management skills of all the participants are mobilised to assist in solving individual problems.

The Inter-Firm Comparison (IFC) process was described in the subsection on inter-firm comparison in section 3.2.

Business clinics are essentially discussion groups where participants discuss their own problems and their progress in solving them. They are run by a consultant or management development institute.

We will describe the approach as developed in an ILO study.[14] The IFC/BCA has three main stages:

Stage 1: Participants receive an IFC report which compares the performance of their individual enterprise with the other, similar, enterprises.

Stage 2: Areas where improvement is needed are pointed out through comparison and analysis of the reports and performance of the other enterprises.

Stage 3: Follow-up action takes place in the form of business clinics.

One of the advantages of this approach is that it is especially attractive to small- and medium-scale entrepreneurs. The approach has a good chance of success if the following conditions are fulfilled:

● The industry concerned must be experiencing a degree of pressure on profits or productivity.

● There must be a "godfather" who is concerned about the way things are developing, who perceives the need for increased professionalism in management as a response to the threats facing it, and is willing to give his support to trying this approach.

● There must be a "champion", an innovator who is interested in this approach as an addition to his present range of training and consultancy techniques.

IFC as an entry point

IFC acts as an entry point when entrepreneurs have to be persuaded that the services of a management development centre or consultant really will help to solve current problems.

When entrepreneurs receive an IFC report they almost always find out from it that their firm's operation is unsatisfactory in one or more respects. If they want to improve their business, and cannot solve the problems alone, they have to look for help. If a management development or productivity centre has been associated with the IFC, then it is likely that they will go there to ask for help. Thus IFC provides a point of contact between entrepreneurs and the institutions which would like to help them.

How is IFC used?

IFC is used to find out where organisations should concentrate their efforts to improve their performance. Without IFC a manager can only guess which parts of the organisation are performing well or poorly, and where priorities for improving performance should be. A set of figures showing industry averages can indicate immediately whether the organisation is doing better or worse than average. The areas that are better than average can be given low priority. It should be fairly easy to obtain significant improvements in areas that are worse than average, so management should concentrate on these. If IFC data are already available, this preliminary phase can be reduced to a few hours. Once the procedures for collecting data have been established, it is easy and inexpensive to collect and process further data.

Business clinic concepts

A distinctive feature of the business clinic approach is that it emphasises project-based learning. This means that the participants, who are trainees in this situation, carry out an assignment (a project) in an actual enterprise, usually (but not necessarily) their own. The project must deal with a real problem and the trainee is responsible not only for analysing the problem but also for taking action to solve it.

Project-based learning combines naturally with IFC. The entrepreneur uses the IFC report to identify an area of weakness and defines a problem which has to be solved if the business is to prosper. So there is a ready-made project. If the manager can then get some help and advice from a management development centre, this will be a strong motivation to work on the problem. In this way IFC creates a demand for project-based learning.

Thus, project-based learning is a technique for self-development. Its effectiveness can be considerably increased by carrying it out in a group context, and this is the basis of the BC concept.

An advantage of the BC approach is that it combines psychological pressure to perform well, to be a "member in good standing" of the group, with a degree of support which encourages each member to "keep on trying". Another advantage, of course, is that in a group of people in the same type of business it is probable that there are other members who have encountered and solved the same, or a similar, problem previously. Information available through the group can usually get the members' projects off to a good start.

In the BC context, the trainees are the problem-owners. The trainer, or trainers, are other members of the group, sometimes the consultant, sometimes other entrepreneurs. In one way the BC approach takes some of the work off the consultant's shoulders, since a great deal of the advising and helping takes place between the group members. In another way, however, it puts additional responsibility upon the consultant in the training role, as the benefits can only be obtained if those present actually start working as a cohesive group, rather than just as a number of individuals. This means that the consultant needs to be skilled in group leadership.

It is usually found that by the third meeting a group spirit is starting to develop. Members are beginning to know each other, to appreciate what contribution they can make to the group activities, and what contribution to expect from the others. They are all starting to feel like members of the group, and to define their own role in the group. However, until the group spirit or group dynamic develops, it is the responsibility of the consultant/trainer to hold the group together.

Running the business clinic

Since a business clinic is an arrangement whereby a group of people meet to discuss the results of an IFC, there should normally be a series of six to eight such meetings, which will follow a general progression. The discussion centres first on the general problems indicated by the IFC, then moves to identifying their causes, then to devising remedies for the problems, and then to implementing the remedies. Each member of the group will have a problem (or problems) which all discuss. The organiser must have certain skills in handling such meetings and using discussion techniques. The group leader has to ensure that all the problems are discussed, without frustrating members who feel they still have something useful to contribute or that their problem was not given proper consideration.

An example taken from a business clinic for road transport organisations will serve to illustrate this approach.

Case study: IFC/BC for road transport organisations

At the first session, after describing how the business clinic functions, make sure that all the members have a copy of their IFC report and of their original data report (i.e. the information they supplied). Then write on a blackboard or flip-chart the names of the main cost ratios (fuel costs/100 km, lubricating oil costs/100 km, tyres and tubes costs/100 km, maintenance costs/100 km, and crew costs/100 km — leave out battery costs). Opposite each of these write the median value of each ratio, as determined by the IFC. Then explain to the group that these are the median (or average) values for the basic costs of operating buses. Then all the participants calculate how much higher or lower their own firm's costs are than those of this imaginary "median" firm. This calculation requires simple logic and arithmetic.

	Median	Firm A	Firm B
Fuel costs US$/100 km	12.50	12.63	13.32
Lubrication costs US$/100 km	0.25	0.48	0.38
Tyre costs US$/100 km	5.20	4.81	6.65
Maintenance costs US$/100 km	13.20	13.60	14.49
Crew costs US$/100 km	18.30	18.98	17.33
Total	49.45	50.50	52.17
Km travelled/month ('000)		375	323

Firm A is fairly close to the average. Compared with the "median" firm it is wasting only (50.50 − 49.45) × 375,000/100 = US$3,937 per month. It looks, from the figures for fuel, maintenance and particularly oil costs, as though its vehicle fleet is getting rather old.

Firm B, on the other hand, has costs (52.17 − 49.45) × 323,000/100 = US$8,785 per month higher than the "median" firm. Its lower crew costs, compared with the higher values for other costs (as compared with the median values) suggest that its wage rates are only attracting second-rate drivers.

After suggesting to participants that they should compare the median results with their own firm, point out that the ratios are the *median* ratios, not specially chosen "good" ratios, and that all the participants, unless they are working in particularly difficult circumstances, should be able to get their performance up to the standard of the median.

Next, discuss such questions as where participant firms save or lose compared with the median firm and ask for opinions about the reasons. Concentrate on the good results, as these are more stimulating in group discussions.

During the first two business clinic sessions it might be difficult to get the participants to enter into the discussion and contribute ideas. However, subsequent sessions should be much easier. Participants will know each other and become accustomed to talking about their business and what they are doing to improve it.

It is advisable to end the first two or three business clinics by asking the participants what action they propose to take as a result of the meeting, or before the next meeting. This is an effective way of using the psychological pressure of the group. If participants intend, for example, to find out why they are getting a short tyre life, then they are more likely to actually carry out their intention if the group expects it.

Another effective way of speeding up the development of the group spirit is to identify a problem common to most of the group members and get two or three members of the group to form a "task force" to see what can be done about it. For example, defective battery mountings are a common cause of short battery life. In this case a useful task force exercise would be to find a metal-working enterprise that would be willing to fabricate and fit properly designed battery mountings at a reasonable price. One or two quick successes in such tasks early in the business clinic series are very effective in bringing the group together, even though the cost savings they bring about might be quite small.

If a technical topic turns out to be of general interest (such as the care of tyres or maintenance of fuel injection pumps) the trainer should try to arrange for a specialist from a suitable supply firm to talk to the participants. If a management topic comes up, for instance a topic in costing, then a class session can be arranged.

The frequency of the meetings can be varied as the participants wish. At the start of the series, meetings might be fortnightly or even weekly, while participants seek advice from each other about preparing and starting up their individual cost-reduction projects. Later, when the projects have been implemented, and participants have to wait to see from their cost data how effective they have been, one meeting per month will be sufficient.

A business clinic series should not be expected to continue longer than six months. If participants cannot solve their problem within six months it is likely that it is far too difficult for them, and they will either have to call in a consultant or else just learn to live with it. Experience with groups of the business clinic type is that after about three months most participants have either solved their problems or at least have made substantial progress.

IFC operations and cost control

All the information given in IFC reports is presented in the form of ratios. Ratios permit comparison between the results for organisations of different sizes, help to maintain confidentiality, and express the results in numbers of reasonable size, which are easy to understand and work with. Therefore, at the start a decision must be made about what ratios to calculate and report.

The success of any enterprise depends on its strategy (how well its decisions on choosing the market and capital investment correspond to the realities of the outside world), and the effectiveness with which its strategy is executed.

The management of this second factor is essentially short-term. The manager compares periodic reports on the performance of various aspects of the enterprise with what they ought to be (formally specified in the budget, or in the manager's own expectations) and takes action if the data show that performance is not up to the standard expected.

In carrying out this short-term control function the manager will only be interested in factors that can be changed within a few weeks or a few months, and which do not require large capital investments or major changes in enterprise policy. Therefore, the information provided in the periodic reports should only refer to these factors. The manager will be interested in knowing about vehicle crew overtime hours worked, for example, because this is affected by crew scheduling, and can be changed in the short term. As a general rule, the periodic reports should only contain information about variable costs, not about fixed costs.

When IFC is used for management control, the system uses values based on industry performance. Therefore, the ratios used must refer only to operational factors, in the same way as the periodic reports.

IFC ratios for road passenger transport

Below are some of the important productivity ratios used by bus operators. The first three ratios measure the effectiveness with which the firm uses its income-generating asset, i.e. its vehicle fleet; the remaining ratios deal with operating costs. In order to design a set of ratios, it is important that every ratio should be described by:

— the name of the ratio;

— the units of measurement;

— the data required;

— the way the ratio is calculated;

— a brief discussion of the significance of the ratio.

1. *Vehicle availability percentage*

Data required: No. of vehicles registered (V).

No. of days in reporting period (D).

No. of vehicle-days spent under maintenance or repair during the reporting period (VRD).

Calculated as: $(V \times D - VRD) \times \dfrac{100}{V \times D}$

This ratio measures the effectiveness of the firm's maintenance. In a well-run firm with good routine maintenance (and thus few time-consuming major repair jobs) it can be as high as 85 per cent. For many bus firms in developing countries it is lower than 50 per cent. It can be improved by doing routine maintenance at night, but at the cost of paying overtime rates to the mechanics. High vehicle availability rates might be associated with high maintenance costs. The optimal balance between vehicle availability and maintenance costs will depend on the relative costs of capital (financing extra vehicles) and labour (mechanics' wages).

2. *Vehicle utilisation percentage*

Data required: V, D and VRD, as in ratio 1.

Vehicle-days worked (VDW).

Calculated as: $VDW \times \dfrac{100}{V \times D - VRD}$

This ratio is a measure of how many vehicles are available but standing idle. Depending on the age and condition of its fleet, a bus company will normally keep some 2 to 5 per cent of its vehicles in reserve in case of breakdowns on the road.

3 (a) *Revenues/100 km — US$/100 km*

Data required: Revenue during report period (R) and total km run during report period (km).

Calculated as: $R \times \dfrac{100}{km}$.

3 (b) *Load factor percentage*

Data required: Details of ticket sales, possibly spot checks in buses. Bus companies usually have their own ways of calculating this ratio.

The load factor depends upon the bus routes and the times and frequency of services, which are usually set after negotiation with the regulatory authorities and often cannot be changed at short notice. This factor is included because bus firms normally keep records of it and are accustomed to working with it. The load factor is the "physical" counterpart of the "financial" ratio (3a); the two are obviously closely related.

The ratios which follow deal with operating costs. The calculations are simply made as type of cost $\dfrac{100}{km}$.

4. *Fuel costs/100 km — US$/100 km*

Data required: Fuel costs during the reporting period.

Fuel consumption depends on the type of service — stage buses will use more fuel per kilometre than express buses. Also, buses in hilly areas will use more than those in flat areas. Factors within the manager's control include:

- *Driving habits.* Excess speed wastes a good deal of fuel, and faulty use of the gear box and accelerator pedal wastes even more. Stage bus operators in Europe have found that further training (of their already-trained drivers) gives savings of 2 to 5 per cent in fuel costs. Training of untrained drivers can save much more.

- *Excessive idling.* One operator in the Philippines has reported a 4.5 per cent saving in fuel costs simply by reducing excessive idling.

- *Losses during refuelling.* Pilferage and spillage can be a surprisingly large cause of wastage. Automatic shut down nozzles on fuel pumps can help a great deal, and many operators fit the vehicle fuel tanks with extra large diameter entry necks, to eliminate foaming during filling.

- *Maintenance.* Lack of maintenance to fuel pumps and fuel injectors can increase fuel consumption by up to 8 per cent; these items should be overhauled every 12 months. Incorrect engine timing can also increase fuel consumption quite considerably.

- *Radial-ply tyres.* In addition to greater safety and longer life, radial-ply tyres give fuel savings of 5 to 8 per cent in bus operations, as compared with standard tyres.

5. *Lubricating oil costs/100 km — US$/100 km*

Data required: Lubricating oil costs during the period.

Lubricating oil and oil filters should be changed according to the vehicle manufacturer's specifications. It is a false economy to try to make them last longer, and so is using inferior quality oil. Apart from this, excessive lubricant cost is mainly caused by pilferage and spillage.

6. *Tyre and tube costs/100 km — US$/100 km*

Data required: Tyre and tube costs during the period.

This ratio is easy to calculate and simple to understand. It also permits some degree of international comparison. Excessive tyre wear is mostly caused by:

- bad driving: excessive cornering speeds, fierce acceleration, hard braking; scuffing against kerbs;
- incorrect tyre pressure;
- incorrect front wheel alignment (note: radial-ply tyres are particularly sensitive to this).

7. *Battery costs/100 km — US$/100 km*

Data required: Battery costs during the period.

Battery life is a ratio which is easy to understand, and is more useful for comparative purposes than ratio 6, tyre life, as it is independent of driving standards.

The main causes of short battery life are careless topping-up and faulty handling in storage. Faulty or poorly maintained mounting brackets which allow the battery to rattle about when the vehicle is in motion can also seriously reduce battery life.

8. Maintenance costs/100 km — US$/100 km

Data required: Maintenance costs during the period.

Maintenance costs are paid in order to keep vehicles available for service. Therefore, ratio 8 should be evaluated in connection with ratio 1, vehicle availability. It might be a firm's policy to cut maintenance costs at a sacrifice of some percentage points of vehicle availability. Since this policy will normally result in a high incidence of road breakdowns, extra vehicles will need to be kept in reserve, so that ratio 2, vehicle utilisation, will also be relatively low. By the same token, high values of ratio 8 should be accompanied by high values of ratios 1 and 2. If ratio 1 is low and ratio 8 high, it is likely that the firm's fleet of vehicles is becoming too old. A high value for ratio 1 combined with a low value for ratio 8 could mean that the firm has very efficient mechanics, but might also be due to a recent large purchase of new vehicles, needing little maintenance.

9. Crew costs/100 km — US$/100 km

Data required: Crew costs during the period, including crew members employed per vehicle shift worked or crew members per bus and crew hours worked per 100 km.

Crew costs per 100 km are affected by several factors. One is the length of time required to travel 100 km, since workers are paid by time rather than by distance. Another factor is the operator's staffing policy. Some operators might prefer to employ more crew members and pay less overtime, others might prefer to employ fewer crew members and pay more overtime. The set of ratios given above allows these differences to be taken into account.

Misunderstandings sometimes arise about the collection of data and the calculation of ratios. If this happens, it means that the figures are not comparable. It is therefore vital that potential misunderstanding be eliminated right from the beginning. The best way to avoid misunderstanding is to hold a meeting with *all* the participants before the IFC exercise starts. The purpose of this meeting is *(a)* to discuss the proposed IFC ratios; *(b)* to decide the precise specifications of all the data to be reported, and how they are to be collected.

Presentation of IFC reports

IFC reports provide all the participants with a set of numbers (ratios) summarising their own firm's performance, together with another set (a "reference set") summarising the performance of other, similar firms. The participants are thus able to compare the two sets, and see how their firm's performance compares with that of other firms.

The usual format of such reports is shown in figure 4.7. It includes the names of the ratios, the units of measurement (e.g. percentage vehicle availability or fuel costs per 100 km), etc. The participants can easily scan across each line and note how their ratio compares with the others.

It is recommended that the median be used as the representative or typical value. The advantage of the median is that it is relatively unaffected by extremely high or extremely low values. Such extreme values can occur if one company is working under unusual conditions — for example, a bus company operating in hilly country will have higher fuel costs per 100 km than companies operating in flat country. Odd results can also occur if a firm sends in faulty data, which can happen sometimes. When this happens, using an arithmetic mean (or average) will give a misleading result, while using the median will still give usable results.

Figure 4.7.   Sample report from small group

INTER-FIRM COMPARISON REPORT

Covering the period
. . . . to . . . .

Ratio		Representative values			Firm code					
		Low	Median	High	A	B	C	D	E	etc.
1.	Vehicle availability (%)									
2.	Vehicle utilisation (%)									
3 (a)	Revenues/100 km (US$)									
3 (b)	Load factor (%)									
4.	Fuel costs (US$/100 km)									
5.	Lubricating oil costs (US$/100 km)									
6.	Tyre and tube costs (US$/100 km)									
7.	Battery costs (US$/100 km)									
8.	Maintenance costs (US$/100 km)									
9.	Crew costs (US$/100 km)									

Source: C. Guthrie, 1985, p. 30.

Setting up an IFC business clinic programme

Before starting an IFC business clinic programme, it is important to check the three conditions mentioned previously, i.e. if firms are experiencing a degree of pressure on profitability; if there is a "godfather" to sponsor the project; if there is a "champion" interested in using this approach.

When it is certain that these conditions exist, the consultant's first step is to work out the starting strategy. The key point in developing this strategy is to make the first IFC/business clinic group a success. Occasional later failures will not then do the programme much harm.

For this reason the first group should be selected very carefully. The participants should come from a sector that is experiencing a squeeze on profits, but a squeeze which is not caused by basic economic factors.

Another factor to be kept in mind is that the IFC/business clinic approach focuses on making improvements in the use of resources, and that the participants themselves bring about these improvements. The participating firms should, therefore, be well established and fundamentally sound, and their managers should have reasonable knowledge and experience of running the business. The approach is not ideally suited to the needs of new entrepreneurs.

If the sector appears promising for this programme, the consultant should discuss the idea of inter-firm comparison of productivity ratios with the more prominent businessmen, preferably those who are active members of the trade associations. The breakthrough comes when someone says: "Why don't you do something like this for us?" The consultant now has an ally, possibly a godfather, who will persuade friends to join, and so bring in other allies. A meeting of potential participants can now be arranged, preferably in collaboration with the association, at which the IFC/business clinic approach can be described and the idea of holding such an exercise suggested.

The actual operation of the IFC/business clinic exercise then proceeds as already described. That is, meetings are held with participants to agree on the productivity ratios to be used; the data to be collected are precisely defined; the participants are helped with their data-collection problems during the first few reporting periods; IFC reports are prepared and distributed and the business clinics are conducted.

* * *

In this chapter we have discussed how to *manage* a productivity improvement process. We have briefly analysed the main strategies and methods, the different types of programmes and their major variations. Many other variations exist in practice; our purpose here was simply to introduce the methodology and to give some examples of its successful application.

---

[1] Stephen Moss: "A systems approach to productivity improvement", in *National Productivity Review* (New York, Executive Enterprises Publications), Summer 1982, pp. 270-279.

[2] Alan Lawlor: *Productivity improvement manual* (Aldershot, United Kingdom, Gower, 1985), p. 95.

[3] Robert Abramson and Walter Halset: *Planning for improved enterprise performance. A guide for managers and consultants* (Geneva, ILO, 1979), pp. 7-19.

[4] Y. K. Shetty: "Key elements of productivity improvement programmes", in *Business Horizons* (Bloomington, Indiana, Indiana University, School of Business), Mar. 1982, pp. 15-22.

[5] Lawlor, op. cit., pp. 100-107.

[6] Magsikap B. Mole: "Productivity improvement programmes: A case study", in *Manpower Forum* (Manila, Meralco Foundation), Oct. 1981, pp. 45-51.

[7] R. B. Freeman: "Blue Circle industries PLC", in *Europroductivity Ideas* (Brussels, EANPC), Jan. 1984, pp. 16-19.

[8] George Boulden: *Programming for improved performance (PIP)*, Workshop manual (Rugby, United Kingdom, ALA International, 1985), pp. 1-38.

[9] Salvador M. Panopio: "Survey on the circles programs in the Philippine setting", in *PDC Info Digest* (Manila, Development Academy of the Philippines), Dec. 1984, pp. 34-59.

[10] Roberto A. Vasquez et al.: *Productivity improvement circles. A manual* (Manila, Development Academy of the Philippines, 1983), pp. 8-40.

[11] D. Scott Sink: "Performance action team process: An update of continuing developments", in *Productivity Management* (Blacksburg, Virginia, United States, Virginia Productivity Center), Winter 1985, pp. 1-6.

[12] Patrick E. Haggerty: "Technology, people and productivity", in *Dimensions of productivity research* (Houston, Texas, The American Productivity Center, 1980), Vol. II, pp. 1199-1203.

[13] Low Sue Foung: "Sanyo Electronics' 3 Ps approach to higher productivity", in *Singapore Productivity News* (Singapore, National Productivity Board), Aug. 1985, p. 3.

[14] Colin Guthrie: *Interfirm comparison and business clinics in road transport*, SED/10/E (Geneva, ILO, 1985), pp. 1-40.

PRODUCTIVITY IMPROVEMENT TECHNIQUES $\quad$ 5

The techniques used in carrying out productivity improvement programmes are mostly for collecting information and increasing the effectiveness of work. The methods used fall into two groups:

— the technical approach — engineering techniques and economic analysis;

— the human approach — behavioural methods.

Since most of the techniques are well described in the literature on industrial engineering and management and also in training programmes, our task here is simply to summarise and when necessary to illustrate their application. (Useful references are: Mundel, 1970; *Industrial engineering handbook*, 1971; ILO, 1979; Sudit, 1984; Lawlor, 1985; and Tracey (ed.), 1985.)

5.1 Industrial engineering techniques and economic analysis

Work study

Work study is a combination of two groups of techniques, method study and work measurement, which are used to examine people's work and indicate the factors which affect efficiency. Work study is normally used in an attempt to increase output from a given quantity of resources with little or no further capital investment. This is achieved by systematically analysing existing operations, processes and work methods.

The basic procedure of work study is as follows: [1]

● Select the job or process to be studied.

● Record from direct observation everything that happens in order to obtain data for analysis.

● Examine the recorded facts critically and challenge everything that is done, considering in turn: the purpose of the activity, the place where it is

121

performed; the sequence in which the elements are performed; the person who is doing it; the means by which it is done.

- Develop the most economic methods, taking into account all the circumstances.
- Measure the amount of work involved in the method used and calculate a "standard time" for doing it.
- Define the new method and the related time.
- Install the new method and time as agreed standard practice.
- Maintain the new standard practice by proper control procedures.

Table 5.1 is an example of the best areas for application of work study for productivity improvement.

Method study

Method study (often called motion study, method analysis or methods engineering) is the systematic recording and critical examination of existing and proposed ways of doing work in order to develop and apply easier and more effective methods and to reduce costs. It is used to *improve* processes and procedures, plant layout, design of plant and equipment; to *reduce* human effort and fatigue, use of materials, machines and manpower, and to *develop* better physical and working environments. The basic stages of method study are shown in figure 5.1. Method study is a complex technique that combines several simple tools, mostly charts and diagrams and other recording techniques. Table 5.2 summarises the most common tools used by specialists in method study.

An example of the application of the method study techniques and tools mentioned is given in table 5.3.

The commonly used method study tools are:

- analysis of films;
- memotion photography (memory and motion — a way of using film to analyse movements);
- micromotion analysis;
- question techniques (general and specific questions which help to indicate purpose, place, sequence, person and means).

Work measurement

Work measurement establishes the time a qualified worker needs to carry out a specified job at a defined level of performance. Whereas method study helps us eliminate unnecessary *movement*, work measurement helps in investigating, reducing and subsequently eliminating ineffective *time*, during which useful work is not being performed.

Work measurement is also used to set standard times for carrying out work. Thus work measurement helps to:

- compare the efficiency of alternative methods;

Figure 5.1.   Method study procedure

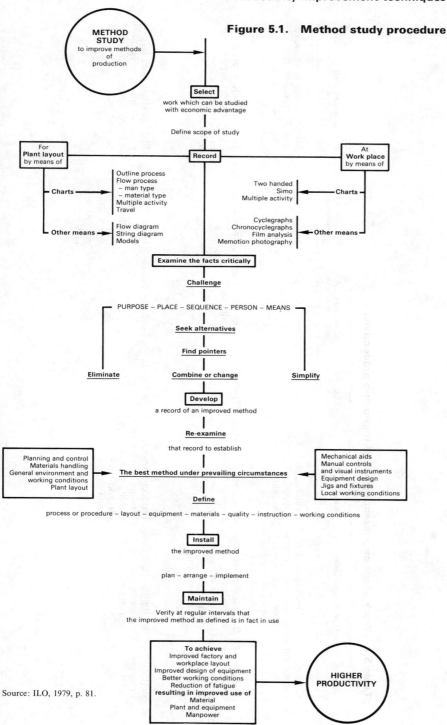

Source: ILO, 1979, p. 81.

Table 5.1. Work study as a direct means of improving productivity

Approach	Type of improvement	Means	Cost	How quickly can results be achieved?	Extent of improvement in productivity	The role of work study
Capital investment	1. Development of new basic process or fundamental improvement of existing ones	Basic research Applied research Pilot plant	High	Generally years	No obvious limit	Method study to improve ease of operation and maintenance at design stage
	2. Install more modern or higher-capacity plant or equipment or modernise existing plant	Purchase Process research	High	Immediately after installation	No obvious limit	Method study in plant layout and to improve ease of operation when modernising
Better management	3. Reduce the work content of the product	Product research Product development Quality management Method study Value analysis	Not high compared with 1 and 2	Generally months	Limited — of the same order as that to be expected from 4 and 5. Should precede action under those heads	Method study (and its extension, value analysis) to improve design for ease of production

4. Reduce the work content of the process	Process research Pilot plant Process planning Method study Operator training Value analysis	Low	Immediate	Limited, but often of a high order	Method study to reduce wasted effort and time in operating the process by eliminating unnecessary movement
5. Reduce ineffective time (whether due to management or to workers)	Work measurement Marketing policy Standardisation Product development Production planning and control Material control Planned maintenance Personnel policy Improved working conditions Operator training Incentive schemes	Low	May start slowly but effect grows quickly	Limited, but often of a high order	Work measurement to investigate existing practice, locate ineffective time and set standard of performance as a basis for — A. Planning and control B. Utilisation of plant C. Labour cost control D. Incentive schemes

Source: ILO, 1979, p. 31.

Table 5.2.   Method study tools

Charts:	To indicate process SEQUENCE	– Outline process chart
		– Flow process charts
		    ● Man type
		    ● Material type
		    ● Machine type
		– Two-handed process chart

	To indicate a TIME SCALE	– Multiple activity chart – Simo chart
Diagrams:	To indicate MOVEMENT	– Flow diagram – String diagram – Cyclegraph – Chronocyclegraph – Travel chart

Source: Adapted from ILO, 1979, p. 88.

— balance the work of team members;

— determine the number of machines one can operate or monitor;

— provide information, using set time standards, on which the planning and scheduling of production can be based;

— set standards for machine use and labour performance;

— provide information for labour-cost control and for fixing standard costs;

— provide information on which tenders, selling prices and delivery promises can be based.

Work measurement provides the basic information necessary for designing, planning, organising and controlling the work, especially in industries where the time element is important. The basic procedure of work measurement is as follows:

● Select the work to be studied.

● Record all relevant data, the methods and elements of work.

● Examine the recorded data and make a detailed breakdown to ensure that the most effective methods and movements are being used; separate unproductive elements from productive ones.

● Measure the quantity of work involved in each element in terms of time.

● Compile or compute the standard time for the operation.

● Define precisely the series of activities and methods of operation for which the time has been compiled and derive the standard time for the activities and methods specified.

Table 5.3.   Typical problems and appropriate method study techniques

Type of job	Examples	Recording technique
Complete sequence of manufacture	Manufacture of an electric motor from raw material to dispatch Transformation of thread into cloth from preparation to inspection Receipt, packing and dispatch of fruit	Outline process chart Flow process chart Flow diagram
Factory layout: movement of materials	Movements of a diesel engine cylinder head through all machining operations Movements of grain between milling operations	Outline process chart Flow process chart — material type Flow diagram Travel chart Models
Factory layout: movement of workers	Labourers servicing spinning machinery with bobbins Cooks preparing meals in a restaurant kitchen	Flow process chart — man type String diagram Travel chart
Handling of materials	Putting materials into and taking them out of stores Loading lorries with finished products	Flow process chart — material type Flow diagram String diagram
Workplace layout	Light assembly work on a bench Typesetting by hand	Flow process chart — man type Two-handed process chart Multiple activity chart Simo chart Cyclegraph Chronocyclegraph
Gang work or automatic machine operation	Assembly line Operator looking after semi-automatic lathe	Multiple activity chart Flow process chart — equipment type
Movements of operatives at work	Female operatives on short-cycle repetition work Operations demanding great manual dexterity	Films Film analysis Simo chart Memotion photography Micromotion analysis

Source: ILO, 1979, p. 84.

The most important techniques of work measurement are:

(1)   Work sampling.

(2)   Stop-watch time study.

(3)   Predetermined Time Standards (PTS).

(4)   Standard data.

(1) *Work sampling* ("activity sampling", "ratio-delay study", "random observation method", "scrap-reading method", "observation ratio study", "statistical work sampling") helps us find the frequency of occurrence of a certain activity by statistical sampling and random observation. It is widely used in

industry to compare the efficiency of two departments, to provide for an equitable distribution of work in a group and to help managers become aware of the percentage of ineffective time and the reasons for it.

Work sampling is based on probability and uses observation methods, and statistical instruments such as curve of normal distribution, sample size and random techniques and the monogram method. These methods can be found in a number of statistical or industrial engineering manuals and books. (Useful references are: Carroll, 1960; *Industrial engineering handbook*, 1971; Miles, 1972; Barnes, 1975; and Clark and Clark, 1983.)

(2) *Time study* is a work measurement technique for recording time and speed of working for the elements of a specified job carried out under specified conditions, and for analysing the data so as to compute the time necessary for carrying out the job at a defined level of performance. The main steps in time study procedures are as follows:

— obtain and record all the information available about the job, the worker(s) and the environment;
— record a complete description of the method, breaking down the operation into "elements";
— examine the detailed breakdown to ensure that the most effective methods and movements are being used, and determine the sample size;
— measure with a timing device (usually a stop-watch) and record the time taken by the worker(s) to perform each "element" of the operation;
— assess the effective speed of working relative to the observer's subjective judgement;
— extend the observed times to "basic times";
— determine the allowances to be made over and above the basic time for the operation;
— determine the "standard time" for the operation.

The basic time study equipment includes a stop-watch, a study board, time study forms, a small calculator and measuring instruments such as a tape measure, steel rule, micrometer, spring balance and tachometer.

Time study also requires the extensive use of such techniques as *rating* in order to assess the rate of working and to relate it to a standard pace. If the standard pace is maintained and the appropriate relaxation time is taken, a worker will achieve *standard performance* over the working day or shift. The standard time for the job will be the sum of the standard times for all elements of which it is made up, due regard being paid to the frequency with which the elements recur, plus a margin for relaxation.

(3) *A Predetermined Time Standard (PTS)* is a work measurement technique whereby times established for basic human movements (classified according to the nature of the movement and the conditions under which it is made) are used to build up the time for a job at a defined level of performance. It is used to analyse the work content when the cycle of operation is very small, involving micro-motions. PTS systems are thus techniques for synthesising operation times

from standard time data for basic movements. By examining a given operation and identifying the basic movements of which it is composed, and then referring to PTS tables which indicate standard times for each type of motion performed under given circumstances, it is possible to derive a standard time for the operation as a whole. PTS systems can be applied in two main ways: direct observation of the worker's movements; mental visualisation of the movement needed to accomplish a new or alternative work method.

Although several PTS systems exist, the most widely used one is methods-time measurement (MTM).

(4) *Standard data* banks containing work elements which occur repeatedly in the workplace are useful to avoid carrying out time studies for all new jobs. Instead, by breaking down the job into elements and referring to the data bank to derive the normal time for each element, it is possible to calculate the total time needed to perform the new job and to determine its standard time by adding appropriate allowances. The reliability of data can be increased by standardising as many elements as possible and by making sure that all factors have been considered. To develop a standard data bank the following steps are recommended:

— decide on coverage (work areas, processes, work elements);
— break the various jobs into elements, through *job analysis*, identifying as many common elements as possible;
— decide on the type of reading (stop-watch time study or MTM);
— determine the factors likely to affect the time for each element and classify them into major and minor factors;
— when using stop-watch time study, use actual observation to measure the time taken to perform the activity;
— record the observations on special forms depending on the system of measurement (stop-watch or PTS).

The recording system associated with work measurement should include at least the following data:

Information	Source
Hours of attendance of each worker.	Clock card or time sheet.
Standard time for each operation.	Job card or work study office.
Times of starting and finishing each operation.	Job card or work sheet (via shop clerk).
Quantities produced.	Job card or work sheet (via shop clerk).
Scrap or rectification: quantities and times.	Scrap note or rectification slip (via inspector and shop clerk).
Waiting time and non-productive time.	Waiting time slips or daily worksheet (via shop clerk).

A system of timing workers and recording their output is required for the full application of work measurement techniques associated with an incentive scheme.

Work simplification

This is a philosophy and set of procedures introduced in the 1930s, based on the realisation that the people who actually do a job are often the best placed to improve it. Instead of an army of specialists in time study, work measurement and methods analysis, it is often better to train workers to think creatively about their jobs and then give them incentives to make improvements.

Work simplification consists of three elements: the philosophy, the pattern and the plan of action.

The philosophy is that people know best how to do their own jobs and therefore should be involved in job improvement. They should be trusted by management, and workers themselves should want to be involved in job improvement. They should be trained. To ensure success in work simplification, it is essential to build trust in the organisation and to demonstrate management commitment to the philosophy.

The pattern of work simplification means developing the tools and techniques of an organised approach, which is not the same as making flash improvements based on snap judgements.

Typically, work simplification uses the following six steps:
● Select a job to improve.
● Get all the facts.
● Make a process chart.
● Challenge every detail, asking all possible questions; list possibilities and improve necessary details.
● Develop the preferred method.
● Introduce it and check results.

Work simplification tools include flow process charts, flow diagrams, and economy of movements, as mentioned in the discussion of work study.

Pareto analysis

Pareto analysis is named after an Italian economist who noted the principle, often called the 80/20 rule, that 80 per cent of the results come from 20 per cent of the effort. It is a useful tool for productivity analysis since it concentrates attention on the most important few issues or problems and helps establish priorities.

The principle is used in many production and management areas: marketing, quality control, stock analysis, purchasing, sales analysis, waste reduction processes and so on.

The basic steps of Pareto analysis are as follows: [2]
1.   List the items (products or processes) to be analysed in ascending order of use, cost or occurrence.

2. Determine total use, cost or occurrence.

3. Express the individual use, etc., as a percentage of the total.

4. Produce a cumulative column for step 3.

5. Divide the cumulative percentage column into three groups, say 70 per cent, 20 per cent and 10 per cent. Pareto analysis is sometimes called "ABC" analysis — "A" being the expensive 70 per cent, "B" the moderate 20 per cent and "C" the low-cost 10 per cent.

6. Repeat steps 1 to 4 for the items studied. The previous steps have all related to cost; we now need to relate the "ABC" aspects to the percentage of items contained in each category.

7. Compare the cumulative percentage use/cost/occurrence column with the cumulative percentage item column.

Table 5.4 and figure 5.2 illustrate tables and diagrams used in Pareto analysis.
Pareto analysis could also be considered as an application of management by exception.

Table 5.4. An example of ABC stock analysis

Item No.	Stock group	Usage		Cumulative %	Items	
		Cost (£)	%		%	Cumulative %
1	A	60 000	40.0	40.0	10	10
2	A	44 000	29.4	69.4	10	20
3	B	22 000	14.7	84.1	10	30
4	B	15 000	10.0	94.1	10	40
5	C	5 000	3.4	97.5	10	50
6	C	2 000	1.3	98.8	10	60
7	C	1 000	0.7	99.5	10	70
8	C	500	0.3	99.8	10	80
9	C	250	0.1	99.9	10	90
10	C	250	0.1	100	10	100
Total		150 000	100	100		100

Summary:

Stock group	% of cost	% of items
A	69.4	20
B	24.7	20
C	5.9	60
Total	100	100

Source: A. Lawlor, 1985, p. 168.

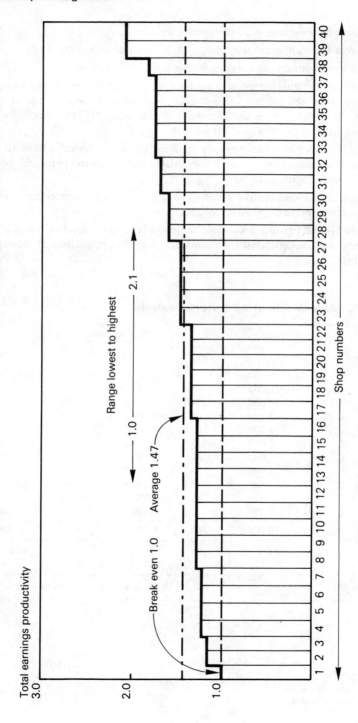

Figure 5.2. An example of productivity audits of 40 shops arranged in ascending order of total earnings productivity

Source: A. Lawlor, 1985, p. 164.

132

Just-in-time method

The just-in-time (JIT) method is the production (or delivery) of the necessary units in the necessary quantity at the necessary time. Clearly, the meaning of "necessary" depends on the context; a government department, a public company and a small private enterprise have different priorities and responsibilities, and their minimum necessary inventory must be calculated accordingly. The main purpose of JIT is to reduce costs in the production process, thereby improving the total productivity of the organisation. This system was developed and implemented in Japan and is aimed at eliminating unnecessary inventories, minimising inventory carrying costs and increasing the ratio of return on investment. However, more important than the reduction of inventory is the improvement in manufacturing that results from operating with low inventories.[3]

JIT removes the security blanket of high inventory and thus exposes operating problems. After introducing JIT, back-up inventories, once considered an insurance against unexpected shortages or delays, are viewed as evidence of lack-lustre planning, even of laziness.

JIT also forces the elimination of the time wasted in long procedures for setting up jobs. JIT is a wide-ranging management philosophy that encompasses greater staff involvement, much greater concern over quality, closer links with suppliers and a new attitude to the way products are made, so that companies make only what is required and only as it is required.

An essential prerequisite to JIT is a comprehensive production control system based on the planning of materials requirements. Introducing JIT will demand new computer systems integrated into existing production and material control, since the less stock is held the more problems arise. Experts at Hewlett-Packard believe inventory hides problems, and if you have not got any problems you are certainly holding too much stock. The move towards JIT production, where stock levels are gradually reduced, will therefore reveal more and more problems, such as machine breakdown or in quality control, which must be tackled promptly.[4]

JIT is not an easy option if a company has not got the discipline or management commitment to fully exploit a production control system. But the results can be rewarding. For example, a Hewlett-Packard plant has reduced standard hours by 50 per cent, cut material scrap by 80 per cent, reduced floor space requirements by 33 per cent, cut process time from 17 days to 30 hours and slashed inventory by 75 per cent.[4] It is no surprise that many companies are showing interest in JIT manufacture, although it seems that a large proportion of managers are still unconvinced. JIT's success depends to a great extent on the high quality of incoming materials. If a supplier delivers a bad batch, the whole production line will stop! Once suppliers understand the consequences of failure, they will be sure to make on-time deliveries of high-quality materials. That is why JIT can succeed only in combination with a sound quality assurance system. A good example is the Toyota production system which embodies two key concepts (figure 5.3):[5]

Figure 5.3. Key elements in the Toyota production system

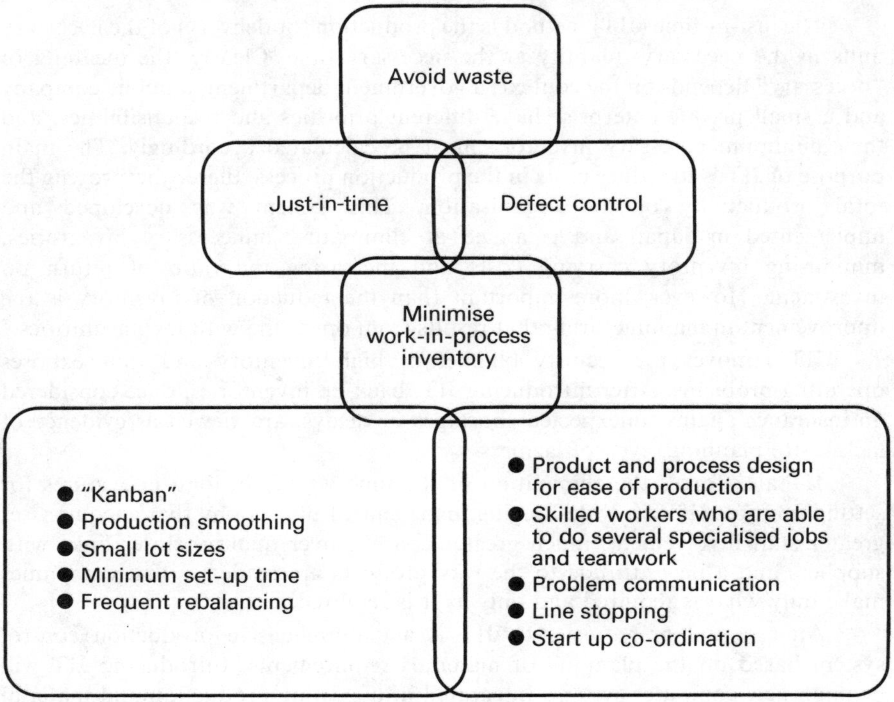

Avoid waste

Just-in-time   Defect control

Minimise
work-in-process
inventory

- "Kanban"
- Production smoothing
- Small lot sizes
- Minimum set-up time
- Frequent rebalancing

- Product and process design for ease of production
- Skilled workers who are able to do several specialised jobs and teamwork
- Problem communication
- Line stopping
- Start up co-ordination

Source: S. Moss, 1982, p. 278.

— JIT production management;
— defect control.

In this model "Kanban" refers to a procedure of using cards to keep inventory status highly visible and of managing production so that necessary units are made in the required quantity and at the required time. This procedure is part of the information system which supports JIT. "Kanban" imposes a discipline on the shop-floor by using standard containers that always hold the same number of a given part, and which must be filled within a certain time.

JIT also depends on production smoothing. Toyota generally fixes the production schedule for the current month and then runs the same volume and mix in the same sequence every day, intermixing different vehicles, rather than running them in batches. This levels the demand for parts specific to a vehicle type. To facilitate production smoothing, Toyota standardises more items of equipment than its American counterparts.

JIT's small lot sizes facilitate production smoothing and are made economical by short set-up times. For example, Toyota has reduced set-up time to five minutes on a line stamping body panels (in the United States it requires six hours).[5]

Much of the success of the Toyota system depends on the willingness of workers to shift from job to job and to work as a team whenever a problem arises.

134

This minimises manning requirements, enhances job security, reduces boredom and improves overall labour productivity.

To implement JIT it is important to win not only management commitment, but that of all the workers as well. It means first of all allowing time for the necessary changes and the restructuring of the production process.

One possibility is to appoint a project leader who will champion JIT's implementation, set up a training programme, make the conversion schedule and form a conversion team. Even after this conceptual training is complete and the organisation has a common vision of the future, no company is prepared to transform its entire factory instantly into a JIT operation. First it is necessary to establish a pilot JIT project, perhaps involving an entire product line, before converting the whole factory.

The main tools of the JIT method are the fine-tuning of the production processes, autonomous groups and a special information system ("Kanban") (figure 5.4).

It should be mentioned that this method includes a number of other techniques such as production planning, work study, quality control, job design and job standardisation.

Figure 5.4.   Just-in-time framework

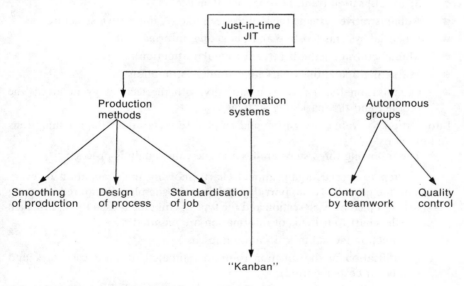

Management through value analysis

An important technique for productivity improvement through waste reduction is management through value analysis. (Some specialists consider value analysis as a modified form of method study, value engineering or method engineering.) Every product can be broken down into its components and each component analysed in terms of its value to the whole. The main criteria of value in such analyses are worth, desirability and utility.

Value analysis aims at achieving many small savings or improvements in efficiency which will collectively be significant. Its usefulness has been demonstrated in manufacturing and many other fields as well. Substantial cost reductions have been achieved in hospital administration, banking, construction and also in public services and government.

Value analysis is an organised, creative approach for identifying and eliminating unnecessary costs in a product or service. All costs connected with a product (or service) in its design, material, manufacturing process, and particularly its specifications and requirements, are analysed for the value each contributes.

Thus, value analysis is an approach to cost reduction, which *emphasises function* rather than method; *identifies* excessive or unnecessary *costs*; *improves* the *value* of the product or service; *provides* the same or better *performance* at a lower cost; and *reduces* neither *quality* nor *reliability*.

For the purpose of analysis an organisation can be broken down into eight main functioning areas:

● Manpower utilisation (personnel policy and motivation for productivity).
● Plant/equipment utilisation (optimum use of plant, operating and maintenance costs).
● Space utilisation (rent, heating, maintenance).
● Administrative systems (new office technology; innovative structures).
● Financial systems (costing and budgeting, information).
● Manufacturing methods (area for regular attention).
● Marketing operations (marketing studies, promotion).
● Organisational structure (compatibility with the technology involved, the product and the marketing strategy).

Information for value analysis should emphasise facts rather than assumptions and opinions.

The following three steps are used in the value analysis process: [6]

1. Prepare special organisational charts showing the occupation of every person on the payroll. To support this, a floor plan/site plan is required, showing the space occupied by each section and the type of equipment used there. For each point on the chart four items of information are required:

— the function (actual task, location and cost);
— quantification of the function (output, estimated time for each task and significant costs incurred);
— the operation of the function (principal elements of the task performed, interaction with other functions);
— the contribution of the function (its purpose and relevance).

This information, along with other information on the cost of each function, produces a communications flow chart and a work flow chart.

2. Compare the cost data on each function with the "value" criteria of worth, desirability and utility, asking these questions:

- Is the function essential to the business?
- Is the function correctly placed in the organisational structure?
- Is the method of achieving the function effective?
- Could the function be combined with another to reduce the cost or be more effective?
- Does the staffing level appear reasonable in relation to the tasks carried out?
- Does the space occupied appear reasonable in relation to the function performed?
- Is the function physically located in the best place?
- Is there an alternative method of achieving the same function that would be less costly or more effective?

Such questioning highlights apparent anomalies and suggests many lines of investigation. All should be followed up.

3. Once the value analysis is complete, prepare a report showing clear, practical recommendations. All major organisational changes should be implemented first, with full consultation with those affected. Small changes can then be made within the functions with less possibility of major disruption.

The following case study on a general hospital will illustrate the use of these techniques. The material is from an unpublished case study: the name of the hospital has been changed.

Case study: A value improvement programme at Norwalk General Hospital, United States

Introduction

A value improvement programme is an innovative cost containment programme for any kind of service, including health-care institutions. It brings physicians, managers and staff together to focus on areas where costs are high compared with other hospitals. The value improvement process compares costs and practices with other hospitals and selects lower-cost practices without compromising quality of care. Action plans are developed by task forces, and changes are implemented and monitored.

Objectives

The objectives of the Norwalk General Hospital (NGH) value improvement programme were to:

- Bring together physicians and key staff in identifying potential areas for cost savings.

Productivity management

- Identify opportunities and practices in other hospitals that could be adopted without compromising the quality of care.
- Achieve substantial cost savings for the hospital and improved value for patients.

The programme

The hospital called in consultants who offered a variety of management development services as part of the value improvement programme. Several people from the hospital were sent on short courses where they learned how to analyse hospital costs and to work with the consultants. Courses were also run in-house on how to analyse costs, hold brainstorming sessions, organise task forces and make convincing presentations.

Eleven therapies and services were prepared for the analysis process; the final choice was based upon estimates of potential cost savings. The therapies and services were broken down as follows:

Initial studies	*Secondary studies*
— cardiac care	— myocardial infarction;
— laminectomy;	— total hip replacement;
— obstetrics (normal delivery);	— chronic dialysis.
— dietary;	
— laboratories;	
— laundry and linen;	
— housekeeping;	
— cholecystectomy.	

Since secondary studies would not present substantial cost savings they were not considered for further analysis. The steering committee decided that the first three task forces would work on laminectomy, obstetrics (normal delivery), and heart surgery.

Laminectomy task force

The total costs (including allocated overheads, depreciation, etc.) for a laminectomy at NGH were calculated and compared with other teaching hospitals. A "patient screen" defining a simple laminectomy was used to ensure that the costs were comparable across hospitals. Key hospital personnel involved in laminectomies and a chairman of the department were asked to serve on the task force. The cost comparisons served as a catalyst to the discussions. The best demonstrated cost (BDC), which is a cost bar comprised of the best elements of all the hospitals, provided a target cost. Analysis of the biggest cost differences identified key areas for opportunity. A chart showing the key areas was prepared:

	Key areas of opportunity		
	NGH cost (US$)	Difference vs. BDC (US$)	% difference
Room and care	1 241	642	53
Supplies	367	238	20
Operating room	383	187	15
Blood and therapy	99	66	5
Pharmacy	208	39	3
Radiology	185	21	2
Laboratories, tests and nuclear medicine	143	17	2
Total	2 626	1 210	100

This analysis revealed that the biggest potential for cost savings was in room and care. The room and care difference was mainly a function of length of stay, possibly because of keeping patients longer than necessary. A detailed breakdown of pre- and post-operation length of stay was presented and discussed. Comparison with other hospitals revealed that it was possible to reduce both by one day.

Supplies were also a major concern of the task force. A detailed breakdown of the supplies used on the floor and in the operating room was made and discussed. There was excess inventory of rarely used supplies and the operating room helped identify those items. It was decided that a reasonable amount should be retained and avenues for selling the excess were explored.

The total annual savings from the laminectomy task force were as follows:

Result	Expected annual cost saving (US$)
Length of stay reduced by two days	60 868
Sale of excess inventory in the operating room	20 000
Total	80 868

Obstetrics (normal delivery) task force

Obstetrics (normal delivery) is an important service at NGH and the number of deliveries is expected to continue to increase. The patient profile for a normal delivery includes a second or later birth, a mother between 24 and 30 years of age, and no complicating conditions. NGH's cost was high compared with other hospitals. The biggest cost differences were for labour and delivery, post partum and the nursery. The length of stay was 2.4 days, which was low; therefore, the task force concentrated on staffing differences.

	Key areas of opportunity		
	NGH cost (US$)	Difference vs. BDC (US$)	% difference
Labour and delivery	418	191	28
Post partum	538	260	37
Nursery	267	65	10
Supplies	211	102	15
Laboratories/tests	33	3	—
Pharmacy	67	50	7
Blood	22	22	3
Anaesthesia	0	0	—
Other	2	−3	—
Total	1 558	690	100

An arrival distribution was plotted for labour and delivery, post partum and nursery by shift by day for a three-month period. Each graph was reviewed and discussed with the head nurse for each area. After careful analysis of the arrival distribution and staffing comparisons with other hospitals each head nurse agreed to the following reductions in full-time equivalent (FTE) staff:

Area	FTEs	Savings (US$)
Labour and delivery	4.6	111 000
Post partum	2.8	39 000
Nursery	1.8	51 000
Total	9.2	201 000

At the task force meeting each head nurse presented the analysis for her department and the possible FTE reductions. In the discussion that followed the physicians mentioned any problems or concerns. Total agreement was reached and the maximum savings of US$201,000 were expected to be realised from staffing reductions.

Although the length of stay was low compared with national statistics, the group wanted to become more responsive to modern trends and offer an early discharge option to patients.

While the task force was working, the finance department developed a plan to reduce fees in the obstetrics area. The task force was therefore able to present these rate reductions to the physicians. This was a very positive conclusion to the task force effort, which achieved substantial cost reductions and passed on some of these savings to patients.

Cardiac arterial bypass graft (CABG)

The CABG task force was also instrumental in bringing significant savings to the hospital. Staff responsible for administration, management, engineering, nursing, surgery administration and heart surgery all contributed to cost reductions in the areas of pumps, supplies, laboratory and X-ray tests, and length of stay. The total costs (including allocated overhead, depreciation, supplies, direct labour and laboratory tests) for a CABG were calculated and compared with other teaching hospitals. An analysis of the length of stay for a CABG patient was also made from patient charts.

Total cost savings from the contributions of the CABG task force were about US$178,000.

Summary

Hospitals using the value improvement programme process have achieved impressive savings. At Norwalk General Hospital the annual savings from the first task forces were approximately:

Task force	Saving (US$)
Laminectomy	81 000
OB normal delivery	201 000
CABG	178 000
Total	460 000

These savings were achieved with full co-operation from physicians and hospital staff, while maintaining or improving the quality of patient care.

Cost-benefit analysis

Cost-benefit analysis is a powerful productivity improvement technique to determine the ratio of the benefits of a given project to its costs, taking into account the benefits and costs that cannot be directly measured in monetary units. This technique can also be used to find the least expensive means of reaching an objective or a way of obtaining the greatest possible value from a given expenditure. It is closely related to productivity measurement and analysis, which was discussed in Chapter 3.

Zero-based budgeting

Zero-based budgeting (ZBB) is an operating, planning and budgeting process which requires all managers to justify their entire budget request in detail from zero (zero-based). This shifts the burden of proof on to each manager to justify spending any money at all, as well as showing how the job can be done better.

ZBB requires that:

— all activities be presented in decision packages (sets of inter-related decisions) that relate input to output;

— each package be evaluated by systematic analysis;

— all programmes be ranked in order of importance.

This productivity improvement technique is mainly aimed at reducing overheads and is used to reallocate resources among overhead activities, properly compartmentalise the overhead costs and carefully analyse each overhead-cost compartment.

The basic elements of the ZBB process are:

— identifying each decision unit (a significant programme, or level of an organisation, or individual department);

— drawing up the decision packages in priority order and making up the total budget request for each unit;

— ranking all decision packages in order of decreasing benefits to establish priorities on the basis of functions;

— allocating resources where most benefits can be expected and preparing detailed line item budgets.

ZBB helps link top management's strategic planning activities with the programming and control functions performed by all levels of the management hierarchy.

Cost-productivity allocation

Most organisations pay close attention only to costs. They track them, control them, and keep them at rock-bottom levels. This could be a mistake for two reasons: [7]

● First, cost should not be detached from performance. Driving costs down for its own sake inevitably drives performance down. This causes productivity to drop in the long run.

● Second, there are many times when costs must be allowed to go up in order to achieve an important performance target.

The key question is where the money will come from if budgets are tight. Cost-productivity allocation is a technique for the reallocation of money to improve productivity. It works against the traditional, across-the-board percentage cuts, which remove the good with the bad. The proposed technique permits the identification of cost items that are critical and finds the small outlay of money needed to improve productivity.

The theoretical background of this technique is the analysis and reallocation of the following four cost categories:

● Cost avoidance — removing or eliminating a cost item that is anticipated and budgeted for but not expended.

- Cost reduction — reducing or decreasing the amount of a cost item that has been budgeted for and is in process of expenditure.
- Cost control — spending, but keeping the amount of a cost item within the budget standard.
- Cost effectiveness — increasing the spending allocated in a budget because it will improve performance or reduce costs in the long run.

A rough distribution of the above cost categories is shown in figure 5.5.

Figure 5.5.   A typical cost-productivity curve

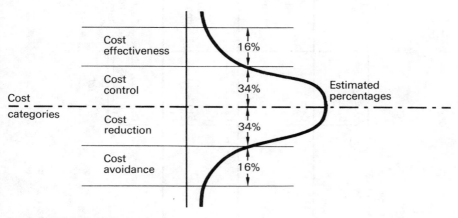

Source: P. Mali, 1978, p. 324.

Process

The process of the cost-productivity allocation is illustrated in figure 5.6.

- List the cost demands in a budget or cost array. The listing may be past, present or future, depending on an individual or a department.
- Arrange the list in order of greatest benefit (return for the amount of cost invested) to least benefit.
- Separate the list according to the cost-productivity curve. Starting from the lowest payoff or benefit, identify in the cost array the percentages for each category; for example, cost avoidance — 16 per cent, cost reduction — 34 per cent, cost control — 34 per cent, cost effectiveness — 16 per cent.
- Redistribute savings (from cost avoidance and cost reduction categories) to cost-effective items.

Figure 5.6. Cost-productivity allocator

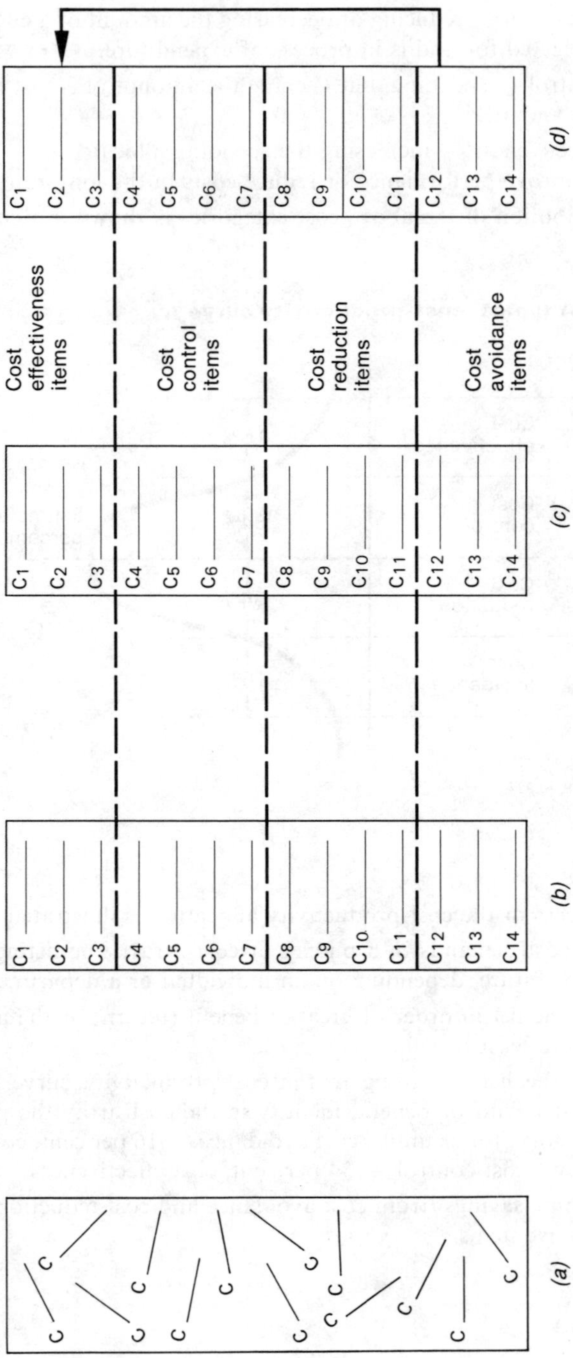
Cost effectiveness items
Cost control items
Cost reduction items
Cost avoidance items
C1
C2
C3
C4
C5
C6
C7
C8
C9
C10
C11
C12
C13
C14
(a)
(b)
(c)
(d)

Source: P. Mali, 1978, p. 324.

5.2 Behavioural techniques

Organisation development

Organisation development (OD) is a planned, managed, and systematic process. Its objective is to change the systems, the culture, and the behaviour of an organisation in order to improve the organisation's effectiveness.

OD deals with organisational aspects of the behavioural sciences and links with human resource development and organisational renewal. Many definitions of OD mention such objectives as helping members of an organisation to interact more effectively. It must always be organisation-wide, directed towards more participatory management, must provide for integrating the individual's goals with the organisation's and must be considered an ongoing process.

Much organisational inefficiency can be traced to individuals who are not interested in the organisation they belong to. Conversely, a lot of personal unhappiness can be traced to feeling inadequately integrated into the organisation one belongs to. The benefit of OD lies in reconciling the interests of individuals and of the organisation and successfully realising both.

While OD will not overcome such deficiencies as outdated technology, inadequate financing or hostile external forces, it will enable organisations to cope more effectively with these negative influences.

OD is based on the assumption that organisations influence human behaviour and individuals influence the behaviour of organisations, but that both can be modified with proper diagnosis and skilful intervention.

Most OD agents or consultants tend to view their mission as helping client organisations become more participatory and consensus seeking.

OD processes and techniques

A model of an OD process is given in figure 5.7.

An OD process is a continuous, circular system, which requires the services of a consultant. To start the process the consultant (who may be internal or external to the organisation) may intervene at any level or in any process in the organisation, but most prefer to start with the most powerful person to gain management support. However, executives should avoid using an OD consultant to take problems off their hands. Neither should they consider the consultant as a temporary staff member who must be closely supervised.

The problem identification and recognition stages allow the expression of dissatisfaction at every level to reveal the problems. Entering into an OD process requires a dialogue between consultant and client. At this stage OD consultants use such common techniques as surveys, interviews and direct observation methods. They also look at the traditional indicators of dissatisfaction such as slumping production figures, delayed shipments, absenteeism, turnover, pilferage, poor housekeeping and grievances. They observe the norms and the whole organisational culture.

Productivity management

Figure 5.7. Model of a typical organisation development process

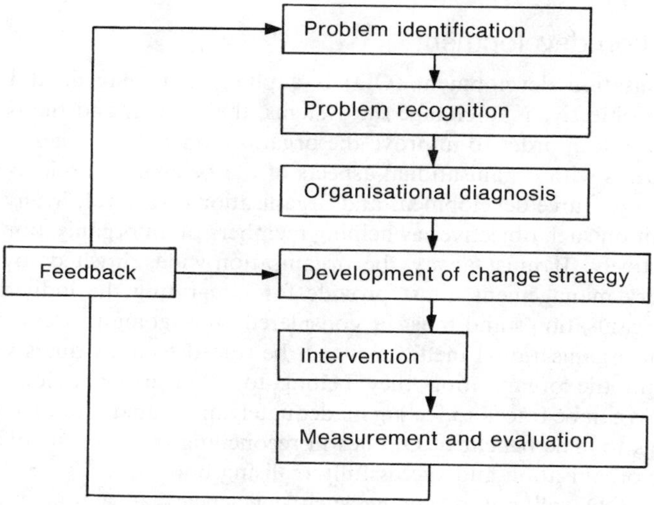

```
                    ┌──────────────────────────┐
           ┌───────▶│  Problem identification  │
           │        └────────────┬─────────────┘
           │        ┌────────────▼─────────────┐
           │        │   Problem recognition    │
           │        └────────────┬─────────────┘
           │        ┌────────────▼─────────────┐
           │        │ Organisational diagnosis │
           │        └────────────┬─────────────┘
  ┌──────────┐     ┌────────────▼─────────────┐
  │ Feedback │────▶│ Development of change     │
  └──────────┘     │ strategy                 │
           │        └────────────┬─────────────┘
           │        ┌────────────▼─────────────┐
           │        │      Intervention        │
           │        └────────────┬─────────────┘
           │        ┌────────────▼─────────────┐
           └────────│ Measurement and evaluation│
                    └──────────────────────────┘
```

Organisational diagnosis deals with the identification of the nature and scope of the problem within the organisation. It typically involves three main elements:

— investigation of the areas of the organisation where change is needed;
— establishment of the objective of the change strategy;
— preparation for the change through research and education.

This diagnostic activity is often undertaken at the highest level in the organisation. At this stage, team building techniques are particularly useful, as they help the members become more effective as a problem-solving or project-planning group. Another important tool is performance factor analysis which focuses attention on the variables that influence organisational behaviour, particularly work performance. The factors analysed are communication, training, motivation and freedom for individuals to do what is effective and expected. Among other tools and techniques which are widely used in OD processes at this stage are management by objectives, reward system analysis, norm modification, force-field analysis, conflict resolution, transactional analysis and brainstorming. The important characteristic of this stage of the OD process is creating a learning environment.

Development of the change strategy is the major decision-making stage of the process. At this stage it is important to select the instruments for change. The change technique may be designed by the original group of inquiry, by a specially appointed design committee, by the company OD specialists or outside consultants or by any combination of these. Interventions may be made in organisational structure or culture and norms, or in management development, product assembly, customer service, sales, or in combinations of these elements.

146

The design should have clearly articulated objectives, a time frame, conditions, budgetary control and reporting arrangements. It is important to start with a pilot programme followed by an evaluation and adjustment of the design strategy and instruments.

Only after this is it reasonable to go into the full implementation of the strategy design (intervention stage). The evaluation and measurement stage has to be a long-term undertaking with procedures for continuous monitoring of progress. The form of this evaluation could be results- and objectives-oriented progress reports, a monthly or quarterly management review, attitude surveys, or programme evaluation review techniques providing feedback to close the OD cycle.

The speed with which the process is implemented throughout the organisation depends on many physical and psychological factors such as the active and skilled use of such techniques as problem-solving groups, job re-design, quality circles and team building. Because of this emphasis on human behaviour, introducing changes through OD is necessarily a learning-by-experience process rather than a purely intellectual exercise. People learn best by doing, and an organisational culture is better developed by working on tangible problems than by discussing abstract concepts.

Brainstorming

Brainstorming is an organised idea-generating process avoiding any premature evaluation, as this so frequently shuts off the production of good ideas.[8] It is an uninhibited discussion in an open atmosphere, in which new ideas (solutions to the problem) are nurtured and new insights developed. All aspects of a subject can be examined without any attempt to limit who says what. This type of discussion generates useful ideas that may not occur to an isolated invidual puzzling over a problem. Not only do more and better ideas emerge, but the group itself gains strength and confidence as it improves its ability to brainstorm effectively.

Process and operating hints

- A brainstorming session begins with the selection of a specific problem or topic. To ensure that everyone participates, the leader calls on each member in turn for comments.
- No criticism is permitted.
- If members run out of ideas, who, what, when, where, why and how questions are used to get the talk flowing again.
- The ideas should be duly noted and written on a flow chart or blackboard kept in full view of everyone.
- The members sort out the various ideas and select the few key ones. These are discussed in detail and listed in order of importance. The whole list is retained for future use.

- Members then select (by majority vote) one or two ideas for in-depth investigation.
- Brainstorming may precede, follow or take place concurrently with the use of other improving tools and techniques.

In the initial stages of brainstorming the leader should anticipate the following problems:

- The member writing ideas on the flip chart (board) is too slow and misses important comments.
- Some members are inhibited in public (in groups of more than seven people).
- Members tend to follow tradition and discuss each idea as it is suggested, instead of waiting for the proper stage.
- Members combine several ideas instead of discussing them separately.
- The ideas suggested deal with trivia rather than the suggested topic.
- Members jump to conclusions and think they have a solution before the problem is thoroughly understood.
- One member tends to dominate the others.
- The leader is unable to keep order and get each member to speak in turn.

The leader should be trained to overcome these difficulties. The brainstorming technique is one of the important components of many productivity improvement methods and techniques such as QCs, PIP, work study, etc.

Force-field analysis

The technique of force-field analysis (FFA) is a tool for analysing a situation that needs to be changed. It facilitates change in an organisation by minimising effort and disruption. FFA can be applied when there is confusion about what improving step should be taken next. It opens up new options for action. This technique boils the problem down to a "do-able" size and helps the group to work together. It can be used by an individual, a small or a large group.

FFA is based on the concept that any given level of per-formance-productivity is the result of equilibrium between "driving or impelling forces" (those factors which support productive action), and "restraining or impeding forces" (factors that inhibit productive action).

Behaviour resulting in productive action can be raised by one or a combination of the following strategies:

— remove or reduce the restraining forces;

— add to or strengthen the driving forces.

Unfortunately, increasing those driving forces that threaten or pressure people is likely to increase resistance. It is often better to work on restraining forces, or to increase those driving forces that do not increase resistance. Another possibility is to consider a new driving force that may be brought into play.

Process

- Define clearly the current "equilibrium condition" — the level of performance-productivity which needs to be improved; determine the desired end result.
- Identify the driving and restraining forces that exist in the organisation, the environment, the jobs and the workers. (A brainstorming or nominal grouping technique can be used — see figure 5.8.) Present the data graphically.
- Make the length of the arrows in the figure proportionate to the magnitude of the force (strength can also be indicated with numbers: 1 — low, 2 — some, 3 — medium, 4 — high, 5 — very high).
- Analyse which of the restraining forces can be removed or reduced and what driving forces can be added or strengthened.
- Test to see if the analysis is sufficiently complex (e.g. if it includes the motivation of influential people, outside forces, policies, administrative procedures and practices, the nature of individual habits and needs, financial and material input).

Whatever is done must significantly shift the balance in favour of the impelling forces. This requires a careful analysis of what is technically, economically, organisationally and politically possible. It is necessary to concentrate on those forces that are easiest to change, have the greatest payoff and, when altered, are least disruptive.

After completion of the analysis, an implementation plan should be prepared for the proposed change (ensure that, among other points, it contains details of the necessary events that must occur).

Figure 5.8. An example of force-field analysis showing forces impeding and impelling performance improvement

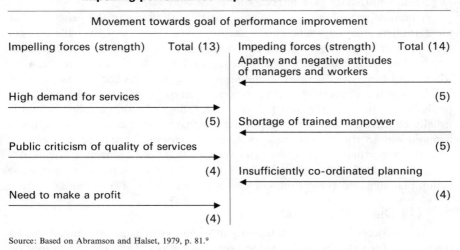

Movement towards goal of performance improvement	
Impelling forces (strength) Total (13)	Impeding forces (strength) Total (14)
	Apathy and negative attitudes of managers and workers
	←
	(5)
High demand for services →	
(5)	Shortage of trained manpower
	←
	(5)
Public criticism of quality of services →	
(4)	Insufficiently co-ordinated planning
	←
	(4)
Need to make a profit →	
(4)	

Source: Based on Abramson and Halset, 1979, p. 81.[9]

Operating hints

- Define the current (equilibrium) condition clearly and determine the desired end result.
- Press the people concerned to identify as many forces as possible. Persist with the method even though it may seem a little silly at first. Persist with identification without worrying about what can or can't be done at this stage.
- Use flip charts.

A limitation of this techique is that the analysis sometimes seems to be too detailed. However, results depend on the quality and completeness of the analysis, a fact which should not be forgotten.

Nominal group technique

Nominal grouping is a participatory approach to fact finding (gathering data), identifying problems and strengths, generating ideas (action planning) and evaluating progress.[10] It can be used effectively in three phases of productivity improvement processes: productivity diagnosis, action planning and evaluation. It also has an indirect advantage in that the frequent, intense participation of organisation members enhances the change process, thus facilitating the implementation phase.

In this technique members develop their views (solutions) independently. Then their ideas are shared with other members of the subgroup in a structured format. Suggestions are discussed for clarification and each subgroup reports its findings to the larger group.

Nominal grouping has certain advantages over other interventions such as interviews, questionnaires, observation and interacting groups in action planning. It is superior because it is much faster, ensures tight control of the time the process takes, is less expensive, and involves more people in a shorter time. It also appears to generate more data than interviewing.

Nominal grouping is also superior to brainstorming in the generation of ideas. It offers great satisfaction and a sense of involvement, as it gives all members the opportunity for equal participation and prevents any one member from dominating the discussion. It is more congruent with the creation of a climate where communication is open. Nominal grouping initiates the process of team building as the nominal grouping process itself is open and everyone shares preliminary data from the outset. It creates a feeling of group ownership, and is usually effective in bringing a sceptical participant "on board" and ensuring a commitment to the improvement programme. Nominal grouping participants have the opportunity to pinpoint priority items that need immediate attention.

The nominal grouping process itself has the three classic phases of diagnosis, action planning and evaluation. It requires the services of a consultant.

(1) Diagnosis phase

The process begins with a meeting in which participants are introduced to the reasons for initiating a planned improvement effort. They are encouraged by the general manager and the consultant to be honest and open in giving their views. The first meeting deals with two questions:

- What are the strengths of the organisation that have helped it to reach its present state of productivity-effectiveness?

- What are the problems that are preventing the organisation from reaching higher productivity-effectiveness?

The participants are divided into subgroups of six to eight, grouped according to rank (all top managers might be in one group) and/or function. Homogeneous grouping is important because different levels of status and position inhibit the performance of certain group members if personal relations between managers and subordinates are seen as a problem. Then each subgroup proceeds as follows:

- The members of the subgroup all respond separately to the two questions, by writing their own views on cards (one card for each idea, strength or problem). This is done individually. The time allowed is 20 minutes.

- Subgroups select one member to serve as the recorder and speaker.

- Each speaker asks members of the subgroup in turn to read out one strength from their list, and the speaker writes it down on the flip chart. If anyone else has noted the same strength, a checkmark is placed by the item. The process continues, one item at a time, until all strengths are recorded on the flip chart. Discussion of each item is discouraged until all items are recorded. The same process is followed for the problems identified by the group members.

- After both lists are complete, discussion is allowed in order to synthesise, clarify or add items.

- All subgroup members are again given two cards and asked to vote for the five strengths they think are most significant and the five problems they feel are most crucial and should receive highest priority.

- Each subgroup reports the top five items on each list to the group as a whole. The consultant then explains that the data will be classified and the results will be presented so that the organisation can proceed to develop strategies and improvement plans. Another option would be for the subgroups to develop cause-effect diagrams.

After classifying the results of the diagnosis, the consultant discusses them with top management. Together they plan how to build on strengths and overcome the problems.

(2) Action planning

It is possible that a shared approach using nominal grouping will be applied in developing action plans to overcome top priority problems. This approach may even be applied in an attempt to eliminate disruptive friction among managers so as to develop a management team with unity of purpose.

When nominal grouping (and brainstorming) is used as an aid to action planning, it is necessary to move into interacting groups to discuss and develop final action plans.

(3) The evaluation phase

After six or 12 months nominal grouping could be used again as a primary intervention in the evaluation phase to pinpoint strengths and problems. A comparison would then be made with the findings at the beginning of the improvement programme. If the improvement effort has been successful, the top priority problems should be, at least partly, resolved. The new problem set will be different. Perhaps some of the previous problems will now be considered as strengths. The evaluation phase also serves as the starting-point for the diagnosis phase of a new cycle.

* * *

There are many other productivity improvement techniques which are similar or which overlap with those discussed above. Some of the techniques which have not been discussed here include general planning techniques, critical path network, different types of scheduling, management by objectives, programme evaluation and break-even analysis. They can all be found in textbooks, manuals or management encyclopaedias (see, for example, Grant, 1972; Bittel (ed.), 1978; and Taguchi, 1986). However, what is described here gives the necessary understanding of the processes and benefits of the commonest techniques used in productivity improvement programmes.

----

[1] ILO: *Introduction to work study* (Geneva, 3rd (revised) ed., 1979), p. 35.

[2] Alan Lawlor: *Productivity improvement manual* (Aldershot, United Kingdom, Gower, 1985), pp. 165-168.

[3] Richard C. Walleigh: "What's your excuse for not using JIT?", in *Harvard Business Review* (Boston, Harvard University Press), Mar. 1986, pp. 38-54.

[4] Chris Wyles: "Computers: Think big, but start small", in *Works Management* (London, Trade News Ltd.), Feb. 1986, pp. 35-37.

[5] Stephen Moss: "A systems approach to productivity", in *National Productivity Review* (New York, Executive Enterprises Publications, Summer 1982), pp. 270-279.

[6] Michael Speirs: "How to manage value", in *Management Today* (London, Management Publications Ltd.), Jan. 1985, pp. 82-87.

[7] P. Mali: *Improving total productivity* (New York, John Wiley, 1978), pp. 323-325.

[8] Alexander Hamilton Institute, Inc.: *Quality circles: New approach to productivity*, Modern Business Reports (New York, 1981), pp. 64-67.

[9] Robert Abramson and Walter Halset: *Planning for improved enterprise performance. A guide for managers and consultants* (Geneva, ILO, 1979), pp. 80-82.

[10] D. C. Mosley and T. B. Green: "An analysis of nominal grouping as an organisational development intervention technique", Support material for the European Foundation for Management Development (Denmark, Scanticon Asrhus, 1973).

CONCENTRATING ON VITAL AREAS

PART III

CONCENTRATING ON VITAL AREAS

IMPROVING THE USE OF CAPITAL RESOURCES 6

In Chapter 4 we discussed how to organise productivity programmes within an organisation such as an enterprise. Many organisations run several subprogrammes simultaneously — one subprogramme might concentrate on energy conservation, another on reducing scrap and materials wastage and yet another might concentrate on improving product quality and value to the customer.

How can we choose which opportunities to take? How can management decide, for example, whether energy savings promise a better return than reducing scrap? Moreover, which type of approach — action learning, OD/PIP, PIC, etc. — should we apply to which area? Table 6.1 illustrates these choices and indicates that each of the different approaches could be applied to each of the areas.

When all the necessary factors have been identified and analysed it is not difficult to combine different components of the above-mentioned approaches to design a tailor-made programme. The aim of the next two chapters is to discuss what needs to be taken into consideration in planning a productivity improvement process tailored for particular areas.

6.1 Waste reduction and energy conservation programmes

Some important principles

Significant productivity improvements usually come from saving materials and energy. Raw materials account for about 40 per cent of total national production costs on average; if we include energy, this figure increases considerably.

Poor operator practice, bad layout and inadequate storage space can aggravate problems in handling materials and lead to excessive movement. A significant objective of any productivity improvement programme should be to

Table 6.1. Matrix of inter-relationships of productivity improvement areas and programmes

Types of programme / Productivity areas	Quality of labour force management	Quality of goods and services	Maintenance of equipment and facilities	Materials and energy
OD/PIP				
Action learning				
PAT process				
PIC				
Business clinics/IFC				

suggest methods of maintaining the volume of production while reducing consumption of energy and materials, and substituting cheaper materials and spare parts for costly ones. Alternatively, a productivity programme should suggest ways to produce more from a given quantity of raw materials. Improving productivity also depends on optimal choice and utilisation of materials and energy sources.

Typical manufacturing companies spend between 30 and 80 per cent of sales turnover on purchasing raw materials and energy. Yet frequently less than three-quarters of what is bought actually goes into the finished, full-value article.

A waste of 5 to 10 per cent of raw materials and energy occurs in the course of the hundreds of operations performed in a month. There are numerous reasons for this, and management can do little about it. Nevertheless, managers can still control the waste of 2 to 3 per cent of materials and energy that occurs during the last five minutes to one hour of the production process, and which arises from a few well-known causes. It is the operators and foremen who actually control the utilisation of materials, energy and machines, but managers, production engineers and quality assurance staff still have three important responsibilities in this field:

● To make it physically possible for operators and foremen to reduce the waste that occurs at their process from a very few known causes.

● To delegate responsibility so that operators and foremen can control the operations for which they are responsible.

● To ensure that the results are being achieved.

If these responsibilities are accepted, several important principles of waste and reject management follow:

— information on waste or reject performance needs to refer to the small percentage arising from one or two clearly understood causes;

— the only true control arrangements are those which enable an operator to adjust production on a minute-by-minute or hour-by-hour basis;

— the data collected should be processed to indicate clearly what should be done or whether any action need be taken at all;

— information to be used by departmental managers should not be more than 24 hours old: a reasonable target is to have the previous 24 hours' performance indicators by 10 o'clock each morning; in other words, information is between four and 28 hours old;

— independently produced operating statements showing monthly variations should verify and evaluate the degree of control being exercised;

— performance should always be measured against actual materials use, even if less than 100 per cent use is acceptable.

Experience shows that the correct application of these principles can bring considerable benefits without any changes being made in basic equipment or methods.

Energy conservation and materials waste reduction must be tackled at several levels, from the organisation level down to that of the operator.

The following is a suggested check-list of measures to improve use of materials:

At the design stage, ensure:

— that the design is such that production requires the minimum use of materials;

— that physical deterioration and depreciation of plant and equipment are minimised.

At the process or operation stage, ensure:

— that the process used is the best one;

— that operators are properly trained and motivated to carry out their functions effectively;

— proper handling and storage at all stages from raw materials to finished products, eliminating all unnecessary handling and movement;

— proper packaging to avoid damage in transit to the customer;

— proper use of scrap and other waste materials.

Energy conservation programmes

Most of the energy used in industrial production and services finally escapes into the atmosphere. The thermal efficiency of most industrial furnaces ranges between 20 to 40 per cent, while boilers have a thermal efficiency of between 70 and 90 per cent. Energy can be conserved by re-using wasted heat or redirecting misused energy.

The success of any conservation programme depends largely on the commitment of everyone within an organisation, and on the habits and life-styles of its managers and workers. People, therefore, are the key to an effective conservation programme. Since workers take their cue from management, management must initiate energy conservation efforts.

At the technical level contributions to energy conservation must be expected from specialists in civil, mechanical, fuel, heat, ventilating and electrical engineering. They must consider what can be changed and what equipment to buy. Managers and supervisors must rely on the technical skill of the engineers to collect much of the basic information necessary for planning improvements.

To obtain the benefits of energy conservation, a series of practical management tasks has to be carried out near the point of control, usually the machine or workplace. Appropriate analytical tools facilitate an understanding of the process and help in finding ways to improve performance. They usually make it possible to improve the operation before making more permanent changes. The organisation's policy on energy conservation should be based on:

— proper organisational set-up;
— staff training;
— collection and analysis of operational data on energy;
— setting up of energy conservation targets by the manager responsible.

Managers should communicate regularly with staff on energy conservation problems, spell out their policies and procedures, announce the launching of the programme, check and monitor the programme's status and investigate why certain targets are not being attained. Managers should also support the programme by personally displaying energy conservation efforts.

An energy conservation programme should systematically investigate and assess the actual situation and promote energy conservation measures, draft practical plans, organise their implementation and evaluate results. The mechanism for action could be an energy management department, a committee, a project team and so on. For example, Japanese enterprises typically support their self-motivated small groups by setting up energy conservation promotion committees with the factory manager as leader. These committees draft practical plans and evaluate their results.

In the Philippines Enercon (Energy Conservation) committees are primarily responsible for formulating and implementing energy conservation programmes. An energy co-ordinator or full-time energy manager may be appointed to report to top management. Some Enercon committees are even headed by a company president or vice-president. Typical Enercon committee functions include planning and participating in energy-saving surveys; developing uniform record-keeping, reporting and energy accounting; conducting research and developing ideas on how to conserve energy; suggesting tough energy conservation goals and communicating ideas on how to achieve them; developing ideas and plans for enlisting staff support and participation; and planning and conducting a continuing programme of activities to stimulate interest in energy conservation efforts.[1]

Energy conservation requires the co-operation of all workers. To make the programme a success it is important to create a climate which is favourable to generating suggestions at all levels, encouraging ideas and promoting awareness; all the workers should understand why the programme cannot function without them. To involve workers in energy conservation programmes, it is important to explain how escalating energy prices will affect the survival of the enterprise *and their own employment*; to stress their crucial role in energy conservation; to show inconsistencies between excessive energy consumption and the values held by workers.

When explaining to workers why they should conserve energy, make sure that the goals are realistic and attainable. Consider sharing the gains from energy conservation with workers; foster reasonable competition between departments and shifts; eliminate unnecessary fears that the measures will be at the expense of working conditions; and recognise the efforts and accomplishments of individuals and departments.

Training is also a good tool, not only to raise awareness, but to answer technical questions on how to conserve energy.

Energy management

A systematic energy management process effectively promotes energy conservation. Depending on the level of energy costs in the final product, the technology, the policies and the type of organisation, three stages of action are possible: a "housekeeping stage", an information collection stage; and an investment stage.

Housekeeping stage

This can start immediately, and needs little preparation. It is based only on existing experience. Housekeeping means tightening up the use of materials and energy. There is almost always some slack in the system somewhere. Housekeeping activities at this stage include arranging information posters, notices, booklets, etc.; appointing an energy conservation manager, a department warden, and forming an energy conservation and waste reduction committee to secure participation, involvement and commitment.

Information stage

At this stage auditing is needed to help answer such questions as: "What energy do we consume?" "Where does it go?" "How efficiently do we use it?"

This stage involves the installation of instruments to measure electricity, liquids and gases. Since few firms have these, specialists from trade associations, trade research or specialist fuel consultants are usually required to conduct audits and make recommendations. At this stage it is important to set targets for energy consumption and waste reduction, to improve permanent instrumentation for better control of quantities and efficiency, and to form other energy conservation and waste reduction groups.

Investment stage

This is the stage for decisions about capital expenditure for energy conservation equipment and technology. When replacing equipment, energy conservation and better use of materials now need to be considered.

Procedures of energy management

This section is taken from an ILO project in Bangladesh. It is relevant to energy management in any context.[2]

Energy conservation starts with the following energy management procedures:

— measuring energy use;
— analysing the cost of energy per unit of product;
— setting targets;
— taking action to cut energy costs;
— measuring the results of the programme.

Data about energy consumption come first from electricity and fuel bills. It is desirable to express the amount of energy used as consumption rates. Consumption rates, the amount of energy used per product lot, are expressed by the relation of energy used to output.

Collection and analysis of energy-related data

Quantitatively it is better to get the data about energy flow by metering the input of electricity, fuel, and so on, and then measuring the amount that is productively consumed. The difference is the amount wasted. At the same time, one must record and analyse productivity, a temperature, a pressure and a time corresponding to this energy flow.

These data tell us where and how much energy is lost, which is useful when determining priority. A good measure of energy flow is the quantity per process and facility.

Preparation of measuring equipment

Since few factories have the necessary equipment, they cannot measure energy consumption by process and facility but only for the whole factory. For example, few industrial furnaces and boilers are equipped with fuel-flow meters. Few boilers are equipped with feed water meters or steam-flow meters even though they may have fuel-flow meters. In this situation, identifying energy conservation/consumption requires know-how based on experience.

When installing equipment make sure it has these measuring devices, and periodically inspect and maintain them.

Understanding energy flows

There are several types of graphic display that help people understand where energy can be saved and how well the energy conservation programme is working. Figure 6.1 shows daily output, a fuel service amount and the fuel consumption rate of a factory for a month. Such a control chart is basic to energy management.

Figure 6.2 shows the correlations between the output rate, fuel service amount and consumption rate, using the data in figure 6.1.

Figure 6.1. Fuel consumption rate chart

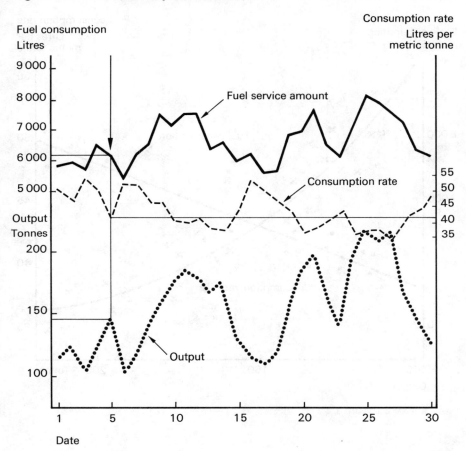

Source: R. Takahashi, 1985, p. 7.

This chart indicates that although *actual* fuel consumption increases as output goes up, the fuel consumption *rate* decreases. The chart also shows that actual data are scattered from correlative curves. However, if the curves can be equalised with lower ones, this will indicate that fuel consumption can be reduced.

Energy supply flow chart

An energy supply flow chart is used to show how energy is branched and supplied. The chart needs values such as pipe diameters and lengths, flow rates, steam pressures, etc., inscribed, so that it can be effectively used to help prevent losses of radiant heat.

Figure 6.2. Correlative chart of output and fuel consumption rate

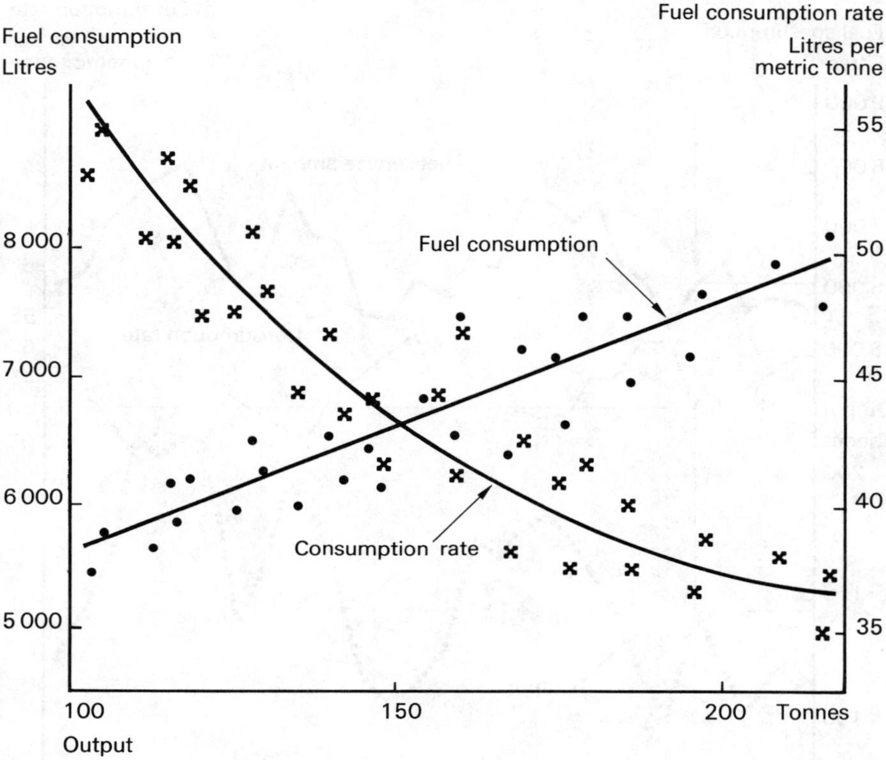

Source: R. Takahashi, 1985, p. 8.

Heat balance

It is important to analyse heat balances to know how energy is used, and where, and in what form, energy is wasted. Figure 6.3 shows an example of steel material heating with improvement points added.

Comparison between energy supply and demand

Comparison between energy supply and demand, expressed in terms of temperature and pressure, indicates any possible reduction in supply. If supply is surplus to requirements it indicates that more efficient methods of energy conservation should be introduced.

Figure 6.4 compares steam pressures. If the service pressure in area "C" can be reduced, steam pressure surplus overall will increase and the pressure level of the steam supply can be lowered.

Figure 6.3. Energy flow by heat balance

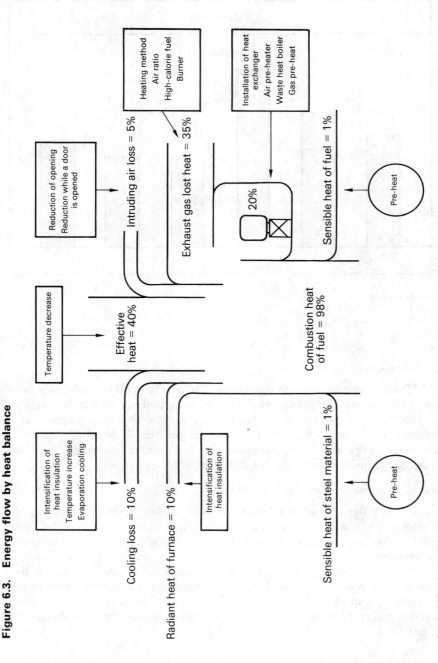

Source: R. Takahashi, 1985, p. 9.

Figure 6.4. Comparison of required steam pressures

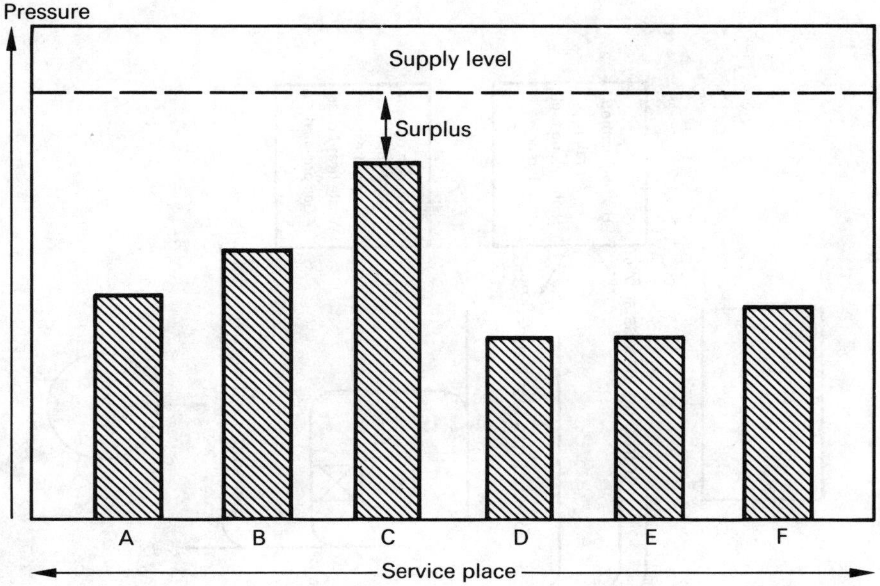

Source: R. Takahashi, 1985, p. 10.

Recommendations

If present excessive energy consumption is to be brought to public awareness, many points where energy conservation must be carried out need to be identified. It is necessary to decide on the priority of carrying out energy conservation measures. For this purpose the following factors should be totally reviewed: amount of energy used; energy consumption rate; sum of investment; pay-back period of the investment; degree of difficulty; effects; continuity.

First step (intensification of energy control)

The first step is to intensify energy control without additional expense. This includes review and observation of standards of operation, service, manufacturing, facility control and repair. The main aim is to eliminate useless, irregular energy consumption.

"Useless" consumption occurs when a light is left on, or combustion air is excessive, or a motor is overloaded, or too much fuel is burned in order to heat some material quickly. This damages facilities and equipment and consumes excessive energy. "Irregularity" refers to a situation where operational standards are not fixed.

Second step (introduction of energy conservation equipment)

This step is aimed at introducing special equipment for energy conservation. Examples would be: a heat exchanger to recover waste heat, an automatic combustion control unit, a high-efficiency lamp, and an automatic flash for outdoor illumination.

Although investment increases in this second step, it can be expected to reap considerable benefits. But unless energy management in the first step has been intensified, the second step may not be very effective.

Third step (improvement of the process and systems)

Normally, this step is associated with expanding or introducing up-to-date, efficient facilities. For example, it could be process omission (continuous casting in the steel industry); one of heat in cascade, conversion of manufacturing methods (new suspension pre-heater kiln in the cement industry), continuity (continuous annealing in the steel industry) and so on. However, large investments are normally required to undertake this kind of modernisation.

Case study: Ewekoro Cement Works, Nigeria [3]

Through successive projects over a period of about ten years, the ILO and UNDP assisted Nigeria in productivity improvement and management development. Efforts were made to strengthen the National Productivity Centre and other agencies.

One of the productivity problems in Nigeria was the need to improve the use of resources. The case presented here was typical in its emphasis on training workers, thus creating local know-how and experience in coping with problems of energy management.

Cement production: Ewekoro Cement Works produced 502,000 tons of cement in 1984. The process of manufacturing cement is as follows. Raw materials (limestone and shale) are ground and mixed together with water to form cement "slurry". For the wet process line the slurry is tested, blended and passed directly into the kiln where it is gradually heated up: as the temperature rises the moisture in the slurry evaporates and chemical changes turn it into clinker. In the semi-wet process line, the slurry passes through a filter press which squeezes out most of the water leaving a "cake" of raw material. The cake is cut into small pieces called "nodules", which are heated and dried. They then pass into the kiln, which is fired with fuel oil, to produce cement "clinker". This is cooled and ground to a fine powder and becomes cement. At this stage, about 5 per cent of gypsum (calcium sulphate) is added to control the setting time of the cement. The finished cement is mechanically packed into paper bags and bulk tankers for dispatch to customers.

Initiating a waste reduction programme

A joint team from the Nigeria Productivity Centre (NPC) and the ILO contacted the company in the middle of 1984 to initiate a productivity improvement programme, within the framework of the National Productivity Scheme 1982-86.

In an introductory meeting where the programme was introduced and discussed the General Manager briefed heads of department and urged them to co-operate. A steering committee was set up with eight members: the deputy general works manager as chairman; the production manager; the technical manager; the chief electrical engineer; the chief mechanical engineer; the stores controller; the training and development manager and the process control engineer. Their terms of reference were:

— to establish a company strategy of productivity improvement, check its feasibility, and get it widely accepted;

— to create appropriate motivation and readiness for change and a climate conducive to high productivity;

— to develop a company productivity improvement plan and to launch preparatory steps;

— to liaise effectively with all staff members: both general and specific productivity improving activities were undertaken by numerous teams, units and people;

— to facilitate and follow through the implementation and evaluation of the programme.

The steering committee had a number of sessions: introductory, diagnostic, improvement, team work and leadership, etc. They normally met once every two weeks. During a diagnostic session, it was decided to start with the kiln side, where most of the productivity problems had arisen.

It was therefore decided to set up an action group of 21 members, all of whom were either familiar with the problems or could help solve them. At the diagnostic meetings of the steering committee the following productivity problems had been identified, in order of significance: inadequate standards and data; need for better maintenance and better supervision during maintenance; need for improvements in the skill of artisans and operatives, in the time management of the labour force, and in attitudes to work; inadequate communication between departments; transport problems.

The action group independently diagnosed the problems with the kilns and rated them as the steering committee did. The diagnoses made by the two groups were discussed and ranked by the members of the steering committee as follows:

Problem	Average rating
1. Lack of spare parts	1.6
2. Maintenance procedure	3.4
3. Attitude to work	6.0
4. Preventing and reducing acts of negligence	7.2
5. Insufficient skill (of operatives and craftsmen)	8.0
6. Reconditioning of spare parts	8.2

Problem	Average rating
7. Modification of equipment and parts	9.0
8. Power failure	10.0
9. Managerial skill related to delegation, follow-up and feedback	10.2
10. Reducing air inleak	10.4
11. Press cloths — need for local substitute	11.4
12. Communication	10.6
13. Standardisation, especially of Nos. 1, 2 and 3 kiln cooler spares	11.6
14. Motivation — boss/subordinate relations	11.8
15. Major transformation of obsolete equipment and plant	13.4
16. Pre-heater nodule/water level control	15.8
17. Absenteeism	16.2
18. Transport	17.0
19. No planned job rotation/incentives for good long-timers to stay on the job	17.2
20. Poor blending	17.6

The problems were then divided into those that could be solved within the works and those that could not. Those that could be solved within the works were subdivided into those that would yield immediate results and those that would take a long time before showing results.

It was then decided to start with three main tasks:

— reducing air inleaks;

— control of pre-heater nodule bed/water-level;

— supply of spare parts.

The action group split into three subgroups, one for each task.

Work in subgroups

The work in the subgroups involved the use of productivity improvement techniques which have been described in Chapter 5. The techniques used at the Ewekoro Cement Works included brainstorming, force-field analysis, Pareto analysis, and cause and effect diagrams. In addition to discussing problem-solving techniques, the subgroups worked on analysing the selected problem area and on developing ground rules for effective team work.

Activities of the subgroups

1. The subgroup responsible for spare parts identified the following problems as the most important: forecasting; inventory control; procurement; storage.

An analysis of kiln stoppages for the first nine months of 1984 was carried out (see table 6.2). It was found that lack of clinker cooler spare parts for No. 3 kiln (the biggest) was responsible for 54 per cent of the downtime of the kiln.

167

Table 6.2. **The Ewekoro works productivity improvement programme: Major causes of kiln stoppages from January to September 1984**

Reason for stoppage	No. 1 kiln		No. 2 kiln		No. 3 kiln	
	Downtime (hours)	% contri-bution	Downtime (hours)	% contri-bution	Downtime (hours)	% contri-bution
Pre-heater repair	228	18	205	12	1	—
Clinker conveyor repairs	110	9	232	13	529	19
Power failure	214	17	194	11	57	2
Cooler repairs	189	15	84	5	1 541	54
Brickwork	173	14	—	—	390	14
Maintenance	230	18	66	4	283	10
Low slurry stock	33	3	96	5	9	—
ID fan repairs	20	2	514	29	18	1
Kiln drive repairs	11	1	379	21	27	1
Press/noduliser repairs (belts, presses, etc.)	53	4	1	—	—	—
Air failure	1	—	1	—	1	—
Total downtime and % downtime	1 262	19	1 772	27	2 856	43

Source: NPC, DR/NIR/82/010.

An inventory of the spares required at the kiln side was taken with special reference to those that were vital. This was to determine priorities in spending the inadequate import licence allocation.

Ways of reducing spare parts requirements through standardisation, modification and reconditioning were identified. Previous efforts at modifying parts were intensified and these soon started to yield some dividends as the running time of No. 3 kiln increased from an average of 52.3 per cent in 1984 to 65 per cent in January 1985.

2. The subgroup responsible for the pre-heater nodule bed/water level. This group identified problems in the pre-heater to include: poor chemistry of feed; poor blending; inadequate dust on nodules; air inleak.

Members of the group took advantage of a repair stoppage of a kiln in January 1985. This permitted a major overhaul of the pre-heater which dramatically reduced fuel consumption.

3. The subgroup responsible for the air inleak. This action team used a cause-effect diagram and a brainstorming session to tackle the problem and to find various causes and effects of air inleak into the kiln system.

Air inleak to the kiln system reduces the efficiency of the internal draught fan which transfers the heat inside the kiln from the source. Because of the condition of the ductings and of the kilns themselves, they had air inleak as high as 60 per cent.

Figure 6.5.   Cause and effect diagram of air inleak into the kiln system

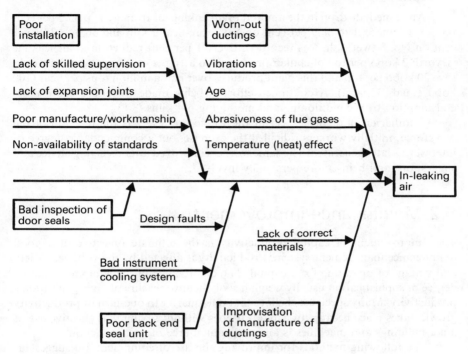

Source: NPC, DR/NIR/82/010.

Initial action plans and team ground rules were laid down. After drawing the cause and effect diagram (figure 6.5), it was decided to work on No. 1 kiln (a semi-wet type) because it was down for repairs. The plant efficiency manager was asked to analyse the air flow in the kiln to determine the amount of air that was leaking into the system. It was discovered that cold air was leaking into the system and the necessary preventive action was taken.

Improvement action

The jobs to be carried out in the areas inspected were assigned. The chief mechanical engineer and his deputy were informed of areas that would require special attention during the repairs. The supervisors of the production handymen and the masons were similarly informed. When the kiln was stopped, workers cleaned out all the suspected areas in order to expose all the gaps, cracks and other defects.

The service department started the repair work, which was progressively monitored by members of the team. Some jobs could not be taken on because of lack of spares and materials, but arrangements were made to do them as early as possible. A gas analysis was carried out after a 48-hour run. Further plans were mapped out.

Results

An immediate drop in the amount of in-leaking air from 64.1 to 53.5 per cent on No. 1 kiln, 55.1 to 38.9 per cent on No. 2 pre-heater kiln and 56.6 to 35.1 per cent on No. 3 (wet) kiln was recorded. Every 1 per cent reduction in air leakage is worth 2 kobo per ton of clinker produced, so a 10 per cent improvement would save 20 kobo per ton and this plant produces over half a million tons per year (100 kobo equals 1 naira). A continued effort is being made to reduce spare parts consumption by reconditioning and modifying old kilns.

Another encouraging aspect of the whole exercise was the reaction of the workforce; initially workers ridiculed the exercise, but a commendable degree of interest was later generated. The same workers improved after receiving advice and suggestions and being more personally involved.

6.2 Maintenance improvement

Improvement of capital productivity is the ultimate objective of a good maintenance management system. Productivity is affected by the volume, variety and vintage of operating fixed capital. The quality, age of the equipment and its degree of sophistication usually weigh heavily in any measure of an organisation's productivity. Many specialists believe that one-quarter to one-fifth of productivity growth takes place because of capital. It goes without saying that effective use of land, buildings and machines is an important source of cost reduction.

The following methods for improving the use of equipment are suggested:

— designing the optimal technological process;
— choosing the most appropriate equipment;
— scheduling machine use;
— organising the maintenance service;
— training the operatives.

It is not uncommon to find a 50-70 per cent rate of machine use, due to poor planning and lack of preventive maintenance. In one comparatively successful productivity improvement drive, downtime on critical production equipment was reduced from an average of 19 hours per week to 4.4 hours per week. There were no changes in equipment or personnel, just improved performance from the maintenance crew, which resulted from better management.

This illustrates why maintenance is gaining increasing attention in asset management as an important productivity improvement area. This is also due to increases in the price of simple as well as sophisticated machinery and equipment, which constitute added costs for importing countries. In developing countries maintenance and asset management are particularly important, for the following reasons:

● The "state of the art", i.e. sudden popular demand for a transition from a predominantly subsistence economy to an industrial one.

● The brain drain, which results in the depletion of management and technical personnel.

● The lack of interest on the part of overseas suppliers in training local personnel in the maintenance of equipment and in making spare parts readily and cheaply available.

● The indifference of international and government lending agencies to maintenance requirements. The tendency is to be satisfied with budget provisions for depreciation of assets without due regard for adequate maintenance costs. Usually the amount budgeted for maintenance covers only the expected cost of replacement parts and does not take into consideration long delays and work stoppages due to unavailability of spare parts.

A good maintenance system is normally achieved through:

— the clear objective of reducing the frequency of failures and shortening the time length of repairs;

— covering the whole life span of all equipment and facilities — at the project engineering stage, during operation and at the time of failure;

— involving all personnel, from top management to operators, in various maintenance measures.

In designing a maintenance system four major types of maintenance should be taken into consideration:

— preventive maintenance;

— breakdown maintenance;

— corrective maintenance;

— maintenance prevention.

Preventive maintenance includes routine and periodic maintenance. The first involves daily or weekly inspection of equipment by users, cleaning, adjustments, oiling and minor replacements. The second requires maintenance people to adjust equipment according to maintenance standards. It involves regular inspection for any abnormality, adjustment, replacement of worn out parts, and repair of damaged parts.

Breakdown maintenance means the repair of equipment after failure. It is appropriate only when there is spare equipment, otherwise production will be disrupted.

Corrective maintenance means improvement in equipment design to prevent failure or, in case of breakdown, to facilitate repair.

Maintenance prevention is an attempt at a maintenance-free system. It refers to equipment which is easy to repair and not to equipment which is unsafe to handle. This will incur no maintenance cost to an organisation when conditions are perfect. However, equipment costs are usually very high. Despite the high cost, this approach is realistic and practical in a number of cases for developing countries.

How to design a maintenance system

The following are some practical guide-lines to designing a maintenance system for an industrial enterprise:

● Identify all critical facilities and critical spare parts.

● Establish an equipment record containing parts, specifications, history and the special characteristics of each item.

● Set up a diagnostic system to ascertain the condition of equipment while it is operating. This involves assessment of many factors, such as maintenance timing, measuring methods, signal processing techniques, statistical analysis techniques, mean time between failures, repairs and fault-free analysis.

● Determine the frequency and kind of maintenance needed by each piece of equipment to meet operational requirements. Base this on the results of diagnosis.

● Evaluate the economy of a maintenance system based on total maintenance cost. For instance, the amount of preventive maintenance can be determined by balancing costs of breakdown maintenance and preventive maintenance. In the same manner, the value of corrective maintenance can be defined by balancing downtime cost and corrective maintenance cost.

● Establish a procedure which sets in motion a planning function to anticipate breakdown or equipment failure. Set a pool of competent people to determine the cause of the trouble and the appropriate repair or corrective work, including parts, tools, materials and manpower skills requirements.

● Schedule and assign the repair, corrective, or preventive maintenance work to appropriate personnel.

● Design a spare parts management system and establish a systematic procedure for obtaining parts, tools and materials.

● Establish control elements (staff and equipment) to meet maintenance plans and carry out maintenance activities adequately.

● Establish a maintenance information system to record what has been done and provide feedback on design, performance and cost.

● Establish a system for maintenance evaluation based on standards. Various productivity indices provide useful guide-lines in assessing maintenance performance.

● Establish a system for maintenance manpower skills development and motivation.

These guide-lines could be used in any productivity improvement programme stressing maintenance improvement as one of the target areas.

Shop-floor level roles in maintenance

Success in the initiation and implementation of maintenance improvement programmes is a product of total organisational participation. However, the shop-floor level is of particular importance in this kind of programme. The following description of the Japanese approach is an example of shop-floor participation in maintenance. It is described by George Logan, a United States consultant, who visited over 85 Japanese plants to study their experiences.[4]

Typical machine operators learn many machines in great detail, working closely with the maintenance staff and the manufacturers' representatives to become as expert as they can. This is encouraged by management, and the workers take great pride in keeping their own machines operating. Operators who can keep their machines running can meet or exceed standards, and operators who can do their own repairs avoid the delays involved in getting help. If operators know that a problem is developing and that they cannot solve it themselves, they immediately notify the assistant foreman who does the repair during the break. On the rare occasions when the assistant foreman needs help, the maintenance man is called. If the machine is down, the maintenance man and the assistant foreman fix it immediately. (The assistant foreman will not need to call for help again on this problem.) If it is less serious, the adjustment is made during a break, at lunch, or at the end of the day. The maintenance man is a mechanically inclined individual with wide experience, who is trained by the equipment suppliers and by the engineers within the company, and is motivated to be more knowledgeable about every piece of equipment than the operators or the assistant foreman. On the rare occasions when he cannot do the repair, the equipment suppliers send in an expert to do it and to train the maintenance man so he can handle this situation next time. When the equipment supplier has to be involved, this is considered a major crisis since production is down. The foreman and production manager get involved in finding solutions and, if the equipment supplier is called, to exert pressure for immediate attention. If repeat problems occur, the equipment maker may be asked to compensate the company for the time lost.

If the equipment supplier says that a part should be replaced every 1,000 hours, the 1,000 hours becomes a target that the Japanese strive to beat. They will follow and exceed the maintenance recommendation, experimenting with cleaning and lubrication, modifying operating practices with reduced output, and so on.

With regard to critical expensive parts, everyone, from the operator up, will study and work on modifications that can be made to that part in order to extend its predicted life and prevent failures. They may buy the part from the supplier and, unknown to the supplier, modify it to extend its life. They may also buy parts from another vendor or make them themselves. By monitoring the critical part they will extend the life of equipment.

With regard to continuous lines which might be shut down by a failure, the Japanese have a task force assigned to study the line. The primary goal is to avoid ever having to shut the line down, but of equal importance are the dry runs to cover every possible contingency. The emergency teams rehearse every potential failure — who does what, with what, and in what order. It is a crisis and they treat it that way — a failure represents downtime and reduces their competitiveness. After such a failure, every detail is analysed, studied and restudied. Suppliers' products which might be at fault are subjected to close inspection and either the supplier must improve or the Japanese customer will find a more co-operative supplier.

The policy of rotating key staff makes assistant supervisors and key operators knowledgeable about the entire plant. This cross-fertilisation is further encouraged by formal presentations on problems and solutions which are made to the entire staff of the organisation.

If workers feel there is a problem with new equipment or products, they will raise questions. This is the often-discussed Japanese approach at its best — it may be in a quality circle, or it may be a totally informal discussion activity. No one is obliged to participate, but everyone who feels there is a problem asks the opinion of friends, co-workers or superiors. Over a period of time a consensus is reached. It is not a formal consensus but everyone agrees that there is a problem, and often a direction for the solution is agreed upon. When a solution is instituted the result is that it is supported by everyone involved.

Training in maintenance improvement

It is important to improve participants' awareness in any productivity improvement programme aimed at maintenance. However, awareness training should be combined with careful skill training of all concerned. This is especially relevant to maintenance because of the technicalities involved. Any training programme should centre on developing technical skills and improving awareness and attitudes. As an example, we will consider the case of corrosion prevention as an important component of maintenance improvement.

In order to improve awareness and attitudes, it is important to discuss the economic impact of corrosion. It is responsible for tremendous wastage of materials and labour, estimated at about 4 to 6 per cent of GNP. For example, in 1975 corrosion cost the United States about US$70,000 million, or 4.2 per cent of GNP. Of this total, about 15 per cent or US$10.5 thousand million was avoidable. About 3.4 per cent of the United States energy demand was generated by corrosion; one-sixth of this was estimated to be avoidable.[5]

In developing countries relative corrosion loss is estimated to be much larger than in developed countries, especially in tropical regions. About 25 per cent of these losses could be avoided.

Education about the negative economic impact of corrosion is thus vital. Managers, workers, engineers and designers must all be trained in anti-corrosion techniques.

A case study from India will illustrate the great productivity potential of maintenance improvement.

Case study: Improving the availability of shot-blasting plant (India) [6]

The objective of this case study was to increase the availability of plant which was critical for shot-blasting the surface of switchgear components to increase their life after painting. The operation is done by blasting the surface with grit. Since this is the first stage of the assembly line, its failure causes a serious

Figure 6.6. Cause and effect diagram for the plant

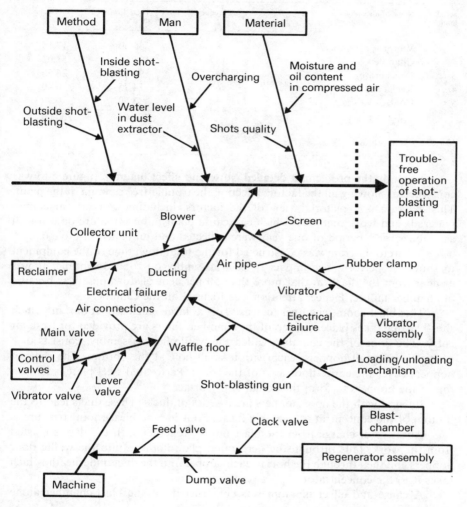

Source: S. Jakate, 1985, p. 5.

bottle-neck in production. This plant's contribution towards downtime was found to be as high as 8 per cent in a span of one year. The problem was analysed with the help of Pareto and cause and effect diagrams as follows:

Failure analysis

The plant comprises five major assemblies, namely: vibrator assembly; chamber; regenerator assembly; reclaimer; and control valves.

Table 6.3. Failure data for the plant

Serial number	Name of assembly	Frequency	Total downtime (hours)	Percentage
1	Vibrator assembly	8	66.50	17.18
2	Chamber	18	197.50	51.02
3	Regenerator	44	94.75	24.50
4	Reclaimer	6	24.75	6.40
5	Control valves	3	3.50	0.90
	Total		387.00	100.00

Source: S. Jakate, 1985, p. 5.

To study the problem, a detailed cause and effect diagram (figure 6.6) was constructed, showing all the factors affecting the trouble-free running of the plant. This diagram is a pictorial view of the factors, including workers, machines, materials and work methods, which can cause plant failure. Failure data for all assemblies for a period of one year were collected and tabulated in table 6.3.

A Pareto diagram was constructed for the total downtime of the equipment to show the performance impact of each assembly on total downtime. It was evident from the diagram that more than 50 per cent of downtime was because of chamber failure. Hence, attention was focused on the chamber.

The blast-room chamber consists of a large enclosed room in which shot-blasting takes place. On top of the chamber, filters are provided for fresh air entry. The floor of the chamber, called the waffle floor assembly, consists of a multitude of small hoppers, each with a small hole at the bottom. The rows of hoppers cover the entire floor area of the room. Perforated steel plate is laid on top of the hoppers to form the actual floor surface.

Integral with the floor hoppers are a series of ducts. These ducts lead to the bottom of the concentrator assembly located outside the blast-room structure.

Abrasive discharge from the blast nozzle, together with the debris blasted from the work, falls through the perforated plate flooring into the waffle floor hoppers and then through the hole in each hopper into the duct underneath, which takes it to the concentrator.

A cause and effect diagram was constructed for the blast-chamber alone (figure 6.7).

Failure data pertaining to chamber assembly were collected (see table 6.4) and a Pareto diagram was constructed (figure 6.8). From this Pareto diagram, it was obvious that it was the floor which frequently got choked up leading to the breakdown of the plant. The downtime due to this was as high as 85 to 90 per cent, indicating that this factor needed immediate attention.

Solution

As mentioned above, the waffle floor is a bed of small pockets connected underneath by separate ducts leading to a common opening. After a lot of study

Figure 6.7. Cause and effect diagram for the chamber

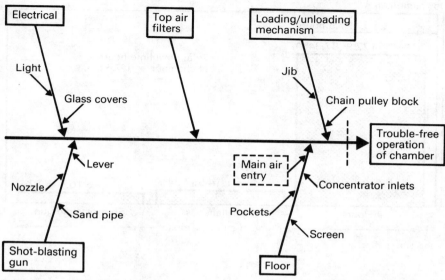

Source: S. Jakate, 1985, p. 5.

and a check on the condition of the floor, the possibility of local failure was eliminated by clearing out the pocket holes and replacing the perforated steel plate by plate with larger perforations. The duct openings were also thoroughly cleared. It was observed that the main air entry to each row was full of shot, which completely blocked the initial passage of air to the row. This had not been noticed earlier because the entry from one side was covered by rubber sheets. Since the air entry was partially blocked, the suction capacity of the reclaimer blower was considerably reduced, as the air flow from one end helps to carry the shot along with it up to the reclaimer. It was also observed that blockages always started from the row where the main air entry was choked and then spread to other rows, because they are interconnected. Earlier, whenever the plant failed, only the floor, pocket and rows were cleaned and nothing was done to the main air entry. The

Table 6.4. Failure data for the chamber

Serial number	Name of assembly	Frequency	Total downtime (hours)	Percentage
1	Floor	11	172.5	87.34
2	Shot-blasting gun	4	10.5	5.32
3	Miscellaneous	3	14.5	7.34

Source: S. Jakate, 1985, p. 5.

Figure 6.8. Pareto diagram for the chamber assembly (before improvement)

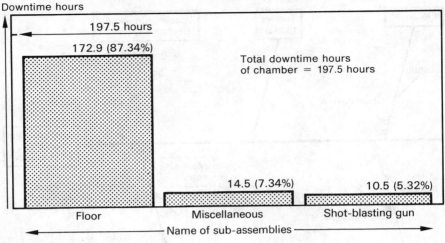

Source: S. Jakate, 1985, p. 5.

waffle floor used to fail frequently since the basic cause remained untouched. After the cleaning of the main air entries for each row, the plant was put under continuous observation for one year. Again, failure data for the plant were collected as shown in table 6.5.

The improvement is shown graphically by the Pareto diagrams for the plant before and after the study (figures 6.9 and 6.10). Analysis showed that the total downtime for the plant had come down from 8 to 4 per cent and for this particular assembly from 51 to 5.4 per cent, thereby substantially increasing plant availability.

Table 6.5. Failure data of the plant after this case study

Serial number	Name of assembly	Frequency	Total downtime (hours)	Percentage
1	Vibrator assembly	22	105.50	52.16
2	Regenerator	25	45.50	22.50
3	Reclaimer	11	20.50	10.14
4	Control valves	4	19.75	9.76
5	Chamber	5	11.00	5.44
	Total		202.25	100

Source: S. Jakate, 1985, p. 5.

Figure 6.9. Pareto diagram for the plant (before improvement)

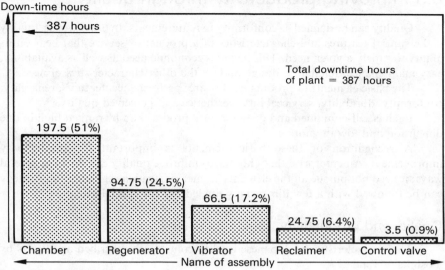

Down-time hours

387 hours

Total downtime hours
of plant = 387 hours

197.5 (51%)

94.75 (24.5%)

66.5 (17.2%)

24.75 (6.4%)

3.5 (0.9%)

Chamber Regenerator Vibrator Reclaimer Control valve

Name of assembly

Source: S. Jakate, 1985, p. 5.

Figure 6.10. Pareto diagram for the plant after one year of improvement

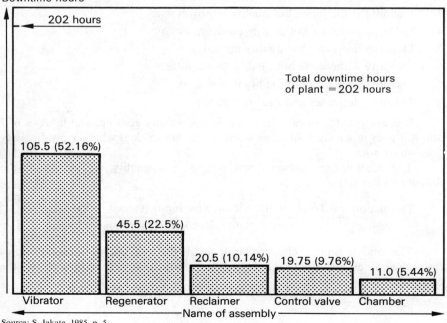

Downtime hours

202 hours

Total downtime hours
of plant = 202 hours

105.5 (52.16%)

45.5 (22.5%)

20.5 (10.14%) 19.75 (9.76%)

11.0 (5.44%)

Vibrator Regenerator Reclaimer Control valve Chamber

Name of assembly

Source: S. Jakate, 1985, p. 5.

6.3 Improving productivity through quality

Quality can be defined as conformity to requirements. In other words, quality is the sum of features and characteristics of a product or service that bear on its ability to satisfy a given need. This includes economic need as well as availability, easy maintenance, reliability, design and all the other characteristics of need.[7]

The basic elements of product quality are: performance, features, reliability, conformity, durability, serviceability, aesthetics and perceived quality.

Each is self-contained and distinct, for a product can be ranked high in one dimension and low in another.

A recognition of these basic elements is important for productivity improvement. An enterprise that chooses to improve quality can do so in several ways; it need not pursue all the elements at once. Instead, a segmentation strategy can be followed with a few dimensions singled out for special attention.

Quality and productivity

The characteristics of Japanese quality control are described as follows by Yoshikazu Tsuda.[8]

In a production process there are eight possible relationships between change in quality and change in quantity. They are:

1. Quantity increases and quality improves.
2. Quantity increases but quality is the same.
3. Quantity is the same, but quality improves.
4. Quantity increases but quality deteriorates.
5. Quantity decreases but quality improves.
6. Quantity is the same but quality deteriorates.
7. Quantity decreases but quality is the same.
8. Quantity decreases and quality deteriorates.

It is evident that in cases 1, 2 and 3 productivity goes up, and in cases 6, 7 and 8 it goes down. But, in cases 4 and 5 it is not evident whether productivity goes up or not.

The relationships between productivity and quality are shown in the following formula:

$$\frac{\text{Production}}{\text{cost}} = \frac{\text{Total amount of effective input (valued in money)}}{\text{Total quantity of products satisfying quality level q}}$$

The total amount of effective input equals the total amount of input minus the value of excessively rapid depreciation, which is not acceptable to the customer.

Figure 6.11.   Relationships between quality and productivity

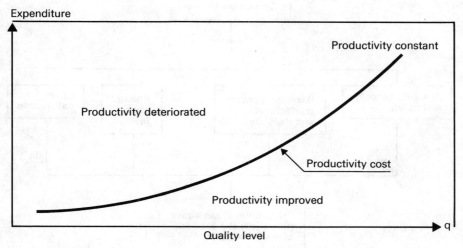

Source: Y. Tsuda, 1980, p. 45.

Here, production cost changes as quality changes and therefore cost change influences productivity changes. In cases 4 and 5 productivity does not change if changes in quality and quantity of product are located on the production curve, because the production curve is obtained by changing the quality level under fixed production conditions (see figure 6.11).

If the changes are located on the inside or outside of the cost curve, productivity deteriorates or improves according to those locations. Here, the outside of the cost curve is the region of productivity improvement. Thus, it is clearly seen that quality is one of the important factors and areas of productivity improvement, and quality management is an important tool of productivity management.

Total quality control concept and quality management

Numerous quality control methods and procedures have been developed (e.g. statistical quality control, statistical process control) and have demonstrated their achievement in raising standards. Quality assurance programmes and audits have been introduced with positive results in many industrialised countries.

Most of these programmes, however, are diagnostic. Quality improvement can relate to the physical attributes of a product, or to the information on a document which enables subsequent operations to be performed correctly the first time. However, production requires a system which reproduces quality, and this is known as Total Quality Control concept (TQC) or Company-Wide Quality Control (CWQC).

Productivity management

Figure 6.12. Customers' needs identification

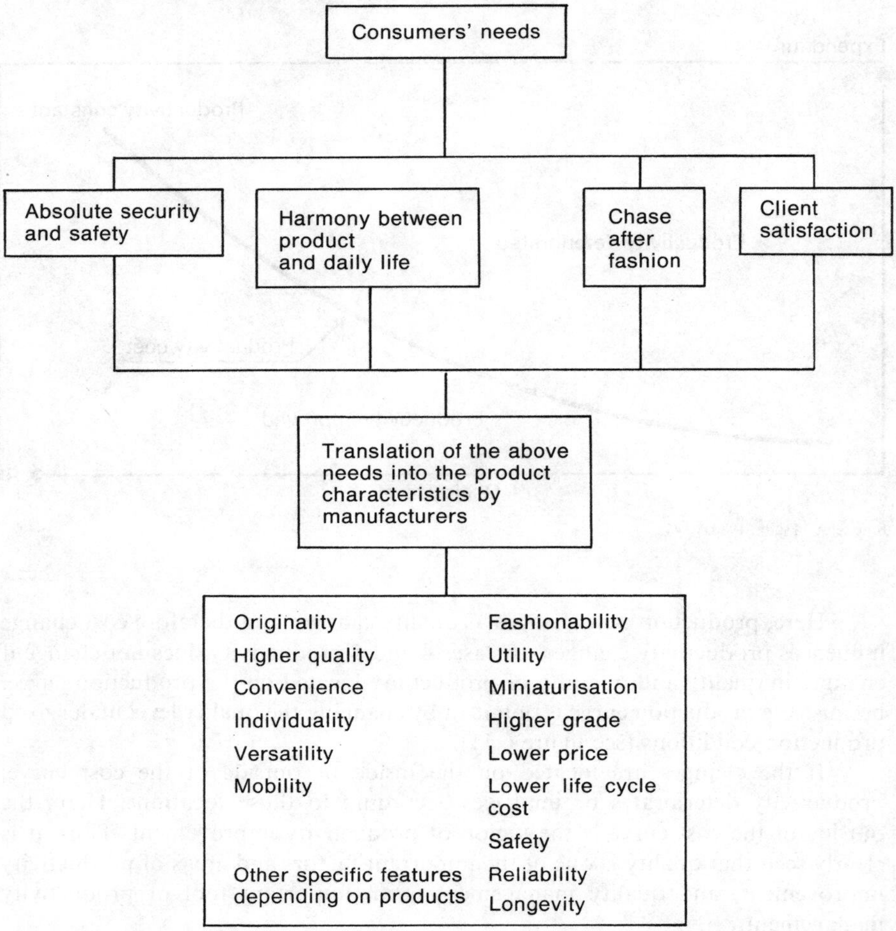

Source: Adapted from I. Miyauchi, 1980, p. 27.

Total quality control ensures that the product meets customers' needs, ranging from the physical use of the product to its aesthetic characteristics. Product life cycle assurance procedures are necessary within the total quality control policy and programme, which generally consists of the following components:

— identification of customers' needs;

— quality assurance;

— reliability;

— quality assurance procedures in the market.

Let us briefly consider these components. The customers' needs should be classified. Depending on the products, such aspects as luxury, finish, reliability, durability, low price, etc., are relevant. Analysis of the results of market research could be demonstrated by figure 6.12, adapted from I. Miyauchi, 1980.[9]

After identifying the customers' needs, the producer should integrate them into the products, using the TQC system to ensure that they are met in production. The main phases of quality assurance succeed each other as follows:

Phase	Quality assurance function
Market	Customers' needs identification
Planning	Quality target definition
R & D, design	Quality target validation, design
Pre-production	Quality standard setting
Reliability test	Test for reliability and easy maintenance
Production	Quality control during production
Sales	Quality control prior to and during sales
Customer	Quality control in use after sale (feedback from customers)

In most industries reliability is the most critical customer need. In companies that are functioning well, the requirements to satisfy this need are implemented at the stage of product design and met by specific tests. Testing is aimed not only at confirming design quality, but also for such customer benefits as:

— improvement of quality design to meet the customers' needs and ensure quality by consistent feedback during testing;

— identification of possible causes of failure while in use;

— assessment of the standard of the manufactured product and the implementation of a better quality manufacturing process.

Quality testing

Tests can indicate the various environmental conditions and constraints to which products are exposed when used by customers. They can also prevent recurrent quality problems through analysis of the feedback data from the field; they can identify the failure mechanism and establish corrective action for new designs, identify any malpractice or malfunction revealed and indicate the corrective action to be taken during the manufacturing process. Finally, results of accelerated durability testing predict the life of the product. Such tests are performed under stringent environmental conditions for components which are critical for safety and for customers' needs.

Quality assurance procedures in the market must cover the pre-sale, on-sale and after-sale stages.

Quality assurance for the pre-sale stage is normally a function of marketing and includes the following elements:

— a planning conference for new products, to identify the customers' needs;

Productivity management

— a design review to ensure that customers' needs are fully integrated into product design and hardware;
— training of staff for distribution networks, emphasising the specific features of new products;
— a periodic quality survey and audit for the product in inventory.

Quality assurance for the on-sale stage ranges from production to use and service, and includes:
— sale of products which correspond to customers' needs;
— inspection and quality assurance for export goods;
— prevention of deterioration during packing, transport and handling;
— full information and instructions for use;
— making customers familiar with the quality of the product.

Quality assurance for the after-sale stage is the most common function. However, several elements are often neglected. Among them are:
— surveillance and monitoring of newly marketed products so that any quality problems can be rectified immediately;
— quick response to complaints from customers;
— prevention of recurrent claims;
— quick response to requests for service or repair, quick diagnosis of faults, and improvement of after-sales service;
— periodic patrol-type services to get feedback from customers.

A good example of the successful implementation of a total quality concept is the strategy used by the Industrial Electronics Group (IEG) of Hughes Aircraft Company. They recommend the following steps: [10]
— develop a clear and easily understood definition of a total quality concept;
— explain the need for organisational improvement;
— develop models of excellence;
— evaluate and analyse current operating status;
— develop improvement strategies.

The TQC, or commitment to excellence, used by IEG aims to satisfy customers by giving them a quality product, excellent service, affordable cost and a timely delivery. Every organisational unit within IEG has customers, so every unit and individual must be dedicated to customer satisfaction. This definition of TQC is easily understood, and meets the prime objective of stressing the importance of the total involvement of everyone in the organisation.

To gain commitment to the concept, workers must be convinced that the future success of the organisation hinges on it and that their job security depends upon their individual performance.

To make every IEG worker understand the need for total quality, management had to implement broad communication strategies to define the nature and uses of IEG products, and to describe the current and future business pressures that have an impact on those products. An example of communication techniques for implementing such strategies is given in the box in the form of the IEG excellence model.

Excellence model: Employee communications

To attain excellence in employee communications, the organisation must utilise communication techniques that:

- Communicate the organisation's objectives, goals, priorities and values to all employees.
- Ensure that supervisors clearly define the tasks and responsibilities of each of their employees.
- Ensure that supervisors give employees timely evaluation of their job performance.
- Communicate the organisation's expectation of quality to all employees.
- Ensure that policies and practices are clearly communicated and understood by all employees.
- Stimulate frequent face-to-face discussions between managers and their employees.
- Inform all employees of the organisation's accomplishments, achievements and other important issues related to the work environment.
- Involve employees in the development of organisation policy and procedures.
- Encourage employees to express their ideas and recommendations to improve the operation of the organisation.
- Provide timely feedback to employees regarding the organisation's consideration of their ideas and recommendations.
- Solicit information from employees relative to their career goals and aspirations.
- Provide employees with information they can use to make personal career decisions.
- Inform employees of job openings within the organisation.
- Encourage employees to voice their problems and concerns.
- Give timely consideration and response to employee problems and concerns.
- Continually monitor what information employees want to receive.
- Regularly measure the effectiveness of communication techniques.

Source: T. Day, 1984, p. 19.

The most difficult aspect was making organisation units identify specific tasks. IEG management had to conduct an organisational self-audit in each division. The results of these self-audits were the basis for operating improvement.

A self-audit consists of three of the processes used for implementing a total quality control concept: i.e. developing a detailed model of excellence, evaluating and analysing current operating status, identifying areas that require improvement.

Productivity management

An excellence model is a specific description of excellence in a given operation, task or issue. It is a set of specific behaviours or activities that can be observed, described and measured along with their cause and effect relationships. An example of an excellence model for producing a quality product is given in the box.

Excellence model: Produce a quality product

To attain excellence in producing a product of high quality, our organisation must:

- Have a clear understanding of our product(s), its capabilities and applications.
- Ensure that all of our employees understand the product, its capabilities and applications.
- Understand our customer(s).
- Understand the requirements of our customer.
- Have a clear definition of the acceptable quality level of our product.
- Have a clear understanding of what our customer defines as the acceptable quality level of our product.
- Have an effective means of measuring the quality of our product.
- Continually solicit our customer's views and evaluations relative to the quality of our product.
- Continually communicate to employees the importance of producing a quality product.
- Continually emphasise to employees that they contribute to product quality in the successful performance of their jobs.
- Identify and then build upon the operating factors that sustain and contribute to product quality.
- Identify and then minimise or eliminate the operating factors that decrease product quality.
- Utilise techniques that solicit and stimulate employee innovation, ideas and recommendations that improve product quality.
- Utilise techniques that solicit customer ideas and recommendations to improve product quality.
- Give serious and timely consideration to employee and customer ideas and recommendations.
- Utilise effective techniques to test and evaluate new ideas and recommendations.

Source: T. Day, 1980, p. 18.

A similar excellence model could be developed for any aspect of an organisation's operations. A model defines excellence, facilitates monitoring and measurement, and provides the organisational units with a list of specific activities to use in diagnosing and evaluating their operational status. It could also be used to identify activities that are not being performed or are being performed inadequately. Thus, the model identifies areas of improvement.

A detailed diagnostic guide to the self-audit process is given in Day, 1984.[10]

In this approach, the system of improving quality is geared towards prevention; that is, it concentrates on preventing defects and errors, not on testing for them. The slogan of a quality improvement programme should be, "Do it right the first time". The cost to the company of *not* doing things right the first time is the "cost of quality".

Below are the important categories of the cost of quality; there are two types — the costs of non-conformity to needs, and the costs of conformity.

External failure: Costs generated by defective products being shipped to customers (internal or external). These include customer complaints and warranty claims.

Internal failure: Costs associated with defective products that fail to meet quality requirements, e.g. scrap, rectification and correcting problems.

Appraisal: Costs associated with testing to assure conformity with requirements, e.g. inspection and statistical quality control.

Prevention: Costs associated with designing, implementing and maintaining the quality management system.

These costs occur in every activity of every business, and in all forms of administration and services, not just industry.

As we have already said, one of the important aims of total quality control management is to build quality into the product, not only to inspect quality. This approach leads to a concept of quality management which recognises each individual worker's contribution.

This concept requires a flexible approach to quality management: as products move through the process from design to market, the techniques of quality management must follow their evolution. This is shown below:

Source: Y. Tsuda, 1980, p. 46.

In other words, the characteristics that denote quality must first be identified through market research (a user-based approach to quality); these characteristics must then be translated into identifiable product attributes (a product-based approach to quality); and the manufacturing process must then be organised to ensure that the products are made precisely to these specifications (a manufacturing-based approach to quality). A process that ignores any of these steps will not result in a quality product.

There are two main ways to improve product quality: to adopt more severe selection and inspection criteria; and to improve the production processes, including design, management and quality of labour.

Productivity management

The first way improves the quality of output, but it does not improve the quality and productivity of the whole process. The second way improves the distribution of quality characteristics over all operations first of all, and then quality level is optimised to total cost within the limits of the resources available. The second way thus improves not only the quality of the product but also productivity.

The concept of quality management involves managerial responsibility for standard setting, for quality control and measurement strategy, including the methods and techniques used, and for quality supervision and improvement.

In designing any kind of quality management system, programme or set of systematic actions, four important principles of quality management should be taken into consideration. They state that:

— quality is defined as *conformity with requirements*;
— *prevention* is the basis for a quality improvement system;
— the *performance standard* is "Do it right the first time";
— the *cost of quality* is the cost of conformity and of non-conformity.

In short, the implementation of a simple quality management programme includes some or all of the following steps:

Step 1: Presentation by the quality team to obtain commitment from top management.

Step 2: Presentation for senior plant managers.

Step 3: Selection of plant quality improvement teams by senior management.

Step 4: Training of the quality improvement teams, using actual case studies and exercises.

Step 5: Selection and training of departmental "discovery teams", composed of three or four people and led by departmental managers or supervisors.

The teams then analyse the flow of work and study all the input (products and paperwork), all the activities performed within the department and all the output (products and paperwork). They identify sources of error and loss in input or output, and study any significant quality assurance activities. These discovery items are then developed into measurements — frequencies, etc., and a measurement-reporting system is set up to cover the most significant items. For all of the measurements to be reported costs are then analysed and grouped into prevention, appraisal, internal and external failure costs. This allows department "cost of quality" reports to be produced; they direct attention to problem areas and monitor the impact of quality improvement efforts. They also help to reinforce quality awareness.

During these activities the following elementary statistical methods, named "Seven tools for quality control", are widely used:

● Pareto diagram.
● Cause and effect diagram.

- Histogram.
- Control chart and graph.
- Scatter diagram.
- Stratification — to separate collected data into homogeneous groups.
- Check sheet, flow chart and document form for easy data collection.

For engineers and research staff, more sophisticated statistical methods could be used. They are:

- Test and estimate.
- Reliability analysis.
- Analysis of variance.
- Experimental design by orthogonal array.
- Simple and multiple variables regression analysis.
- Curve-fitting theory.
- Multi-variant analysis, factor analysis.

Descriptions of these and other statistical methods can easily be found in the specialist literature. Some have already been demonstrated in previous parts of this book.

Quality circles

Good impulses for quality improvement have come in recent years from Japan, where a successful new approach to motivation and participation has been applied. This approach is called *Quality Circles*, and it is spreading quite quickly to many industrialised and developing countries.

A Quality Circle (QC) is a small group of volunteers from the same shop who meet regularly once a week in order to identify and analyse actual or potential work problems, to suggest solutions to management, or to act on the solutions themselves.

It is worth remembering that the QC concept is based on a perception of the meaning of the word "quality" that covers more than product standards and defects. The QC concept includes the quality of everything that an organisation does. For example, it includes the quality of management and work organisation, productivity, customer satisfaction, reliability, value for money, after-sales service and support, customer information and training, ease of maintenance, speed of service, as well as organisation image and customer confidence in it.[11]

QC activity was launched in April 1962 in Japan. Conferences, conventions, symposia, seminars and training programmes were organised to promote and disseminate company-wide quality control through QCs. Japanese education in quality control began with seminars intended to increase awareness of the importance of the subject. By the end of the year over 35 companies had commenced QC activities. By 1980 more than 100,000 QCs had been registered in Japan. There were about 980,000 QC members in 3,150 enterprises. However, not all QC circles are officially registered.

Productivity management

During the past ten to 15 years QC activities have spread from South Asian countries to Brazil, the United States and many European countries. A 1982 study showed that 44 per cent of all companies in the United States with more than 500 staff had QC programmes. Nearly three out of four had started after 1980. A good estimate is that over 90 per cent of the Fortune "500" companies now have QC programmes in their structure.[12] This is an indication of the advantages of QC activities.

An exciting feature of QCs is that they provide an orderly approach to bringing together both human and technical resources. The goals are to improve the quality of the product, the quality of working life and organisational efficiency.

Citroen, the French automobile company, provides an example of the bringing together of human and technical resources. It is a company that prides itself on excellence in engineering and has always concentrated on techniques such as work study, value analysis and statistical quality control. However, management has come to realise that it must also emphasise the recognition of people for their achievements. The company has set up quality circles and task forces, realising that total quality is no longer just a technical objective, but also a human one.

QCs can involve staff from any level of an organisation in the process of finding solutions to problems or issues that affect workers' ability to conduct their work activities successfully. Thus, the basic ideas behind QC activities carried out as a part of total quality control are that QCs:

— contribute to the improvement and development of the enterprise;
— respect the human dimension and build up a happy, bright workshop which is rewarding to work in;
— develop the full potential of the participants.

There are few basic requirements for establishing a QC but they are important. First, and absolutely essential, is a management style which cares about people and their feelings. Next is the support management is prepared to give to the programme: it should be free, strong, enthusiastic and steady throughout.

Launching a QC requires some financial investment, which should be considered as long-term investment in human development. Some companies report that returns range from three to six times the amount invested within the first two years of the programme. However, many Japanese companies make no attempt to calculate the return on investment. They consider the development of workers a sufficient return for the sum invested.

While QCs are being introduced, management and workers should be prepared for change and managers must be prepared to deal effectively with the natural fear of change — their own and the workers'. Supervisors, for example, should be prepared to give some authority to QC members and to listen to their advice. The Belgian Confederation of Employers in Fabrimetal provides an illustration of proper management support. They offer help to their members in starting QCs only when the following implementation strategy is respected: [13]

- A meeting with the entire board of directors and all members of the next management level, to inform them in detail.
- A separate meeting of top managers to consider the consequences of working with QCs, so as to find out whether they are really in favour of the principles and philosophy.
- Another combined meeting to discuss ways of motivating staff.
- The appointment of a steering committee to get the process really started, and at the same time starting with a pilot group of departmental chiefs in a top-down approach.

This sequence means that management is already working with the QC principle before QCs are discussed at the shop-floor level.

Another absolute requirement for implementing the QC programme is the thorough training of every key individual before the QCs begin to meet.

Finally, the QC is a voluntary programme. No one should be forced or even urged to participate. Many motivational schemes have failed because workers were compelled by management to participate.

Setting up QCs

The first thing to do is to make a comprehensive evaluation of the situation in the organisation. The evaluation should cover management style, productivity and quality trends, labour-management relations, morale, absenteeism, market position, and so on. All this forms a base from which to measure the results of introducing QCs.

The next step is to create a steering committee to investigate the QC concept and determine if it will benefit the organisation in question. This committee should include a decision-maker from every major department (but not departmental chiefs), union representatives, supervisors and workers.

Some organisations find it useful to include at least one person who is absolutely opposed to the QC idea. Such a person could challenge the other more enthusiastic members to find practical answers to the problems and so ensure that no unpleasant surprises come up.

The steering committee studies the QC concept and makes its recommendation. The key people in the QC programme are the co-ordinator, the "facilitator", the group leader and the subgroup leader. Of these the most important is the "facilitator". All positions in the QC programme are voluntary except for the steering committee members.

The co-ordinator's position is administrative and investigative. The co-ordinator keeps the steering committee informed about progress, brings problems to their attention, and acts as the liaison between all the "facilitators" and the company's department managers.

Most Japanese companies have completely decentralised their QC programmes. They come almost entirely under the control of the group leaders after the "facilitators" have made sure the leaders are qualified to train their own people.

The "facilitators" have great influence on the QCs. They explain the concepts, enlist volunteers, provide training for group leaders, explain the work of the QCs to managers, and help QC members to solve problems. Good "facilitators" encourage and stimulate by asking questions rather than by giving answers. They should have a working knowledge of the tasks performed by the QC members.

Group leaders could be supervisors (United States, European companies) or experienced workers (Japan). Unlike the "facilitators", the group leaders actively participate in the QCs. However, they must be prepared to face challenge to their ideas.

Subgroups are created to work on special tasks that are part of a larger problem. As a rule, subgroup leaders are appointed by the supervisor, who chooses people who have demonstrated ability during the regular meetings. The subgroups remain together until they accomplish their task and then they return to the parent group.

During the initial phase it is important to organise good training programmes for all the key people mentioned above, particularly for the group leaders.

There are five distinct phases of QC development. They are:

— organising the QC;
— the initial phase;
— monitoring and problem solving;
— innovation and self-improvement;
— autonomy in quality control.

The first two phases deal with organising groups of workers into QCs and training them in simple problem-solving techniques. In their work areas they have to identify, analyse and solve problems of quality, housekeeping, wastage, productivity and safety. During the third phase, the QCs begin to develop a "monitoring mentality". The QC members use simple control techniques to maintain and monitor their working environment.

Next is a self-improvement phase. As the QCs begin to mature, they seek ways of making systematic improvements, not just solving separate problems. The fifth, autonomous, phase is reached when QCs are established within an organisation and are trusted by management; they have access to all the necessary information, training aids and techniques necessary for progress. They may spend time in self-study. During this phase they should be given the opportunity of communicating with professional, educational and technical institutions. They should also be permitted to attend conventions to meet QC members from other organisations and exchange experiences.

The basic QC techniques

The most common activity of a QC is identifying and solving problems. Techniques relevant to this are therefore incorporated into QC activities. The most important of these techniques are:

- brainstorming;
- data collection;
- data analysis;
- Pareto diagram;
- cause and effect analysis;
- histograms;
- evaluation techniques;
- presentation techniques.

Detailed descriptions of these techniques can be found in many management manuals and, particularly for QCs, in David Hutchins's *Quality circles handbook*.[11] Practical examples have been described in previous chapters and are given below in case studies in this chapter.

Some common characteristics of QCs

QC activities and programmes are normally associated with developing human potential and have the following characteristics:

- participation is voluntary;
- leaders get participation from everybody;
- members help each other to develop;
- projects are QC efforts, not individual;
- training is provided for workers and management;
- creativity is encouraged;
- projects are related to members' work;
- management is supportive;
- quality and improvement consciousness is developed;
- compensation is paid at overtime rates if the activities take place outside work-hours;
- very simple techniques are used;
- the QC is a democratic group.

Advantages of QC activities

There are many benefits from QC activities — not only quality improvement. For example, Philip C. Thompson describes some of the effects of QCs at Martin Marietta Corporation in the United States. These effects were demonstrated by comparison of hourly-paid members before and after joining QCs in 1980: [14]

- 45 per cent reduction in the rate of unpaid lost time hours;
- 58 per cent reduction in the rate of grievances;
- 57 per cent reduction in the rate of occupational injuries;
- 68 per cent reduction in the rate of safety incidents;
- 59 per cent reduction in the failure of workers to use equipment in the best way.

These are impressive improvements. In another company, Central Azucarera de la Carlota in the Philippines, the results of the activities of 113 QCs are also quite significant: late arrivals and absenteeism were reduced by 33 per cent in 1982 and by 48 per cent in 1983, compared with the 1981 average; workers have become more courteous to clients; machine downtime has been reduced by 30 per cent, resulting in greater machine utilisation; productivity and quality have improved. [15]

David Hutchins suggests that, in the early stages, a QC programme should produce a yield somewhere in the order of three or four to one benefit to cost ratio. [16] This should improve during the second and third years due to the amortisation of start-up costs, together with the continued benefits accruing from some of the early QC projects. In addition to tangible benefits (quality and money saved) there will be further gains which, often, will far outweigh the value of the cost-cutting projects. They include, for example, lower labour turnover, fewer grievances and higher morale. These and other evident effects of QCs raise the question of rewards to QC members. But many experts agree that QC members should never under any circumstances be paid directly in cash for any QC achievement since a direct reward is alien to the entire philosophy of QCs, which is to develop a sense of identity and achievement in organisation problem solving.

However, this does not mean that QC members cannot be rewarded at all. Reward is normally given in the form of:

— recognition;

— attendance at conventions, seminars, workshops;

— exchange visits to other organisations, even abroad;

— power to decide how some of the savings may be spent.

Finally, QCs could also take part in suggestion schemes on the condition that any award given would not be taken as a direct cash benefit but would be spent by the QC in a way the members decided.

When QCs do not work

Almost all countries have experienced QC failures. The following reasons for failure are most often mentioned:

- Lack of top management support and commitment.
- Unrealistic expectations on the part of management.
- Unimportant problems selected for solution by QCs.
- Culture problems. Not every organisation should attempt to implement QCs since the QC is a participatory management technique. In organisations with an authoritarian culture QCs are doomed to fail.
- Lack of maturity. QCs are most successful in mature organisations where there are large numbers of workers and supervisors in the same location. It is much more difficult to organise and maintain QCs in smaller, less centralised organisations with a high proportion of technical or professional staff.

Figure 6.13. From QCs to other forms of participation

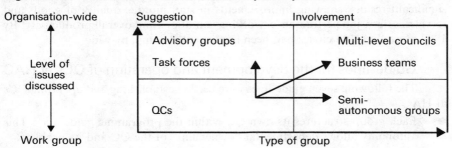

Source: E. E. Lawler, 1985, p. 70.

- Lack of proper training for QC members.
- Lack of management planning in setting up the QCs.

In summary, QCs encounter many threats to their continued existence. Because of these threats, it is not likely that managers will institutionalise and sustain programmes over a long period, especially in western cultures. Given the many forces and pressures that develop during QC activities it is not surprising that the typical programme reaches a point at which it begins to decline. At this point management must intervene to set up a new programme.

QCs can be used in many sensible ways. They can serve as group suggestion programmes, or special projects to deal with critical organisational issues. A QC programme can also be used as a transitional vehicle in a move towards a more participatory management system and culture.

Some companies embark on a QC programme, discover its limitations, and then start a course of action to further develop the participatory culture of the organisation. A possible model of such a transitional process from QCs to other forms of participation is illustrated in figure 6.13.

QC activity may lead group members to want to become an integral part of the decision-making system. For example, group members become frustrated when they are unable to initiate needed changes and they then tend to move outside the limitations of the QCs. Thus, the transition of a QC into a self-managing team is also a possibility. QCs can prepare workers for this type of structure by fostering the development of their skills and knowledge.

Case study: Quality circles programme at Hughes Aircraft [17]

In 1976 Hughes Aircraft Company (HAC) implemented the "Hughes Circles" programme, on the premise that workers will take more pride and interest in their jobs if they have opportunities to contribute systematically to improving their work environment. According to the mission statement presented in "Hughes Circles — Guide-lines", the approach is to promote and use methods that provide workers with an opportunity of participating with management in identifying and solving problems that affect the performance of the company.

Monitoring of four pilot QCs for approximately one year demonstrated significant results, showing improvements in staff morale, quality of goods and services, safety, job performance, working conditions and overall productivity. By 1982 more than 500 circles had been implemented company-wide.

Guide-lines for the development and operation of QCs at HAC

The following seven guide-lines were used in establishing and operating QCs at HAC:

- Each group structures its own QC within the programme guide-lines. This autonomy allows departmental "ownership" of the QC and its problem.
- Circle membership and participation is voluntary.
- The work-group supervisor is the QC leader when feasible.
- The "facilitator" — always a staff member of the company — is not from the same work area but may be from the same department. The benefits of having a "facilitator" from a different, but related, work area are threefold:
  - an outside perspective is provided on the problems discussed;
  - objectivity is enhanced since the "facilitator" is not affected daily by the problems under discussion;
  - members sometimes initially feel more at ease with the "facilitator" than with the leader who is usually also the area supervisor.
- The leaders and "facilitators" participate in training workshops before implementing their QCs; there are also follow-up workshops stressing specific techniques. They work on a wide variety of problem-solving techniques, group dynamics, climate-setting techniques, quality control statistics, and "people-building" techniques. Training of leaders and "facilitators" is viewed as an on-going process.
- Circles are composed of from three to 12 members.
- Circles hold weekly one-hour meetings in company time.

Before implementing the QCs, it is necessary to secure management support.

Six general requirements are made of departmental management. These are that managers:

- allow QC activity;
- assist the QC leader in finding meeting space and other resources as needed;
- attend QC meetings and presentations;
- reply promptly to QC requests and inquiries;
- give explanations of why QC recommendations are accepted or rejected;
- recognise the efforts of all participants in the circle.

The QC process

An orientation meeting is held with all departmental staff to acquaint them with the history, aims and concepts of QCs. During this meeting line managers express support for QCs and indicate the type of resources and assistance to be made available to them. When a sufficient number of people have volunteered to participate, the QC is ready to start.

The first QC meeting sets the timetable for future work, identifies the QC objectives and establishes the ground rules. A brief overview of the techniques used in problem solving is usually given by the "facilitator". The agenda for the next meeting is planned.

The problem-solving process consists of the following six steps:

Step 1: Identify potential problems and select the most significant.

Step 2: Gather and analyse data.

Step 3: Select possible solutions.

Step 4: Define implementation strategies.

Step 5: Present possible solutions to management.

Step 6: Follow up on the implementation of solutions.

At the discretion of management, the QC may take an active role in the implementation of the solution, or it may simply monitor the impact of the solution after management has initiated its implementation. An example follows:

Area: Manufacturing of hybrid and microwave devices.

Problem: Excessive assembler error, part scrappage, and re-work.

Discussion: During a number of brainstorming sessions on the possible causes of the problem, QC members identified inadequate lighting, dirty projector screens, warped slides, and lack of colour-coded planning documents. In addition, they felt strongly that minor changes in the assembly planning documents would result in clearer assembly procedures. The participants decided to study and document the incidence of assembler error, part scrappage, and re-work that appeared to be related to problems in the assembly planning documents. The "facilitator" taught members how to document their findings and write up their recommendations.

Resolution: In meetings between QC participants and supervisors from the planning department, agreement was reached on the process for submitting the circle's documented suggestions. The new process allowed the circle leader/area supervisor more immediate access to planning so as to get recommended changes reviewed. A request was made to the environmental health and safety department to conduct a lighting check, to supplement overhead lighting, and to replace the existing station lighting. One of the QC members volunteered to clean screens on projectors. Warped slides were replaced and all assembly documents were coloured.

Observable results from the QC programme at HAC

The positive results of QC activity fall into two major categories: the growth and development of individual workers; and the creation of a more viable, collaborative work group. In particular, QC leaders report a noticeable increase in information-sharing among their staff, increased co-operation and willingness to make an extra effort when working with other departments due to better understanding of how jobs "fit" into the total company; the development of workers' skills in needs analysis; and increased staff appreciation of those showing initiative on the job.

Problems are less identified with individuals. Application of action research in the work group focuses attention on the system rather than on individuals' failings as the source of problems, and allows individuals to develop new strategies for handling old problems and issues.

Participants feel less "cut off" from the company, since they are actively involved in seeking information and clarifying complex issues; they are more aware of the impact of organisational issues upon workers.

Working with interdepartmental issues is emerging as a strong QC theme. There is clearly a skill-building process inherent in inviting outsiders to the QC in order to discuss problems of mutual importance, and in negotiating specific points with the outsiders.

By ensuring that workers at all levels can bring their problems to top management, QCs reduce potential conflict situations. Members state that it gives them personal satisfaction to know that their suggestions have been adopted by the company.

Participants report that they understand the difficulties of the management process more fully, particularly when they need to consider the most viable strategies for effecting change in their work environment.

Managers report that supervisors seem to have a better rapport with their workers. Supervisors and others who serve as QC leaders routinely report that they feel that their ability to work with their staff has been enhanced. They indicate that they are able to see problems from new angles and that they can think through the steps needed to solve them.

* * *

In this chapter we have discussed three major areas of productivity improvement: materials and energy savings, maintenance of equipment and facilities, and quality management and control. These areas are normally under the control of the enterprise and, when managed properly, can give immediate results in productivity improvement.

However, the most important area for productivity improvement is the management of people. Good staff management is in fact the main instrument for tapping productivity resources in all areas. This vital aspect of productivity is the subject of the next chapter.

[1] "The key to an effective energy conservation programme", in *PDC Info Digest* (Manila, Productivity and Development Center, Development Academy of the Philippines), Sep. 1983, pp. 23-28.

[2] Ryoji Takahashi: *Energy management fundamental course lecture text book*, ILO/UNDP project BGD/83/001 (Geneva, ILO, 1984-85), pp. 1-13.

[3] National Productivity Scheme, 1982-86, DR/NIR/82/010, Nigeria.

[4] George Logan: "Japan has a maintenance secret", in *Manufacturing Productivity Frontiers* (Illinois, Institute of Technology), Feb. 1983, pp. 28-30.

[5] Wenceslao K. Martinez: "The economic impact of corrosion", in *Productive Maintenance* (Manila, Productivity and Development Center, Development Academy of the Philippines), May 1985, pp. 5-6.

[6] Sudhir Jakate: "Improving availability of shot blasting plant — A case study", in *Maintenance* (Delhi, National Productivity Institute), May 1985, p. 5.

[7] P. Hughes: "Quality assurance", in Trevor J. Bentley (ed.): *The management services handbook* (London, Holt, Rinehart and Winston, 1984), Ch. 25.

[8] Yoshikazu Tsuda: *Quality control and quality assurance: The Asian experience*, Papers from APO Symposium, Indonesia, 1980 (Tokyo, Asian Productivity Organisation), pp. 41-68.

[9] Ichiro Miyauchi: *Quality control and quality assurance in the market*, Papers from APO Symposium, Indonesia, 1980 (Tokyo, Asian Productivity Organisation), pp. 22-27.

[10] Terian C. Day: "Strategies for setting up a 'commitment to excellence' policy and making it work", in *Management Review* (New York, AMACOM), May 1984, pp. 16-24.

[11] David Hutchins: *Quality circles handbook* (London, Pitman, 1985), pp. 1 and 10.

[12] E. E. Lawler and S. A. Mohrman: "Quality circles after the fad", in *Harvard Business Review* (Boston, Massachusetts), Jan. 1985, pp. 65-71.

[13] Bernard G. Putnam Cramer: *Quality circles in Europe: Requirements for implementation and expansion*, Paper presented to the Challenges of the Year 2000 for Enterprises and Training, 13-16 November 1984 (Paris, European Institute for Vocational Training, 1984), pp. 2-12.

[14] Robert Zager and Michael P. Rosow: *The innovative organization: Productivity programmes in action* (New York, Pergamon Press, n.d.).

[15] Fred J. Elizalde: "Synergistic approaches to labor-management productivity", in *PDC Info Digest* (Manila, Productivity and Development Center, Development Academy of the Philippines), Mar. 1984, p. 8.

[16] Hutchins, op. cit.

[17] Mary T. Kohler and Everett R. Wells: "Quality circles at Hughes Aircraft", in *National Productivity Review* (New York, Executive Enterprises Publications), Summer 1982, pp. 311-321.

EFFECTIVE HUMAN RESOURCE MANAGEMENT 7

7.1 Management of people

People are the most important and promising area of productivity improvement. In economic and social development, few things are more important than improving productivity. Since all organisations combine two subsystems, technical and human, these subsystems must be balanced and co-ordinated in order to function effectively. In trying to realise this, decision-makers commonly make three errors:

● Too much energy is spent on measuring, collecting and reporting data and not enough is left for practical action to improve performance.

● Too much reliance is placed on straightforward solutions such as new technology, incentive schemes, QCs, etc., which are effective techniques if properly applied but which divert resources in counterproductive ways if they are inappropriate or adopted without commitment.

● For many people, productivity is still synonymous with traditional cost-cutting, or working harder, but not necessarily with a more intelligent approach. This attitude often creates difficult work relationships, drives away the best people, compromises quality, delivery and services, and can compromise future opportunities for the sake of short-term profit improvement.

These and other "technocratic" mistakes lead to situations where the human side of productivity has somehow been left out of the total picture.

After all, equipment and technology are the product of the human mind and can be made productive only by people. The success of any productivity programme depends on human innovative ideas and creativity.

Thus, there is an urgent need to look more closely into the human factor and consider its contribution to the improvement of productivity. Formal analysis of basic productivity factors such as output, input, labour, capital, technology and managerial motivation reveals at once that more than half of these factors are concerned with the quality of the labour force. With deeper insight into other technical factors we see that their quality is also an integral part of the quality of human input.

Many attempts have been made to define the characteristics of high-quality manpower. Among the qualities most often cited are: a sense of commitment, dedication and loyalty to the organisation; achievement orientation; good communication skills; participatory abilities; social commitment; professional skills; and receptiveness to change. Let us look at this question in a more systematic way.

First of all, a high-quality workforce is characterised by productive behaviour. Only the on-the-job behaviour of an operative, engineer or manager can actually produce things in a more or less productive way. This behaviour, in its turn, is the result of complex, but quite distinctive, combinations of personal and organisational characteristics, such as:

— work attitudes;

— knowledge and skills;

— opportunities.

Thus, in order to change the behaviour of a workforce to make it more productive, we have to influence all three of these characteristics in a balanced and co-ordinated way.

A key to productivity is the attitude of people who work together. It is quite clear that a lack of commitment is a very serious impediment to productivity improvement. Attitudes themselves reflect the interplay of many long-term and short-term factors including motivation, culture, management systems, nature of the work and very individual and delicate things such as personal value systems and life objectives.

Many managers reject the idea that it is important or even possible to manage attitudes. "I'm managing results, not attitudes" or "I'm managing behaviour, not attitudes" are frequent statements. Some managers even ignore the existence of attitudes: "You can't see attitudes, you can see behaviour". Some consider that a person's attitude is his own business and that trying to influence it constitutes an invasion of privacy.

Attitudes are largely shaped by systems of personal values or collective values, referred to as social norms.

An important factor which influences work attitudes is culture in a broad sense — national, social, organisational, etc. — which surrounds and shapes any kind of human activity. But the essential point is that culture includes systems of values and that values are among the building blocks of culture; culture and values are in constant interaction.

Let us consider a few examples of how culture influences work attitudes, behaviour and, as a result, performance.

The differences in productivity between north-east Asian economies (Japan, the Republic of Korea, Hong Kong) and also Singapore, and south-east Asian countries (Indonesia, Malaysia, the Philippines, Thailand) are probably mostly due to different work attitudes resulting from the influence of major cultural institutions.

In the north-east Asian workplace industrial relations are more conducive to fostering good work attitudes than in south-east Asia. Industrial relations in Japan place emphasis on trying to make the workplace a pleasant, interesting and satisfying environment in which to make a living. In south-east Asia industrial relations/policies appear closer to Western culture and are less motivating for workers.

The media in north-east Asia are also more effective than their south-east Asian counterparts in fostering good work attitudes. In north-east Asia the mass media are institutions of continuing education, whereas in south-east Asia they are increasingly regarded by the public as entertainment with a low educational role.

In contrast to the West, paternalism thrives throughout Asia. Particularly where the family cannot provide enough security, the employer takes on a paternalistic role. However, with the growth of companies and increasing economic development, paternalism also has adverse consequences for organisational productivity, since it encourages the proliferation of networks of patronage and rewards loyalty rather than performance. The challenge for managers, however, is not necessarily to abolish paternalism as such, but rather to find ways of redirecting it so that it achieves both ends: security for the individual and productive performance.

There is a very interesting new trend whereby Asian management culture is moving away from paternalism and Western management culture is moving towards it. There are many examples of companies consciously introducing new behaviour patterns and carefully blending new elements of organisational culture with traditional ones.

Modifying an organisation's culture can make an important contribution towards solving specific problems. Fundamental to a change in culture is the matter of where the plans are made and how they are put into effect. Thus, the true value of changes made in the context of organisation development is the introduction of joint planning between workers and management. This is based on the assumption that people will be more committed to objectives if they have participated in establishing them. Organisations are human systems after all, and their material components are merely supporting mechanisms or tools that help the human system to function.

Sound management of attitudes towards productivity can create a better cultural orientation, resulting in more effective work. Thus, it is very important to accept that attitudes as well as motivation can be managed.

Skills and abilities can be upgraded through proper manpower planning, selection, job placement and rotation, training and development. These are all good management practice and strategy. Finally, opportunities to use manpower resources effectively depend upon sound management of organisational structure and culture, equipment and technology.

Good management, which is responsible for the development and realisation of the three main components of human resources, is crucial to the effective use of available manpower. However, the term "management" in this context is not restricted to professional managers. Productivity improvement programmes are successful only if they are established and implemented by the joint efforts of workers, technical staff, managers and trade unions. In this connection, it is important to consider the following factors in the effective development and use of manpower as the key to productivity improvement. They are:

— the role of management;
— motivation;
— participation;
— training;
— work organisation, working conditions and productivity improvement techniques at the shop-floor level.

The role of management

Improving organisational productivity starts at the management level since it is primarily the responsibility of managers. Productivity programmes will succeed or fail depending on managers' attitudes, strategy, policy and, most important, practical action. There are two main types of strategy for productivity. The first is based on increasing investment in labour, which is very costly and takes time to yield results. The second is based on better management practice and style. Improving managerial practice is generally inexpensive, and in most cases it generates economic benefits that exceed the cost incurred. Certainly it is important to introduce such management techniques as corporate planning and management by objectives, and to invest in computerised management information systems, new machinery and technology. However, managers must also be assessed on the basis of how well they manage their subordinates.

The manager's role concerns two areas:

— the work and the way it is organised and performed;
— the workers and the environment in which they work: in other words, providing opportunities for productive work.

The first area is concerned with the essentially standard management functions of planning, organising and controlling, together with decision-making on investment, choice of technology, and so on. For example, studies in a number of countries have shown effective working hours to be as low as 25-30 per cent of total work-hours due to a variety of causes which are within management control (see figure 7.1).[1] However, strictly speaking, time lost through bad worker attitudes (absenteeism, lateness, idleness, careless work, accidents, lack of attention and interest) is also a result of poor management, since all the above are under the control of managers.

The second area of the manager's role is concerned with providing good opportunities for the effective use of the labour force.

There are many examples of people (both workers and managers) who are skilled and highly motivated and with positive attitudes, but who cannot fully

Figure 7.1.   Management's control over effective working time

A Basic content of product and/or operation	B Work content increased by design or specification defects	C Work content increased by inefficient manufacturing methods	D Ineffective time caused by poor planning and management	E Ineffective time caused by worker attitudes
● WITHIN THE CONTROL OF MANAGEMENT				
A1 Poor layout	B1 Bad product design prevents use of most economic process	C1 Wrong machine used	D1 Excessive product variety leads to short runs and idle time	E1 Absenteeism, lateness, idleness
	B2 Lack of standardisation prevents mass-production	C2 Wrong manufacturing processes	D2 Lack of standardisation leads to short runs	E2 Careless work leads to more scrap and re-work
	B3 Incorrect quality standards cause unnecessary work	C3 Wrong tools used	D3 Design changes cause stoppages and re-work	E3 Accidents cause stoppages and injury
	B4 Removal of excessive quantities of material	C4 Causes excessive materials handling	D4 Poor work scheduling increases machine and worker idle time	E4 Lack of attention to detail: lack of interest in improving processes, methods and design
		C5 Poor operator working methods — insufficient training	D5 Poor raw materials scheduling increases idle time	
			D6 Machine breakdowns caused partly by poor maintenance systems	
			D7 Poor working conditions result in excessive rest periods	
			D8 Accidents caused by unsafe equipment or processes	

implement their ideas and realise their potential because of organisational constraints. This is not only a waste of precious human resources, but can cause people to lose their motivation, and even *unlearn* a lot of skills and positive work attitudes. It is very important to realise that while machines which stand idle *sometimes* deteriorate, human potential which is not fully or properly used *always* diminishes.

Thus, there is no point in improving skills until the organisation can use them. The same applies to attitudes: a manager must not preach the importance of participation to subordinates until the organisation is ready and able to apply it.

Opportunities development can be achieved through a systematic and balanced improvement of the organisation's structure and culture, management styles and labour-management relations.

An organisation's structure and culture

An organisation's structure contributes to its performance, and must match its products and processes. R & D organisations, for example, seem to perform best with loose, non-hierarchical structures, which permit a certain freedom for researchers and first-level managers. Organisations dealing with complex and diversified products should have project or matrix structural elements. At the same time, the organisational structure, since it influences the organisational culture, should also correspond to the culture of the society. A discrepancy between organisational culture and structure could create additional barriers to productivity. To demonstrate the cultural differences which influence organisational structure, it is interesting to compare the American and Japanese situations:

Traditional American structure	*Traditional Japanese structure*
Hierarchical bureaucracy with specialised and highly structured functions and positions; duties and responsibilities clearly defined in writing for each individual. Organisation built around individual.	Hierarchical organisation with loose, broad general functions and informal job descriptions; strong reliance on internalised work group norms of cooperation, consensus seeking, and high group achievement standards. Organisation built around groups.

Management styles

Much recent research on management styles confirms that participatory, worker-centred methods are effective in enhancing productivity and that democratic supervision leads to higher productivity than authoritarian supervision. One survey in the Philippines showed that 69.5 per cent of workers wanted to be involved in planning their jobs, while 77.5 per cent liked to be consulted by management before decisions were made regarding their jobs.

In a Singapore survey 73 per cent of workers considered that the most important qualities of managers as leaders were: understanding and sensitivity;

ability to inspire and set an example; decisiveness; ability to guide and advise subordinates.

Comparison between cultural influences and traditional management styles reveals the main differences between the American and Japanese approaches:

Traditional American management style	*Traditional Japanese management style*
Maximised return on investment through technological and individual efficiency. Workers dislike work but may be motivated by money if tasks are closely supervised. Organisations' goals are therefore believed to be incongruent with worker goals. Decision-making system is highly centralised, top down, written, with extensive post-decision verbal communication to seek compliance.	People are seen as the most valuable asset in achieving company goals. Organisation and workers' goals are therefore seen as congruent to group goals. Decision-making system is highly decentralised, bottom up, informal, with verbal communication used to seek consensus and written system (ringi) used as post confirmation.

The key dimensions of traditional American management philosophy and practice and the contemporary Japanese management approach are summarised by the following set of terms:[2]

American (traditional) management approach	*Japanese (new) management approach*
Individual	Group
Competition	Co-operation
Us/them	We
Compliance	Consensus
Adversaries	Partners
Blame	Responsibilities/opportunities
Suspicion	Trust
Turbulence	Planned changes
Policeman	Planner/"facilitator"
Reactive	Proactive
Now	Future
Implementation	Planning
Segmentation	Integration
Parochialism	Broad, systems view
Slicing the pie	Enlarging the pie
Human costs	Human capital investments

Certainly these descriptions are too schematic and reflect only the basics of management style. However, ideas in many companies on both sides of the Pacific have started to move towards each other, recognising that any traditional extremes in management styles which have not kept pace with new developments soon become an important constraint on improvement of productivity attitudes, culture and performance.

What is clear is that management has the primary role in setting the tone and nature of the relationships between an organisation and its members.

Almost 50 years ago Chester Barnard convincingly argued that eliciting and sustaining co-operative effort on the part of organisational members was a primary executive function.

Indeed, management's key responsibility is to create not only formal organisational designs and systems, but also an organisational climate that encourages co-operative effort among the staff.

Thus, in its simplest form the new management approach is to value co-operation and to deplore destructive competition within the organisation, to emphasise the recognition and acceptance of mutual interests and goals.

Management should therefore adopt an enlightened personnel policy allowing greater participation, co-operation, job satisfaction and adequate rewards.

There is also plenty of room for management to maximise productive worker efforts through training and development, improving workers' motivation as well as working conditions and climate. These are also managerial responsibilities.

Manpower motivation

The second important issue in the effective use of the labour force is motivation, particularly positive reinforcement which causes behaviour to change in the desired direction. To develop the right attitude, people need to see their work as meaningful activity which gives them self-fulfilment and enriches their professional knowledge and career plans. They must develop a sense of belonging to the organisation. Proper attitudes and behaviour are determined by the workers' system of values, working conditions and the motivation they receive. A survey conducted in some Asian countries indicated that, with proper motivation of workers, productivity can easily be raised to as high as 90 per cent in small and medium enterprises.[2]

The only way to ensure the co-operation of workers is to share with them the gains from productivity both in monetary and non-monetary terms. Recognition and a sense of fulfilment or achievement supplement monetary rewards. However, by themselves they are not sufficient. It helps if there is a perceivable direct link between individual or collective earnings and productivity improvement: workers want to see their efforts result in tangible benefits for themselves.

Thus, a motivational system at the enterprise level is generally based on several important principles:

● It must create an atmosphere of trust, and must open two-way communication between management and workers; both can freely express concerns and opinions and be motivated to work as a team; there must be a positive response to workers' suggestions and problems.

- It must provide security for all workers under productivity improvement schemes.

- It must provide equal opportunities for employment and advancement by promoting workers without discrimination, using performance as the principal criterion.

- It must compensate workers in accordance with their performance and recognise their contribution to the success of the organisation; this means the equitable sharing of productivity gains.

- It must protect the health, safety and well-being of all workers by providing a clean and safe working environment and by running appropriate occupational health services.

- It must upgrade the skills and abilities of workers by providing on-the-job training and professional development programmes.

This list could be even longer. It is easy to break down these principles into two main groups: monetary motivation, and non-monetary motivation.

They both cost money and the best way to raise the money is to improve productivity and then to go into productivity gains-sharing schemes.

Financial incentives through gains-sharing

Successful productivity improvement programmes are first of all characterised by wide sharing of financial and other benefits throughout the organisation. The gains from improved productivity should be shared fairly among all parties concerned — workers, employers, consumers, government. These gains can be invested nationally to improve the standard of living, or at least maintain it while improving the quality of life. Increased national product can be invested, for example, in improving the environment or public services.

The gains from improved productivity should be shared between all "economic agents". For example:

— workers can share in the gains through better pay, better working conditions, a higher standard of living and the job security that comes from a more competitive industry or nation;

— employers can share through better returns on invested capital and upgraded technical capacity that will improve competitiveness in the market;

— governments can share through the possibility of investing gains in better infrastructure, better services, in more employment opportunities and in reducing social inequality;

— consumers share through more goods and services of better quality at lower prices.

The planned distribution of productivity gains is possible within an enterprise since all enterprises keep (or should keep) records of the costs incurred in producing goods and services for sale. The accounting procedures are readily available.

Productivity management

To begin with, it might be worth while to point out that wages can be related to productivity in two quite different ways. First, all or a portion of remuneration may be made to vary with measured changes in performance, as in traditional payment-by-results schemes. Second, the size of periodic increases in general wage levels may be made to depend at least in part on changes in productivity at the national, industry or enterprise level. For the sake of clarity, it is important that these two ways of linking pay and productivity be treated separately.

In the first method, the provisions in collective agreements usually do not attempt to regulate the detail of payment-by-results schemes or other incentive payments. Often the agreements simply specify the basic terms of such schemes or just the guaranteed minimum time rate that workers are entitled to. In some instances there may be a specification of the procedures to be followed when new production standards are established or old ones modified.

The second method, linking increases in the general level of wages with productivity, poses many difficult analytical problems. Because of the complexity and confusion with regard to the issues and the wide differences of view which inevitably arise, we are in favour of the more practical, directly performance-oriented method of linking wages and productivity.

It is still very rare to find collective agreements which relate increases in wage levels to productivity improvements. While productivity at the enterprise or industry level constitutes one of the widely used criteria in wage negotiations, it has not proved practicable to derive simple formulas explicitly linking wage adjustments to productivity changes. One of the exceptions to this pattern is the phenomen of "productivity bargaining" in the United Kingdom. Originally, these agreements were used to "buy out" substantial changes in inefficient work practices (e.g. excessive manning ratios) by means of higher wages. Later, a promise of achieving above-average increases in output was accepted as a justification for exceeding wage increases set by various incomes policy measures.

However, more and more companies are trying to introduce performance-oriented productivity gains-sharing schemes. These attempts are more or less successful. It is believed, for example, that in the United States somewhere up to a thousand big companies are using productivity gains-sharing plans.[3] Hart and Cooley of the United States multinational Clevepak Corporation, is a manufacturer with 550 hourly paid workers. The company recently started using a gains-sharing system, and within one year factory productivity increased somewhere between 22 and 28 per cent, depending on which measure was used.

To be an effective motivator, a bonus scheme must be directly related to achievement in as simple a way as possible, so that the recipients can see immediately how much they have earned from their efforts. The most direct form of performance-oriented bonus scheme is the end-of-project bonus, where a successful piece of work is rewarded immediately by a bonus of suitable size. It is much more effective than waiting many months without any tangible recognition until bonus time at the end of the year when the atmosphere of "everybody gets" will have taken away all the motivational impact.

Let us review the main types of gains-sharing incentive schemes.

Premium payment plans. Often used as a means of motivating workers to achieve a desired standard of performance. In this case pay is calculated monthly on the basis of measured work output per day.

Merit rating schemes. A series of factors is selected to cover the desired behaviour of a group of workers. A range of points is established for each factor and standards are set at various levels to guide assessment. Periodically each worker's performance is assessed and the scores are used to determine the level of pay in excess of basic rates.

Productivity-sharing plans. The principle of these plans is that a certain portion of revenue, such as added value, can be allocated as an "entitlement" for wages and salaries. After deducting the wages and salaries already paid, any surplus is distributed to salary- and wage-earners in accordance with the conditions of the scheme. The main goal of productivity-sharing is to involve all the labour force in the productivity improvement movement.

The following productivity-sharing schemes are well known: Scanlon plan, Zlobin method, Eddy-Rucker-Nickels plans, the Hunter variant of the Scanlon plan, Fein plan and Tanner plan. These plans rely on the willingness of workers and managers consciously to seek improvements and to report them so that they can be acted on. In return, staff receive a share which is usually put at 40 or 50 per cent of the savings. The other 50 or 60 per cent is retained for capital replacement and maintenance and enterprise growth. In case of changes in standards it is suggested that a 67 per cent bonus should be paid to workers and 33 per cent to the person making the suggestion for the changes and improvements.[4]

Group incentives. Sometimes it is impossible to reward workers through a bonus scheme, other than on a group basis: "the group bonus is X and it will be shared out in the same proportion as basic earnings". An advantage of this approach is that pressures within the group ensure an equitable distribution of effort.

An integrated approach, using major parts of these schemes, was introduced by the collective of builders headed by N. Zlobin in the USSR and was subsequently disseminated to a certain extent among the construction organisations throughout the country. The crux of the approach is that the collective of a construction brigade receives a contract for the whole job. If the brigade completes the work on schedule or ahead of schedule, it is awarded a bonus depending on the savings achieved compared with the estimated cost of production.

Of no little importance to the success of the experiment was the fact that all the members of the brigade knew the terms of the agreement, understood their personal role and responsibility for its success, and realised the direct relation between the results of their work and their wages. In these conditions all members of the brigade were careful in their use of all the main factors of production — manpower, equipment and materials.

Payment by results. Here a specified payment is made for each unit of output or the performance of a given operation. There are a considerable number of payment-by-results schemes: they may apply either to a group or an individual; some are based on piecework, on time-based bonuses, or other work results. These schemes set targets for workers by establishing the payment for each piece of work, and provide incentives in the form of increased pay for increased work.

In addition, a more creative approach to productivity gains distribution centres on distributing capital stock. For example, Employee Stock Ownership Plans (ESOPs) in the United States encourage workers to buy shares in their own companies, for which the workers also receive some tax benefit. Thus the workers derive a second income from their ownership of capital. Another similar scheme has been proposed by LO, the Swedish trade union organisation. The plan would tax both wages and profits in order to accumulate funds to buy equity in corporations, the equity to be collectively owned and administered by special boards in each of Sweden's 24 provinces. The boards would be elected, and the profits from the shares would augment public pension funds.

So, creating links between rewards and performance represents a major task for managers. The management of remuneration calls for an anticipatory style. It must develop flexible structures and procedures in tune with the evolving technical, economic, political and social processes, as these have a bearing on remuneration policy and decisions.

A remuneration policy should have the following objectives:

— motivating productivity improvement;
— attracting, recruiting and retaining effective staff.

The process by which remuneration can be determined primarily on a performance basis is represented in outline form in figure 7.2.[5]

The nucleus of this model is the relationship between remuneration levels and enterprise performance. This interdependence provides support for the consumer orientation of workers and the performance orientation of employers, and a recognition of the needs of customers (in terms of competitive prices) and the well-being of the economy. The model is presented as an ideal situation. In developing a remuneration policy, managers might aim at such a model, to provide direction, consistency and flexibility. Clearly, any good productivity gains-sharing scheme can be designed, instituted and implemented only jointly by unions and management within the enterprise. Third parties may be consulted, but the final form and substance must be the joint decision of labour and management.

Non-monetary incentives

In some circumstances, moral incentives can be more powerful than monetary ones. For example, one might work hard and effectively to gain the praise of a respected superior or for fear of criticism, or to be respected by colleagues for fulfilling agreed production norms. Belief in moral motivation started the movement towards more worker participation in management, and it can induce workers to co-operate regardless of monetary benefits.

Figure 7.2. Performance-based remuneration

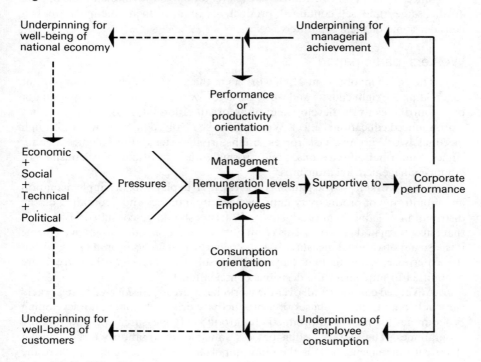

Source: I. Smith, 1983, p. 22.

One of the principal components of Japanese economic success is the Japanese worker's will to work, the work ethic. This is distinct from cultural characteristics, e.g. such typically Japanese modes of behaviour as group-oriented mores and giving priority to the common interest over individual interest. Studies also stress the importance of "intrinsic compensation" (the fact that Japanese workers do not regard their jobs simply as a means of earning an income, but regard work as an arena for the use of aptitudes and abilities), and of the "sense of belonging" (to the whole company rather than to any specific job).

Motivational resources to strengthen workers' positive values and attitudes include the media and other means of publicity. However, non-monetary motivation is not limited to recognition and the work ethic. It also involves workers' participation in decision-making, the quality of working life and working conditions. The latter are of crucial importance for labour productivity. A chemical plant is never going to be a garden city, but there is much that can be done to improve working conditions. Attention to health and injury hazards, to lighting and ventilation, apart from being a moral obligation on managers, almost always pays dividends in higher productivity. Most of this is within the control of managers.

Since all the points mentioned above are not only motivational tools but are at the same time self-contained productivity improvement methods we will consider some of them separately.

Workers' participation

The active involvement of all workers in the process of change is important for creating the right climate and work attitudes for productivity. Participation not only contributes to the development of an organisation but at the same time has a pronounced educational effect. Workers can be involved in many ways: through meetings, work groups, task forces, brainstorming, suggestion schemes, quality circles, informal discussions, and formal and informal mechanisms of labour-management relationships.

Active workers' participation is also essential in planning the implementation and monitoring of productivity improvement programmes and in deciding on the distribution of gains from productivity. Workers should be consulted on matters that affect them in their work. This is not only a moral obligation for management; it is also a motivational measure. If workers participate in decision-making within the enterprise, even though only in a consultative capacity, they are more committed to implement the decisions conscientiously.

Advanced companies all over the world have already discovered that workers can contribute to many phases of a productivity drive: planning and developing programmes for improved productivity, productivity measurement, and training programmes. The workers often possess valuable information which they can share with management. It is therefore important to create a climate where the workers are able to influence the way they do their jobs and to suggest how things can be done better. It is not by chance that in a Singapore survey conducted in July 1985 by the National Productivity Board, 90 per cent of the workers said that they preferred to work for managers who encourage participation.

In an interview, Douglas Wallace, vice-president for social policy at the Minneapolis Norvest Bank in the United States, expressed the following important ideas about the role of people in organisations: [6]

— in any organisation a little participation in decision-making is better than none;

— you can't start off with a lot of participation — that is impractical in a large organisation;

— 5 per cent of the people in an organisation, working in a concerted way, can affect the culture of the entire system;

— the habit of participation in a few can spread to the many.

Douglas Wallace suggested a programme that would involve Norvest staff in formulating policy on social issues affecting the bank. He formed a task force composed of 16 workers representing a cross-section of bank functions and levels. The task force met weekly during the year; they interviewed many bank workers and outside experts. Then they produced a report on their findings and suggestions. To everybody's surprise, top management put into practice all the major policies recommended by the task force.

The bank's top management has found that "employees are a rich source of information and insight on social issues". But, more important, they have found that opening up communication channels in the bank has led to improvement in its overall performance in the most critical area: customer service.

Thus, a "participatory culture" has been introduced, and has contributed to improving the "productivity culture" of all the staff. In turn, management has learned from the staff about aspects of the bank's attitudes and policies that need to be changed if the company is to grow and thrive. Thus, action-learning through participation has resulted in an improved productivity culture and performance.

Participation is successful if workers' organisations get due recognition of their support of productivity improvement programmes. No such programme will succeed without a strong and respected union since only a strong union can be responsible in its commitment and participate effectively in the design and implementation of a productivity improvement programme and in gains-sharing.

Workers are usually involved in the management of enterprises through collective bargaining and joint consultation between management and unions, and in some countries through works councils, i.e. the representation of workers and unions on boards of directors. Works councils do not, however, involve the workers' representative in executive management. There is growing opinion in favour of more participation. In Sweden, for example, this has taken the form of "enabling" legislation, the detailed implementation of which is now being worked out between unions and managers, and the Federal Republic of Germany has legislative enactments to spread worker and union representation on boards of directors. In Norway also, participation is legally established.

The Japanese productivity movement is characterised by two widely known forms of workers' participation: the staff idea scheme or suggestion-box approach, which enables workers to express ideas on improving either their own work, or management practice; and quality control circles, which have already been discussed. These techniques have taken root and flourished in Japanese industry to an impressive extent. For example, in 1981 approximately 1,830,000 workers in 452 firms surveyed submitted a total of 23,532,000 ideas. The number of suggestions submitted on a national scale must be very much higher. Roughly half of the ideas submitted were used in actual business operations, yielding an economic value estimated at 225.3 thousand million yen.

Japan has also developed a considerable degree of joint consultation within the framework of collective bargaining. The commitment of the national trade unions to promoting productivity is reflected in the organisation of joint labour-management consultation bodies, in the organisation of QCs, and in numerous educational activities to promote productivity.

At the APO (Asian Productivity Organisation) symposium in 1980 concerning trade union involvement in productivity improvement, most of the participants, who were from south Asian countries, cited a number of factors which contributed to limited or poor response of workers and their unions to productivity programmes. Among them the following were most often mentioned: [7]

- Employers' attitudes reflecting a master and slave relationship, and autocratic management.
- Workers' apprehension that productivity programmes could lead to lay-offs, longer working hours, heavier workloads.
- Poor climate of labour-management relations.
- Illiteracy of workers and lack of capacity to understand the problems.
- Lack of incentives for involvement.
- Language and other communication barriers including lack of communication channels.
- Lack of a trade union philosophy on productivity.
- A political climate or environment which restricts the exercise of trade union rights.

At the same time, a number of examples were cited of successful co-operation between trade unions and management in productivity improvement. Analysis of successful examples in Asian countries brings out the importance of the range of promotional factors in productivity improvement. Among them are:

- Healthy climate of labour-management relations characterised by mutual trust, respect and openness.
- Assurance of job security, bringing about active involvement of workers in productivity programmes.
- Feeling of the workers that they too have a stake in the productivity programme and that they could have a fair share in the productivity gains.
- Sense of belonging to the enterprise, brought about through workers' participation and supported by good channels of communication.
- Adequate preparatory work prior to the launching of the productivity programme in order to remove all misapprehensions. This could be in the nature of an educational and training programme for both management and labour.
- Good working environment to secure the participation of workers in productivity programmes; provision of supporting programmes for skill development and effective mechanisms for settling grievances.

Workers' participation or consultation does not mean merely giving notice to the workers of company plans and of what is expected from them. Rather, it should mean effective participation in all stages of the programme. This probably requires management to give workers and their representatives access to relevant information.

Productivity training

Only after adequate education, training and development do people become a valuable resource and the most important productivity factor. Therefore, the effectiveness of productivity programmes depends on the quality of the workforce and of managers, and their willingness to contribute to improving productivity. It is not our task here to go into the details of educational and training policy and programmes; this is a special topic and a number of good guides and books are available. Useful references are: Craig (ed.), 1976; Robert-Bittel (ed.), 1978; and Tracey (ed.), 1985. Nevertheless, it is useful to indicate some key points to be taken into consideration during the design stage of productivity improvement programmes.

Three important questions should be considered in this connection:

— which people to develop: workers, technicians, managers;

— what form of development: education and training;

— what to teach: productivity awareness, understanding and skills.

From these a three-dimensional matrix can be built (see figure 7.3), which will help to analyse needs and plan systematic developmental activities for all participants in the productivity programme.

If workers are illiterate, it is difficult for them to contribute to productivity and their ability to participate will increase only with increasing education. Workers, as well as their trade union representatives, must be educated in productivity concepts and their significance, teamwork, positive attitudes, creativity and productivity consciousness. Workers must understand the goals and

Figure 7.3. Three-dimensional human resource development matrix

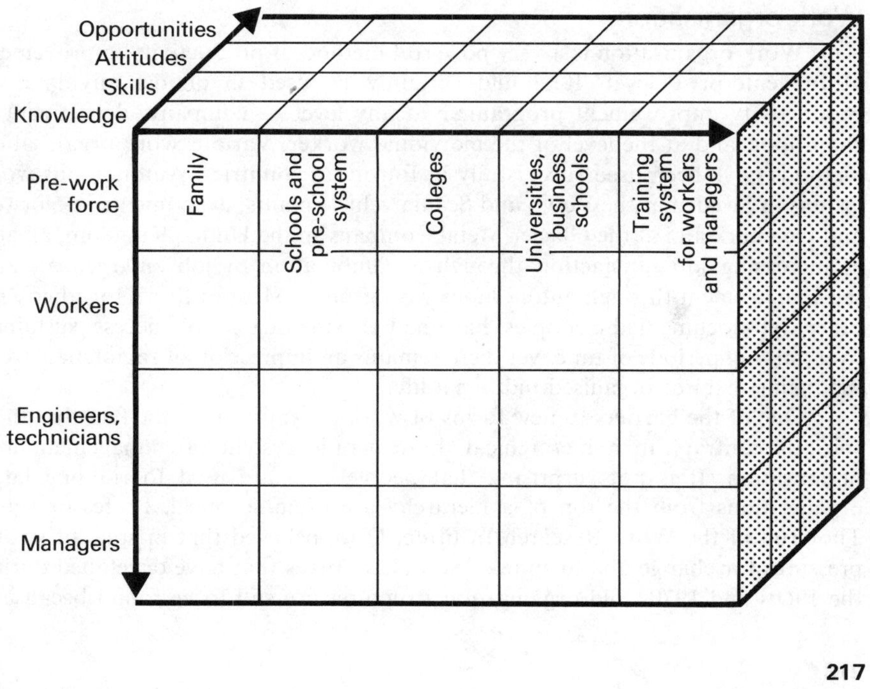

the performance measures. Workers and their supervisors should be given at least one or two weeks' orientation and training in relation to the importance of productivity, its measurement and benefits. They must be given plenty of practice in work-simplification and methods-study approaches.

One of the best approaches is to start exposing workers and supervisors as early as possible to concepts such as labour costs, price determination, the links between productivity and socio-economic problems, quality control and work methods. Such training motivates them towards developing innovations in relation to procedures, work methods and work design.

The same applies to managers. They are the first who have to be trained in productivity improvement programmes and in related managerial skills and awareness.

With the increasing education of the labour force and with changes in its composition, there will be greater demand for more dynamic and educated trade union leadership. If union leadership lacks competence and doesn't have the confidence of the members, this will seriously affect productivity improvement programmes. For example, most trade unions in the Asian region do not have any productivity expertise and therefore they rely on external sources to verify the equity of management's productivity gains schemes. This has deterred some trade unions from being involved in productivity. This means that the education and training of trade union officials and workers' representatives in productivity-related issues is of the greatest importance if worker participation and the role of trade unions in productivity improvement programmes is to be increased.

Work organisation

Work organisation is a very powerful method of productivity improvement at the enterprise level. It should certainly be used in almost any kind of productivity improvement programme at any level — company, departmental, shop-floor, and at the level of the individual worker. Various work organisation methods have been used successfully in European countries. Autonomous work groups in Sweden at the Volvo and Scania vehicle plants, experiments in Norway and Denmark and at the Glacier Metal Company in the United Kingdom, all aim at increasing job satisfaction through a combination of job enlargement and self-management through autonomous workgroups. Most of these, together with other well-documented examples, have had varying degrees of success, sustained over varying periods of time, yet there remains an impression of remoteness from the mainstream of organised industrial life.

One of the barriers to new forms of work organisation is the fact that their spirit is contrary to a hierarchical, bureaucratic system of management and organisation. It is not surprising that people who are used to running large organisations from the top of a hierarchy are often sceptical. Professor Einar Thorsrud of the Work Research Institute, Oslo, believed that in spite of strong pressures for change and in spite of new alternatives that have developed during the 1960s and 1970s, old organisation structures are still to be found because: [8]

- The traditional forms are quite suitable to the mechanisation stage, while mechatronics (a combination of electronics and mechanics) requires new forms.

- The effectiveness of large-scale hierarchical organisations is measured in simple economic terms which do not reveal the wastage of human resources and potential.

- Traditional forms of organisation protect the privileges of people with power and high status.

- The traditional forms include payment systems and planning and administrative routines which need to be adjusted to new forms of organisation. During this adjustment uncertainty may arise about how managerial (power) control is maintained.

Frederich Hertzberg (see bibliography), a management psychologist in the United States, claims that workers are motivated to greater effort by the characteristics of the job (enriched, challenging, interesting) rather than by such factors as the quality of supervision, the level of pay and social welfare conditions. Contemporary job design movements in France, the Federal Republic of Germany, and to a lesser extent in Italy and the United Kingdom, have been partly based on that belief. Moreover, there has arisen a coincident and urgent need to build flexible manufacturing systems (FMS) capable of adapting to changing market demands, and these systems make it possible for job designs to offer challenge and interest. Details of new work organisation principles and techniques can be found in an ILO publication.[8]

However, we will just indicate here the main areas of work organisation and some of the latest development in this field.

Generally, the whole range of work organisation approaches and methods could be classified into two main groups:

— restructuring working time;
— restructuring the job itself.

Restructuring working time refers to time-scheduling; job restructuring is concerned more with the organisation and socio-technical systems of work at the shop-floor level. Let us consider them separately.

Working time

Work organisation methods involving working time have implications which range from conditions of work and quality of working life to the number of hours per day, as in flexitime systems. These methods are used not only to improve labour productivity but also to distribute gains from higher national and sectoral productivity through maintaining employment. If workers displaced by efficiency improvements cannot find other, equally productive work or some other way to maintain their incomes, higher productivity will not increase total output, but will only worsen income distribution.

Productivity management

Below we will consider some experiences in maintaining employment as one of the important forms of productivity improvement, motivation and gains-sharing.

(a) *Part-time work*. In a number of industrialised and developing countries part-time work has become an important option for many enterprises because of the convenient way it benefits both workers and employers. For the employer the benefits include flexibility and low cost; for the worker the opportunity to supplement household income and maintain social contacts, choosing working hours which fit in with family commitments. For example, in the United Kingdom during the past 20 years the number of part-timers has doubled to 4.5 million — a fifth of total employment. Two-thirds of them are women.[9] Some particular uses of part-time working include:

- covering absences, peak trading hours, holiday periods, changes in business patterns;
- minimising disruption caused by split shifts and unsocial hours;
- providing a source of recruitment for full-time vacancies;
- introducing school leavers to working life;
- establishing a pool of trained and committed workers for future promotion.

(b) *Job-sharing* is the division of one full-time job between two or more part-timers and has received a great deal of publicity. It is aimed principally at young people entering employment for the first time. It is a good method for increasing so-called "social productivity". However, it is uneconomic for the most part and has proved unattractive in practice for a number of reasons. It adds to costs (recruitment, payroll, planning, administration and training) without yielding any corresponding benefit. Nevertheless, it has the potential to achieve economic benefits as well, since better total results are frequently achieved by two half-time workers than by one full-time person.

(c) *Shorter workweeks* (shorter hours) are a campaigning issue for many trade unions all over the world. A 1984 declaration by nine members of the European Council of Ministers (United Kingdom opposing) favoured the reduction and reorganisation of working time, including job-sharing and stricter limitation of systematic overtime. However, the experience of companies implementing such schemes seems to show that the employment-generating possibilities from either reductions in basic hours or longer holidays seem very limited.

Some studies suggest that productivity potential is substantial if working time changes are geared to a wider programme of work reorganisation. A reduction in the "working week" may simply result in more overtime with increased costs. So, a *reduction of overtime* would appear to be one of the few promising avenues for increasing the number of jobs. It is commonly felt that overtime working has a depressive effect on productivity.

(d) *Longer vacation time* is another strategy in work organisation and is more readily accepted by workers. In the Federal Republic of Germany, for example, the metalworking, chemical and construction industries have all acquiesced to union demands for six weeks' annual leave. Many companies are introducing extended unpaid leave and study leave.

(e) *Flexitime* also has a good effect in many cases not only on productivity improvement but on the working climate as well. It is more common in white-collar, service occupations. This method is partly a response to social pressure to avoid rush hours, as well as to demands from workers for more control over their jobs and working time.

(f) *Spin-off, contracting out and subcontracting* are important trends towards bringing in more and more special services from outside, because of the flexibility they give in responding to fluctuating requirements. Subcontracts can be made with suppliers or with former staff members, making it possible to concentrate resources on what a company does best. This also provides a number of other openings for spin-off employment, such as by staff secondment, homeworking and freelance work.

Avoiding large-scale redundancy also motivates some companies to explore the above-mentioned contractual arrangements. Sometimes a whole department is converted into an independent subcontractor with individual full-time workers operating from home.

(g) *Working at home* has many variations — full-time or part-time work, staff member of self-employed status, dividing work between office and home or working entirely at home. For example, in the United Kingdom there were close to a million people working at or from home in 1981.[10]

(h) *New retirement patterns* such as flexible, early and phased retirement have been widely used by large companies to reduce unproductive employment. Surveys suggest that many workers would welcome early retirement. Flexible and phased retirement already exists in the shape of part-time work as a way of adjusting to full-time leisure after full-time employment.

Thus widespread changes are occurring in working patterns mainly in response to the following forces:

— the introduction of new technology;

— the need to reshape organisations to fit changing market and customer needs;

— the availability of the right kind of labour;

— the pressure for more leisure and more autonomy;

— the need to contain high overheads, raise productivity and improve quality.

Good management is necessary to achieve positive results from these changes. Below are a few cases which demonstrate some practical solutions and examples of working time management.

"Out-placement" — Hitachi (Japan) [11]

True to its reputation as a master of survival in recession, Hitachi Ltd., the largest electrical manufacturer in Japan, was ahead of others in workforce reduction measures in response to the 1974 crisis. It quickly introduced conventional retrenchment measures (no recruitment, temporary lay-off of the order of 10,000 work-days for one year after summer 1974, and job transfer and company transfer of 7,500 workers). It also embarked on the unconventional measure of transferring some of its surplus labour to other companies totally unrelated to it.

To deal with the surplus labour, reported to exceed 10,000 workers, Hitachi's personnel officers surveyed the labour market, scanning newspaper advertisements and contacting their customers. As a result, they succeeded in placing 1,000 redundant workers in food companies, sports clubs and other leisure businesses, petrol stations and other service organisations.

The company signed a "shukko" agreement with the union for this special measure. Under it, wage differences arising from the "out-placement" would be made up by the company.

"Rings of defence" — Control Data (United States) [6]

To maintain employment stability Control Data created ten "rings of defence". The *first ring* is a long-term R & D strategy in which new products will be regularly introduced (the best defence against lay-offs is growth, and the ability to introduce attractive new products). The *second ring* is control of turnover (being careful not to replace retired workers whenever possible). The *third ring* is the judicious use of part-timers. These people give the company tremendous flexibility in meeting fluctuating product demand. The *fourth ring* is the use of contractors. During the good times the company contracts out work that is not labour intensive and pulls such work back in-house during business slumps. The *fifth ring* of defence is subcontracting with the prison service for cheap labour from prisoners. The *sixth ring* is the use of in-company transfers (moving people from one division to another). The *seventh ring* is offering summers off without pay (some 10 per cent of company workers volunteer to do this in order to be with their children or teacher-spouses). The *eighth ring* is voluntary time off without pay (many people prefer a four-day work-week or would like to take a mini-sabbatical leave). The *ninth ring* is extended public holidays, partly unpaid.

Faced with the need to lay off the equivalent of 4,800 workers in the 1980-83 recession, Control Data made its first attempt at implementing this strategy and finally had to lay off only 600, thus saving 4,200 jobs. In 1985, however, they were forced to lay off workers because they ignored a *tenth ring* — competitive products and high productivity.

"Networking" — Rank Xerox (United Kingdom) [9]

Like many companies, Rank Xerox has been faced in recent years with an increasing burden of overhead costs in maintaining substantial office premises, particularly centrally located headquarters. The scale and continued growth of such expenditure was felt to be unjustifiable in terms of value added. As well as reducing staff numbers, relocating and reducing office space, the company sought further ways to lower overheads whilst maintaining the output and motivation of its staff.

A large number of workers, such as engineers and salespeople, were already operating from outside company premises, so it was a short step to a "networking" scheme for selected staff. Networkers run an independent limited company, working from their own premises, usually their home. The relationship with Rank Xerox is essentially that of a subcontractor.

There are currently some 50 to 60 networking companies in the scheme. The experiment seems to be successful, judging by the accounts of the networkers themselves, the number of "internal" (or core) staff who are expressing a desire to follow suit, and by the cost savings to Rank Xerox.

Nevertheless, considerable thought, time, effort and finance have been necessary to get the project off the ground, both in its initial design and in its management. Issues which have been examined include:

- The type of jobs which are "networkable". Rank Xerox distinguishes between jobs which require a continued physical presence (not networkable) and those for which location is incidental to the required output (potentially networkable).

- The relationship of core staff with networkers.

- The kind of person who enjoys and is capable of running a successful independent business.

- Counselling and training in specialist, business and micro-computing skills for networkers and their spouses.

- Training of core staff, especially network support staff.

- Design of "home office" furniture.

- The deliberate inclusion of networkers in internal company meetings, social events, distribution lists and so on.

- The formation of the Xerox Association of Networkers and Distributed Utilities (XANADU) as a self-help, self-funded organisation to facilitate exchange of business contacts, and to provide group purchasing and services.

It is important to note that the Rank Xerox scheme is only applicable to a relatively small number of people with high-value, portable skills, usually experienced managers with high salaries.

XANADU membership is open to anyone who has left Rank Xerox to set up in business as well as to networkers. It offers the services listed above and is a source of help in setting up in business. There are currently some 250 participant companies, employing 500 people and with a combined turnover of around £5 million.

Department networkers. A new variation on networking now being tried out is to set up specialist departments as independent companies. They can market their services to other customers in addition to Rank Xerox. The fleet control department is now an independent company, though it still maintains an office within Rank Xerox. Similarly, a Rank Xerox department, acting as a separate company, plans to make use of spare capacity in the gymnasium after 4 p.m. by hiring it off to sports clubs. The taxation department (composed of tax lawyers) and a corporate affairs/public relations section have also been "networked".

"Xerox points". A frequent problem in establishing its sales network throughout the world was that Rank Xerox wanted to maintain direct sales in the most profitable areas, and dealers were unwilling to take on the less profitable areas. A project has been started in France, in areas too small to become fully fledged "sales districts", where former Rank Xerox staff are helped to set themselves up as dealers. Such dealerships can be run with lower overheads and offer a desirable life-style to their owners. Currently, some 25 "Xerox points" have been set up; the aim is to have 60 to 80.

There are several common themes in the thinking behind all these initiatives:

— an interest in exploring the possibilities of change opened up by new technology;

— a perception of changing aspirations, particularly the desire for increased independence, and an ambition to harness this to increase motivation and output;

— a desire to introduce some decentralisation and to reduce overheads, including overhead time as well as direct overhead costs.

Job restructuring

Job restructuring comprises another important group of work organisation methods which aim at increasing both productivity and job satisfaction. Increased job satisfaction itself can also result in higher productivity and better motivation. Many managers and workers feel that job restructuring, covering job enrichment and job enlargement, is a promising strategy for improved job satisfaction. Figure 7.4 shows the different ways of job restructuring.[12]

Figure 7.4. Types of job restructuring

Job restructuring			
Job enlargement (horizontal changes)		Job enrichment (vertical changes)	
Increased task length Addition of further similar tasks	Increased product variety through job rotation or other techniques	Increased task variety and complexity, job responsibilities	Increased involvement in departmental and plant activities

Source: J. Prokopenko, 1978, p. 28.

Job restructuring can build up the content of jobs so as to enhance skills, interest, initiative and range of responsibility while reducing frustration and monotony. Job enrichment and job enlargement are concerned with job and work changes through modification of the workers' tasks. Restructuring, the addition of further similar tasks, is often referred to as job enlargement and can be viewed as a horizontal change. One variation of job enlargement is job rotation. Workers are "rotated" between various fragmented activities with some degree of choice. Vertical change involves increased individual involvement through the addition of different tasks and duties; such changes are generally referred to as job enrichment.

So-called "group working", "cell system", "team work structuring", "autonomous working groups", etc., though no longer a new concept in production, still offer a lot of room for expansion and improvement of job restructuring methods since they have many advantages from the point of view of productivity and job satisfaction.

For example, *autonomous working groups* aim at quite different results from mere physical output. They might aim at:

— simply promoting a spirit of collaboration and reviving deeper interpersonal relations;

— serving as a framework for enlarging the possibility of individual action, either through change of job station or through job enlargement;

— delegating complex tasks to work groups.

The autonomy of the work group itself could be viewed with regard to:

— determination of individual methods of production;

— leadership within the group;

— decisions regarding personnel questions;

— all decisions about the organisation of work within the group;

— decisions on production processes;

— decisions on hours of work;

— decisions on accepting additional tasks;

— designation of the group's spokesman;

— influence on the establishment of quantitative and/or qualitative group aims.

In spite of their different origins and technological backgrounds, all groups share the following seven characteristics: [13]

Team: They contain a specified team of workers who work solely or generally in the group.

Products: They produce a specified "family" or set of products.

Facilities: They have a specified set of machines and/or other production equipment which is used in the group.

Group layout: The facilities are located in one area which is reserved for the group.

Target: The workers in the group share a common production target.

Independence: Most of the groups are independent. They can vary their pace of work. Once they have received materials, their achievement does not depend on the services of other production groups.

Size: Most, but not all the groups are small. Most have fewer than 15 workers.

Productivity management

There are five main classes of job design methods to restructure group work. They are:

— task enlargement;
— increased batch frequency;
— job enlargement;
— job rotation;
— job enrichment.

The following advantages and disadvantages of work group methods are frequently cited: [14]

Advantages	Disadvantages
Quantifiable effects	*Additional, one-time costs*
— better product quality, less waste	— preparation for conversion
— higher output	— training for workers
— no losses from tempo modulation	— reduced production in conversion phase
— no standby personnel	— new building and production facilities
— less absenteeism	— more production facilities, tools, buffer installations
	— greater space requirements
Effects difficult to quantify	*Additional, continuous costs*
— production less prone to disturbance, greater ease in overcoming disturbance	— longer training needed for workers (complex job content)
— greater flexibility as regards changes in number of articles, variety range, product changes, changes in manufacturing processes	— greater provision of materials (buffer zones, individual working places)
	— less intensive use of production equipment (e.g. at individual working places)
— lower labour turnover	— greater servicing and maintenance costs (more production equipment)
	— higher wage bill (higher wage groups, longer machining times)
Barely quantifiable effects	
— more attractive workplaces, satisfaction of demanding requirements	
— broader scope for use of workers' abilities	

—   greater field for initiative open to
       workers (sharing ideas,
       proposals for improvements)
—   shorter information routes
—   better climate at work

The introduction of work groups has been found to make a major direct contribution to the humanisation of work, and facilitates the application of other work organisation methods and job design.

"Electronic cottages" refers to work done on home computers linked to an office computer. (Sometimes it is called "remote work", "home work" or "telecommuting".) It is expected to become a viable alternative to working in an office. For example, in the United States at present less than 1 per cent of the labour force is telecommuting, but the figure is expected to jump to 5 per cent within the next few years as the number of computers in offices and homes increases and telecommunications equipment becomes less expensive and more accessible.[15]

This new form of work organisation presents many advantages. Employers can retain qualified, trained personnel who are unwilling or unable to work in the office. They can also recruit people from wider geographical areas and from diverse populations, such as the handicapped and the retired. Less office space is needed with fewer office workers, resulting in savings on rent, utilities, meetings and services. Workers enjoy the flexibility and freedom to use their time as they see fit and save money, energy and stress by not travelling daily to an office.

Telecommuters work either part time at home, spending one or more days in the office, or full time at home. The manager's first task in implementing a work-at-home programme is to identify the staff best suited to it. In addition to performing functions that are easily transferrable to the home, work-at-home candidates should be self-directed, self-motivated, self-disciplined, organised, independent, experienced, mature and customer-oriented when necessary. They should not require a rigid schedule and should have no fear of social isolation.

Case study: Work design team introduces new technology [16]

Automated office technology was introduced at General Foods in the form of word processing during the late 1970s. This development significantly changed the office environment, affected the skills needed for secretarial/clerical jobs, and required managers to make changes in the way they worked. The organisation-development group formulated a strategy for studying administrative work on a unit-by-unit basis. It established a resource group — the work-design team — to lead the process of changing work habits.

Out of this evolved a work-design process: at the invitation of the management of a unit, the work-design team helps the unit study its administrative work and makes recommendations to improve it. Only units whose managers request a work study are examined. Those who want to leave their work environment unchanged can do so. Every salaried worker in the unit participates in the work study from the beginning. This means they decide how to manage the project according to their needs.

General Foods staff have an opportunity to establish the objectives for improvement, describe the work, identify barriers to getting the work done, make recommendations to solve problems, and participate in putting the agreed changes into effect. Once this has been done, they have many options to choose from, including possible new job opportunities.

The purpose of the study is to determine how administrative work should be designed to optimise productivity and increase job satisfaction. It focuses on five areas:

- How paper flows, both within the unit and across functions.
- How work flows between managers and their clerical and secretarial-support people.
- How work is accomplished within a unit.
- How work is organised and assigned within a unit.
- How workers feel about the work and its assignment.

A work-design study takes roughly five months from the beginning to the development of recommendations (see figure 7.5); implementation can require an additional two to six months. The unit first establishes a "contract" or study plan that lists objectives (targets for change), scope (number of workers within the unit and the functions to be studied), and a timetable. In addition, a study team (task force) is assigned to work on the project.

The study team includes a mix of managers, professionals, secretaries and clerks. In addition, the team needs a balance of experience — some members who have a broad knowledge of the organisation and others who are relative newcomers.

A project manager to lead the team during the course of the study is selected from the staff. This person must be a risk-taker (action-oriented) who will be accountable for the results of the team's efforts. Each team member must possess good communication skills, be viewed as creative, and be considered a stable member of the organisation who works well under pressure.

The organisational study conducted in 1980 by General Foods public affairs department could serve as a model for this type of study. The public affairs department is responsible for various company publications, financial communications, executive speeches, media relations and product communications, relations with all levels of government, and related research. As such, its output of paperwork is enormous.

At the time, 44 people worked in the department: 32 managers and 12 secretaries. Although some of the managers shared secretarial staff, the secretarial-managerial relationship was traditional — usually one secretary was responsible for a manager's entire secretarial needs, transcription, telephone communications and so forth.

Since the department was organised by activity rather than workload, some secretaries had a tremendous amount of paperwork while others had less. Also,

Figure 7.5. Work-design process model

Activity	Timetable/resource
1. Develop plan, set objectives, define scope and set timetable. Select study-team members	1 month/work-design team, personnel manager and unit staff
2. Communicate project to the organisation	1-hour meeting/entire unit, unit head and work-design team
3. Collect data by questionnaires, time logs and interviews	10 days
Analyse and consolidate findings, and validate with functional units	1 month Work-design team
Present findings to unit management for agreement and setting of priorities	1½ hours
4. Communicate progress to the organisation	Continuous process
5. Identify solutions and develop recommendations for presentation to unit management. Obtain management's approval	6-8 weeks/unit-study team and work-design team
6. Communicate progress to the organisation	Continuous process
7. Develop implementation plan, timetable and start-up	6-12 weeks/project manager
8. Evaluate implementation against study objectives	4 weeks/work-design team

Source: P. Smith, 1984, p. 40.

there was inefficiency and duplication which stemmed from the department's organisational structure.

Nine members of the public affairs unit were selected for the study team and worked for a month with the work-design team to develop the study plan. Once the plan was ready, a departmental meeting was called to announce the project, explain what would be taking place, and request everyone to participate.

Following the communications meeting, the role of the work-design consultant was to build up an adequate and fair picture of the department's administrative work. Data were collected over a ten-day period through questionnaires and interviews with managerial and secretarial staff. The various functional areas within the department then consolidated the data and validated them with participants. Group meetings were held without the project manager so that workers would share ideas freely. Separate meetings were held with managers to brief them on the emerging issues. Then the information was classified into organisational opportunities to be addressed by the study team and functional data to be handled by the manager responsible.

The work-design team then presented the organisational opportunities to the public affairs staffers, who were asked to identify the study team's priorities and constraints based on such factors as available time, money and people. The study team then turned to the key phase of the entire process: deciding what specific recommendations to make to the department's management.

Once this phase began, each team member spent three to four hours a week on the project, with the work-design consultant serving as a "facilitator" and resource. As the team worked, it kept the department informed through periodic memos. After eight weeks, the team members reached a consensus on recommendations that proposed changes in five areas: work structure, work simplification, new procedures, office technology, and education and training.

Specifically, the implementation plan proposed dividing tasks between a centralised group and an administrative support group. The centralised group would provide word-processing support to the entire department and full administrative assistance to 12 professionals, and the administrative-support group would provide secretarial services for several managers and could handle the administrative activities then being performed by the managers. The team also recommended that the department's research activities be consolidated and that sophisticated new information retrieval equipment be acquired. To support the new operating environment, education and training programmes were designed by the training and development area in corporate organisation development.

The team's recommendations and back-up analysis were presented to the staff. Once approved, the results were presented at a general meeting for the entire department and it was made clear that the study group's recommendations had the full support of the department's management and that the new system would be implemented.

The new structure, implemented in early 1981, resulted in a reorganisation of the department's administrative jobs. Despite initial misgivings, most members of the public affairs department believe that the new system serves them better than the old one. The production centre processes more material more quickly than under the old system. Research information and new data are available on a more timely basis. And some duties, such as maintaining the corporate executive biographies and administering community contributions, are handled by secretaries rather than by managers.

* * *

In this chapter we have attempted to demonstrate the vital importance of staff management for productivity improvement. Managers must promote organisational structures and cultures which emphasise the important role played by workers. They must develop leadership styles which are appropriate for the nature of the business and also for the local culture and conditions. They must introduce effective motivational systems, both financial and non-financial; increase worker participation in decision-making; improve training and development; and pay attention to work organisation and the quality of working life.

In other words, to improve productivity it is not sufficient to invest in machines. It is necessary to invest in labour and management as well, and also in the working environment.

[1] ILO: *Introduction to work study* (Geneva, 3rd ed., 1979), Ch. 3.

[2] Harold E. Dolenga: "Productivity: Problems, paradigms and progress", in *SAM Advanced Management Journal* (New York, Society for the Advancement of Management), Autumn 1985, pp. 39-45.

[3] "Gain-sharing: The west's answer to quality circles?", in *International Management*, Oct. 1983, pp. 31 ff.

[4] Sumer C. Aggarwal: "Productivity: A measure or a mirage?", in *Productivity* (Stamford, Connecticut), Jan. 1981, pp. 457-480.

[5] Ian Smith: *The management of remuneration* (Aldershot, United Kingdom, Gower, 1983), Ch. 1.

[6] James O'Toole: "Employee practices at the best managed companies", in *California Management Review* (Berkeley, University of California), Autumn 1985, pp. 35-66.

[7] APO: *Involvement of trade unions in productivity*, Symposium report (Tokyo, 1983), pp. 17-21 and 140.

[8] George Kanawaty (ed.): *Managing and developing new forms of work organisation* (Geneva, ILO, 1981), pp. 4-7.

[9] BIM: *Managing new patterns of work* (London, British Institute of Management Foundation, n.d.).

[10] Catherine Hakim: "Homework and outwork: National estimates from two surveys", in *Employment Gazette* (HMSO, London, Department of Employment), Jan. 1984, pp. 7-12.

[11] Eiji Mizutani: *Facing challenge to management and productivity* (Bangkok, ILO Regional Office, 1985), pp. 2-6.

[12] Joseph Prokopenko: *Improving productivity in developing countries*, Management Development Working Paper No. 16 (Geneva, ILO, 1978), p. 48.

[13] John L. Burbidge: *Group production methods and humanisation of work: The evidence in industrialised countries*, Research series No. 10 (Geneva, IILS, 1976), p. 18.

[14] Reinhold Weil: *Alternative forms of work organisation: Improvements of labour conditions and productivity in Western Europe*, Research series No. 4 (Geneva, IILS, 1976), pp. 17-18.

[15] Dorothy Kroll: "Telecommuting: A revealing peek inside some of the industry's first electronic cottages", in *Management Review* (New York, AMACOM), Nov. 1984, pp. 18-23.

[16] Pat Smith: "How work design teams introduced new technology to General Foods offices", ibid., pp. 38-41.

PRODUCTIVITY PROMOTION AT THE NATIONAL LEVEL

8

The competitiveness and effectiveness of a nation are not the same as the simple sum of the productivity of its enterprises. National productivity also depends on political, economic, social and cultural forces largely within the control of governments.

Three tiers of government organisation are concerned with promoting productivity in society. The top tier focuses on macro (or national) policies and frameworks. The middle tier is concerned with productivity targets and mechanisms that contribute to national aims for economic and social development. The third tier consists of enterprises and groups of enterprises, professionals and workers who analyse and implement improvements.

These three levels have both *direct* and *indirect* means of action. Direct intervention by government includes running public enterprises, government investment, sponsoring productivity enhancing schemes, etc. Indirect government intervention includes the popularisation of productivity awareness, the sponsorship of education and training, and the support of institutions and institutional mechanisms promoting productivity.

All these means of action influence important macro-productivity factors such as:

— macro-economic structural change, economies of scale;

— labour structure and policy;

— education and training policy;

— technological change, research and development policy;

— the infrastructure;

— the exploitation of the natural environment, raw materials and energy;

— the business cycle;

— the international business and political environment.

Let us consider national and international activities in productivity improvement, taking into account the above-mentioned dimensions.

8.1 National efforts in productivity drives

The effectiveness of national efforts to improve productivity depends largely on the extent to which the most important social forces can be combined and integrated. These forces include:

— government and its institutional mechanisms;
— employers and managers represented by their professional associations;
— workers, normally represented by trade unions;
— other non-governmental organisations.

All these forces play (or should play) a major role in productivity drives at the national level through:

— direct intervention and participation in industry and economic processes, co-ordinating the activities of all the major social groups in productivity promotion;
— improving the quality of both workers and managers through productivity-oriented professional education and training;
— raising public awareness and productivity consciousness.

The role of government in productivity growth

Governments play a vital role in national economic growth and productivity. However, it is important to stress that the actual role played by a government often does not correspond to the real needs. There are many examples where it is necessary to increase direct government intervention in the economy; but there are also many cases of more mature economies where direct government intervention is less necessary and such indirect methods as economic and fiscal policy, strategic planning, legislation and education and training are more effective.

Since governments initiate and control development programmes, government processes are regularly transferred to such programmes. The uncritical adoption of these processes is a major problem in many programmes for the following reasons.

First, government processes of decision-making and implementation are heavily dominated by hierarchical authority, especially in departments which are part of the executive branch of the government. Executive departments often operate as if only those in authority know what needs to be done. Those lower in the hierarchy have little say in this "top-down" process of decision-making.

Second, government processes generally focus on observing procedures rather than on achieving results. Procedures for selecting personnel, for example, focus on whether the norms and practices of government have been adhered to rather than on whether candidates are suitable for the job.

Third, the processes of government are not flexible enough. When tasks and programmes change, governments adapt their processes slowly and with great difficulty. Consequently, processes become standardised and routine, and "precedents" determine the course of decision and action.[1]

We cannot suggest here any "correct" balance between centralisation and decentralisation since this is a matter for every country and its people to decide. However, our approach is that government intervention should be combined with decision-making at the lower levels — sectors, enterprises and even individuals. Good policy and strategy, government stability and strong leadership, capable of implementing its own decisions, are all necessary for economic growth and higher productivity. This is achieved by different combinations of promotional or regulatory policy measures.

The important role of government is to provide the necessary infrastructure and to create opportunities for growth. Infrastructure covers education and training, health, housing, power, water, transport, communications, research and development, and the availability of technology. For example, without tremendous government investment in research and development, the growth of agriculture, highways, airports, water and railway systems would never have been possible in many countries. These systems provide infrastructure to practically all other industries and, therefore, without their growth, the productivity increases of most industries would have been greatly hampered.

Many governments specify their policy in productivity improvement and then carry out a planning process which integrates productivity targets into national development plans. In many developing countries existing capacities remain unused, not only for lack of adequate infrastructure, but also because of the inadequate involvement of all the parties concerned in the planning and implementation process.

Lack of necessary government intervention results in low productivity. Policy instruments available include such possibilities as public enterprise, accelerated depreciation allowance, low interest loans, subsidy programmes, advance exemption and reductions, tax concessions, incentives including tax holidays, and pioneer status for new types of business. All these have been used effectively and with discrimination in many countries to accelerate and redirect capital investment, promoting high rates of economic and productivity growth. But indiscriminate reliance on some of these instruments, especially price controls, has proved unproductive in the long run.

It is clear that while government control and intervention are necessary, they are effective only if they are applied with prudence and with a flexible approach. There is a short list of government instruments which any manager of productivity improvement programmes should understand in order to appreciate the possible positive and negative impacts of government regulations. Enterprise managers cannot control government measures but they can take them into consideration in their planning. The list of relevant government instruments includes:

- national economic plans and policies;
- public enterprises;
- labour legislation;
- pollution control;
- health and safety legislation;

— social welfare;
— commodity price support;
— patent monopoly privilege;
— required audits from enterprises;
— tariffs and import quotas;
— taxes and tax advantages;
— legislation encouraging affirmative action;
— government grants and subsidies;
— regulations on working conditions;
— restraints on competition;
— anti-trust enforcement;
— laws on incentive payments;
— free or subsidised facilities or utilities.

Any of these government instruments could exert a positive or negative influence on productivity growth for specific industries and individual enterprises. So the design of productivity improvement programmes or policies should take into consideration these and other environmental constraints or incentives. Let us now consider some aspects of the government role in productivity improvement.

Macro-economic structural changes, economies of scale

Recent decades have witnessed a significant shift in the economic structure of developed countries: the proportion of high-productive manufacturing industries has decreased and the proportion of low-productive services has increased. For example, if in 1950 the relation between employment in the production and the service sectors was 49 : 51, this proportion is now about 34 : 66 for the United States. This results in a decrease in national productivity. Consequently, the task of increasing productivity in the service sector has become an important national goal in many countries.

Such factors as the recent collapse of oil prices (1985-86) and the prospect of continued price instability, together with the general decline in consumption in industrialised countries, all have a direct impact on employment and productivity, working conditions and industrial relations.

Government economic policy pays special attention to the economies of scale. In general, there is a strong correlation between the size of an establishment and the output per worker. There are many reasons for this. For example, for different types of equipment, cost increases rise proportionately less than equity increases; large-scale production is often necessary for full utilisation of equipment; the cost of large-scale transport rises proportionately less than the increase in volume transported; larger plant makes possible greater division of labour and specialisation of workers.

Economies of scale do not, however, imply any neglect of the potential of the small and medium-sized enterprise sectors for productivity improvement in developing countries. Few developing countries have large industrial sectors and their economic and social conditions are not yet ready to adopt "big business" on a large scale.

Small and medium-sized enterprises often constitute more than 90 per cent of developing countries' economic units and in the manufacturing sector often account for more than one-half of total employment. An advantage of small and medium-sized enterprises in developing countries is their relatively low dependence on scarce managerial, technological and capital resources. Their social importance lies mainly in their ability to use local skills and resources to generate employment, sometimes even to a greater degree than capital-intensive large enterprises. Finally, they offer flexibility, which is very important in the business cycle fluctuations of the modern economy and in a situation of rapid social change.

Government policy and its incentive mechanisms should take into consideration the specifics of the country (the social system, political system, economic structure) in order to make the right mix of economic measures and strategies to achieve national economic and social objectives.

Technological changes; R & D policy

It is vital to maintain (or develop) the optimal relationship between old and new techniques and equipment, and between different production processes which help to improve the effectiveness of fixed capital on the national scale. One of the effective tools in this field is government legislation on depreciation, taxes, and patent and subsidy policies.

Optimum structure and a high quality of R & D in a nation can make a huge contribution to productivity improvement. About half of total R & D expenditure is estimated to be "productive" in the sense of having a direct influence on productivity growth.

One of the problems in this field is maintaining the right balance between basic and applied research. It is very important to close the existing gap between invention and its integration into the production process. A great deal depends upon government policy in this field, e.g. the organisation of R & D institutions, the distribution of funds between them, the priorities in science and technology, motivation, national impediments to the "brain drain" and so forth.

A government can protect the domestic market during an initial period of relatively high cost of new technology by providing low-cost, long-term finance to promote capital investment, and by restricting imports of foreign technology. It can also push companies to adopt the latest technologies and set minimum sizes for new plants.

Infrastructure

Infrastructure includes transport, communications, health services, finance and banking, government controls, local institutions and other so-called non-production services. It is a very important area for productivity improvement for two reasons.

First, enterprise efficiency could be reduced to zero on the national scale if the infrastructure, which assures the distribution and redistribution of goods and services, were ineffective. All functions, services and financial support provided by the government have a profound and direct impact on all aspects of the national economy.

Second, the public sector in the developed market economy countries now employs about 15-20 per cent of the total workforce, and the service sector more than 50-60 per cent. Increasing the productivity of the infrastructure is therefore itself a significant problem.

Natural environment

One shortcoming of the present methods of productivity evaluation is that they do not adequately take into account the use of natural resources. Changes in the value of resources such as land, and consumption of underground resources such as oil and minerals, should be incorporated into productivity measurements. The effects of pollution may also need to be included as a productivity factor (decreasing productivity in the short run but perhaps increasing it in the long term through improving the environment and the quality of life).

Raw materials and energy could also be considered as a significant aspect of natural resources. Their optimal use is an important government responsibility. One of the main goals of government policy is to maintain the accessibility and reasonable price of raw materials and energy, and to balance this with the protection of the environment and industrial demand. Proper government legislation, prices, fiscal and taxation policy, and other environmental protection measures can force consumers (both industrial and individual) to minimise their consumption of energy and materials without prejudicing economic growth.

Business cycle

Changes in productivity arise from a wide variety of causes associated with the business cycle. These changes have an important bearing on production costs as well as on prices, profits and incentives to invest, and therefore on inflation and economic growth, particularly in market economy countries with a low degree of government intervention.

Until now very little could be done even at the national and international levels to prevent some of the consequences of the business cycle which have a negative effect on productivity. However, using sophisticated national statistics, economic research and marketing institutions can now predict business changes and inform industry about them, so that productivity slowdown during business recessions need not be so disastrous as in the past.

Good government long-term planning mechanisms, especially in developing countries, can also help the country to be prepared for business cycle fluctuations and thereby decrease their negative effect.

Using a well-balanced intervention strategy a government can promote individual companies which are trying to open up new sectors. It can reduce the risks involved in initiating change by targeting sectors for new or stepped-up activity and making resources available on favourable terms. It can, in effect, alter the risk/reward prospects by reducing the risk and increasing the reward. In addition, it can even offer negative incentives such as high-cost credit for investment in sectors it wants to discourage. With a national strategy involving both macro- and micro-economic policies, a government can stimulate some sectors more than it depresses others. Public companies can be used to promote and speed up government intervention, which can eventually reshape the industrial profile of a country.

Subcontracting arrangements have also become an important area of government regulations. For example, in Japan subcontracting links are encouraged between large enterprises (including public companies) and small-scale industries. Such arrangements enable big companies to produce at low cost and at the same time increase the productivity of smaller firms.

However, indiscriminate and uncoordinated use of government intervention often results in decreasing economic efficiency. For example, isolated attempts to control inflation often result in depressed output, increased unemployment, declining investment and negative effects on economic growth.

Manpower development and utilisation

An effective employment policy is one of the important factors in productivity improvement since the productivity of the national economy must be assessed from the point of view of the utilisation of all available manpower. Unemployment reduces national economic and social performance independently of the effectiveness of some industries or individual enterprises. Thus any government needs a strong manpower planning system and an executive mechanism to pursue progressive structural changes. It has two main tasks:

● To develop and use human resources as fully as possible.
● To fit the labour force structure (occupational, skill, sex, age, etc.) to the requirements of modern industrial and sectoral change, using government institutions for planning, education, training, legislation and taxation.

Education and training policy

No new technique or modern productivity improvement scheme can be introduced and used effectively without well-trained and educated personnel at all levels of the national economy. Therefore a strong and long-term government education and training policy should be among the first priorities. This policy should promote balance and co-ordination between primary, secondary and higher education, between general and professional education, between specialist training in social and scientific subjects, and so on. Special attention should be given to training managers and supervisors both for industry and for government bodies. These people will be responsible for productivity improvement at all economic levels.

A number of studies have revealed a significant positive correlation between education and productivity. Even a basic comparison of economic performance between different countries demonstrates that the best results, both as regards level of productivity and rate of economic growth, are found in those countries where manpower is better educated.

Indeed, technology is a product of education, culture, creativity, motivation and of management systems. In the long term it is no exaggeration to define productivity as a type of mentality, based on education and culture, which develops the capacity to organise. Thus, education can be seen as a major means of accelerating the development of the workforce and its quality. Figure 8.1 shows the multi-layer links between productivity and education. It can be clearly seen that people are the main productivity resource in the long term and are therefore the most important factor. This factor has unlimited potential for development.

In its broad sense, education covers all types of learning processes in human beings, both formal and informal:

— family education and upbringing;

— formal education in different establishments;

— practical experience;

— experiencing various social and cultural environmental influences.

Unfortunately, almost everywhere — in some countries less than others — this four-dimensional educational process is not co-ordinated or purposefully directed at improving the overall educational level of the population as regards developing a productivity culture. The effectiveness of the educational process can greatly affect the effectiveness of social and economic development efforts and productivity growth in different countries.

Analysis of four major characteristics of the workforce — attitudes, knowledge, skills and organisational opportunities — reveals that education in the broad sense plays a significant role in their development. To ensure that the main components of the educational system are balanced and co-ordinated it is important to consider certain points:

● Does the system include all the necessary components to develop these characteristics?

● If so, are these components and their development well balanced in the educational system?

● Is there a sound planning and co-ordinating mechanism with enough feedback at the national level to provide and maintain the quality of education necessary for the development of the country's economy and, specifically, productivity objectives?

● Are there enough mutually supporting links between formal and informal educational environments?

● Are the educational methods and processes used in compliance with specific cultural and organisational needs?

To answer all the above questions positively, selective strategies should be planned and implemented for developing education as a tool for improving productivity awareness. We have already discussed the type of knowledge, skills,

Figure 8.1. Links between productivity and education

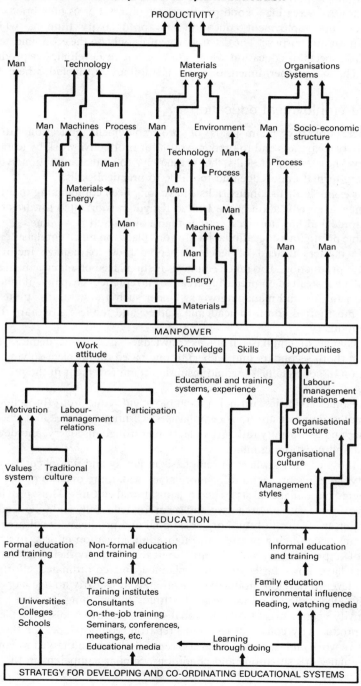

attitudes and opportunities which can be considered as educational objectives directed towards creating a good productivity culture. Let us now briefly discuss two areas, pre-employment education and productivity training, which are important for our purpose. The discussion centres only on the economic, technical and social aspects of education which are relevant to developing a productivity culture. The many other dimensions of education are not included here.

Pre-employment education

There are two main goals of pre-employment education: to create productivity awareness and to prepare youth for productive work by teaching the necessary knowledge and skills. Unfortunately, too much attention is paid to developing formal knowledge and too little to practical skills.

For example British industrialists have long been complaining that business and management education in the United Kingdom is oriented towards teaching how to trade and how to invest, rather than how to add new value.

Some prestigious educational institutions place too much emphasis on purely academic matters instead of teaching people how to manage factories and shop-floor production. Too much emphasis is still placed on management sciences and research instead of on preparing creative entrepreneurs capable of innovating, and of organising and managing work. Under such a system, it is quite normal that the most gifted go on to academic studies, and the less gifted are forced to work in industry.

A change of emphasis from a knowledge-based or academic system of education (both secondary and higher) to one based on problem-solving and the completion of concrete tasks would result in an improvement in the productivity culture.

In some countries formal pre-employment education (in schools and vocational training institutions) emphasises learning by rote, and encourages obedience and conformity rather than learning through discovery, and developing a critical and questioning mind.

In those countries where the emphasis in family and school education is on creativity, young people tend to be more analytical, more open to modern values and progressive managerial styles and organisational cultures. Thus, providing the future workforce with an organised and co-ordinated family and school education is an important factor in future organisational and productivity culture changes. This means encouraging parents, through adult education efforts, to adopt the values of a productivity culture, and to teach them to their children. Some countries have now started to make planned and co-ordinated efforts at the national level to develop productivity awareness at as early an age as possible.

The Icelandic Technological Institute, functioning as the national productivity centre, organised a national campaign in schools with the aim of raising productivity consciousness and preparing young people for their future productive work and careers. Managers went to schools and talked to youngsters about actual work situations and conditions. Similar campaigns in the form of dialogue sessions between industry and higher educational institutions have been held in many countries.

At the national level proper cultural concepts and work attitudes should be built into different training course curricula in schools, colleges and universities. These ideas can be disseminated by the media, thus strengthening the informal education process in their contribution to developing a productivity culture and positive work attitudes.

Management education and training

The most important trends which are forcing managers to adjust their style to rapid change are as follows:

— the transition from an industrial society to an information society;

— the recognition that technology will not be effective unless it takes into account the human factor;

— global economic expansion;

— a change in emphasis from a short-term to a long-term perspective;

— rapid decentralisation of organisations and hierarchies;

— increased reliance on self-help instead of institutional assistance;

— the need and desire of individuals to have a greater role in decision-making within institutions and organisations;

— an increasing number of options from which people can choose.

Each trend calls for a change in managerial style, skills, values and culture to make an organisation effective. For example, there is a growing demand for entrepreneurial strategic planning. Today's executives must be more analytical. They need to look carefully at their workforce, identify the groups and individuals with the greatest potential for productivity improvement and design activities specific to the needs and capabilities of these people. Among the important qualities of the future manager are the ability to manage change, to manage conflict and to apply the systems approach in management.

To develop these managerial skills systematically and sufficiently far in advance significant changes are needed in all the components of the education system. The most important qualities and skills should be taught early, within the framework of family and school education, colleges and universities.

Management education and training continues to focus on such skills as planning, problem-solving, decision-making and other management techniques. But many programmes lack attitudinal and behavioural aspects and do little to build strong productivity values into the consciousness of managers and workers, assuming wrongly that they already possess these attributes. This is one of the important reasons why many managers, especially in large organisations, are more concerned with processes, rules and procedures than with final results. This contrasts with the situation in small organisations, which are usually less hierarchical.

It is necessary to pay more attention to attitude-building and strengthening values and to concentrate on the behavioural aspects of management. The main differences between the smaller, more informal type of organisation and the larger, more hierarchical organisation should be taken into consideration in training and development.

Successful productivity improvement programmes require clear, consistent and frequent communication about organisation policies, productivity plans, and achievements. Today's workers want to know clearly what they are contributing and why, and how they are doing it.

Productivity education efforts should include a constant emphasis on the subject in multi-level meetings and seminars, booklets and newsletters and regular discussions on productivity. Systematic use of educational and training programmes can greatly enhance workers' understanding and awareness of productivity and the need for its improvement.

It is thus crucial for management to provide patient and persistent productivity education for workers, so as to improve their perception of the work environment and their own role, raise their productivity culture and improve their attitudes.

Governments might encourage a more open and regular dialogue between industry and the education system as well as between the components of the education system, at different levels. The use of the media must not be forgotten.

Education and training curricula should include productivity issues stressing a human, behavioural attitude as an important component.

A real, concerted and co-ordinated effort by all institutions dealing with education at all social levels and in all economic sectors is required to achieve this goal.

National mechanisms for promoting institutional productivity

Efforts to raise productivity nationally require effective organisation to bring together all the elements of any production or service system.

Since productivity depends on many factors, both inside and outside the enterprise or sector, it is very important to create the economic, social, political, legislative and organisational conditions that favour productivity improvement. The only institution which can attempt to maintain a balance between all the external and internal factors is the State and its legislative bodies. Therefore, one of the decisive points for productivity improvement on the national scale is mutual understanding between the main social beneficiaries of productivity. This is achieved by means of equitable productivity gains-sharing, strengthening social and job security, labour legislation, real worker participation in management and other progressive changes.

These factors influence many more things than just productivity improvement, but no serious discussion of productivity improvement on the national scale can take place unless they are adopted. However, because of the interaction between productivity and these factors, the development of a national productivity improvement programme and its realisation, even on a limited scale, can have the effect of speeding up their adoption.

To work out a national productivity programme and put it into effect, many countries have established special organisations, both national and regional, or specialising in one sector of the economy. These organisations usually include two main parts (or institutions) which deal with determining the productivity problems and improvement policy required and implementing the productivity improvement policy.

They train, consult and do research. They can also assist other organisations or sectors in planning and carrying out their programmes. Such institutions or centres are (or should be) supported by management, labour, government and other interested social groups. There are about 150 national and regional productivity and management development centres, institutions and associations throughout the world which try, with different degrees of success, to solve the problems of improving productivity. The main issues dealt with by such centres are:

— accelerating the process of working out national objectives that can be adopted by governments, employers and workers;
— developing new productivity measurement systems and tools;
— carrying out applied research;
— developing information and data collection;
— performing demonstration projects;
— offering expertise for interested organisations;
— providing intercompany, intersector and intercountry productivity comparison services;
— offering educational and training activities, both technical and designed to raise awareness.

Specifically, the major long-term activities of many of the most successful national productivity centres are:

— creating a favourable climate within the country so as to include the whole population in establishing national goals and priorities;
— working out a purposeful government (or sectoral) policy for productivity improvement on the national (sectoral) scale, and co-ordinating sectoral policies for optimal use of national resources;
— establishing (or improving the effectiveness of) the government statistical bodies which deal with data collection and analysis at the sectoral and macro-economic levels;
— strengthening legislation on the relation between enterprises (e.g. on takeovers) and between enterprises and government institutions;
— increasing the role of such financial incentives as taxes, credit and incomes policy.

The development of an institutional mechanism which can accept challenge, provide necessary input and forge closer links between interested parties is very important. It can help to integrate national efforts and provide support to institutions engaged in promoting productivity in all economic sectors and at all levels down to the enterprise and the individual.

The role of such national productivity centres in productivity promotion can be illustrated by a few cases from different developed and developing countries with records of high and low productivity.

Case one: Canadian productivity institutions

In Canada productivity improvement activities are carried out by several government departments and agencies at both federal and provincial levels, as well as by privately sponsored organisations, especially industrial associations. The primary responsibility for promoting productivity in Canadian industries lies with the Department of Regional Industrial Expansion (DRIE). It focuses on five priorities: productivity and innovation; market development — export and domestic markets; industrial renovation — adjusting to changing competitive conditions; small enterprises; regional industrial benefits.

The DRIE's major programme is its Industrial and Regional Development Programme (IRDP), which applies to all phases of the corporate and product life cycle. This programme covers:
- industrial infrastructure — studies and specialised public services;
- innovation — assistance for studies, development of new products or processes and encouragement for the introduction of new technologies;
- plant establishment;
- modernisation and expansion;
- marketing;
- industrial renovation.

Financial assistance provided to business includes grants, contributions, repayable contributions, participation loans and loan guarantees. The cost-sharing ratio of supported projects varies from 25 to 75 per cent depending on the type of project and the location of the firm.

Another agency — the Productivity Improvement Service — acts as a centre for information on productivity in general and productivity measurement techniques in particular. Its two major inter-related functions are:
- the gathering and dissemination of information on measuring, analysing and improving productivity;
- the operation of an Interfirm Comparison Programme (ICP) in all industries and in all regions of Canada.

In 1983 the DRIE established an Office of Industrial Innovation to focus on strategic planning of policies and programmes in support of technological development, innovation and the diffusion of innovations.

This provides a meeting place for the private sector to discuss the environment for innovation and to advise on the strategic direction of the DRIE. It is also responsible for analysing and advising on the innovation climate of IRDP and on mechanisms for technology transfer. It provides advice on the design and content of existing programmes, and proposes new programmes and policy initiatives.

An important part of the Canadian productivity mechanism is the Economic Council of Canada (ECC), established in 1963 as a successor to the National Productivity Council. The ECC has done extensive research on the country's productive potential and the factors behind productivity growth in agriculture and manufacturing, commercial policy and regional development. At the end of the 1970s new emphasis was placed on the decision-making process, and more attention was given to the enterprise as the principal decision-making unit. Areas of emphasis were innovation and enterprise behaviour, the service sector and economic growth. Recently attention has concentrated on human resource development, labour-management relations, tax structure and tax incentives to capital investment.

The most recently established (1984) element of the national productivity network is the Canadian Labour Market and Productivity Centre (CLMPC).[2] It is composed of representatives of workers, employers, government — federal and provincial — and universities. Only worker and employer representatives are voting members and the executive committee is composed of six worker and six employer representatives. Funds to the amount of C$27 million have been committed by the Government.

The centre's objective is to bring together the efforts of workers, employers and governments in order to help find the best solutions to the twin challenges of productivity and employment growth, and the closely related goal of more effective development and use of Canada's human resources through a well-functioning labour market. The centre was born from the understanding that higher levels of employment, productivity and international competitiveness could be achieved by consensus and broad participation in the national decision-making processes.

Its bipartite structure endows the centre with access to industrial sectors ranging from the shop-floor to the boardroom.

While the centre is formally independent of government, it does not act in isolation. Four deputy ministers from the federal Government's most powerful economic ministries sit on the centre's board of directors, together with one deputy minister from each of Canada's 12 provinces and territories. Government representatives can make suggestions but have no vote, even though the federal Government provides all funding.

This link with both the federal and provincial levels of government is essential because many issues that concern the centre fall within both jurisdictions. For example, provincial governments are constitutionally responsible for the nation's education, while the federal Government funds many worker retraining programmes. The centre helps to bring these disparate elements together. The centre's main objectives are to:

— gain general recognition of the fact that enhanced productivity is best achieved through equal partnership and shared responsibility between workers and employers;

-    act as an advisory body in matters relating to the operation and administration of the labour market in Canada;

-    develop and advocate policies leading to more and better jobs and an improved understanding of the concept of work;

-    encourage productive practices that can make Canadian industries fully competitive in domestic and world markets;

-    plan for and assist in the implementation of technological change and innovation so as to minimise its adverse effects;

-    promote the sharing of the benefits of technological change.

The centre consists of two branches, the productivity branch and the labour market branch.

Another important federal institution that promotes productivity in Canada is the Federal Business Development Bank, which lends money and organises programmes to improve the management of enterprises. It also lends money to universities and industrial associations engaged in productivity studies and the popularisation of the productivity culture, promoting productivity growth through technical programmes, seminars, workshops, publications, plant tours and industry missions.

Case two: Indian National Productivity Council [3]

In the early 1950s the Government of India invited a series of productivity missions from the International Labour Office (ILO) to demonstrate in enterprises the improvements which can be accomplished through the application of productivity techniques. These missions created a climate in favour of productivity.

The need to launch a nation-wide productivity drive was recognised in 1957 after an Indian productivity delegation visited Japan and saw the phenomenal progress made by Japanese industry through using productivity techniques and procedures. The team recommended that India initiate a similar programme; this paved the way for the establishment of a National Productivity Council (NPC) as an autonomous organisation.

In establishing the NPC, the Government of India accepted the following five principles of productivity identified by the national seminar which was held to discuss the programme. These principles formed the basis of the national productivity drive:

-    The objectives of a productivity drive are to increase production and improve quality by improved techniques and efficient and proper use of the available resources; to raise the standard of living of the people, and improve working conditions and social welfare. The movement rejects increased workloads and speed-up.

-    Increasing productivity will help increase employment by stimulating the development of industry.

- The benefits of productivity increases should be equitably distributed between capital, labour and consumers; they should lead to the renewal and expansion of plant, machinery and equipment.
- The productivity drive may eventually be launched in all the spheres of the nation's economy. It is important to achieve integrated improvement in productivity in all activities of the national economy.
- Increased productivity cannot be achieved without the full co-operation of labour and management. It is necessary to create a climate for increased productivity through joint consultation, the participation of workers in management and the promotion of mutual understanding between labour and management.

Structure of the NPC

As the highest national organisation, the NPC is responsible for India's drive for higher productivity. The council and its governing body are tripartite; the council consists of 75 members including representatives of government, industry and labour, professional bodies and other interests. The Minister for Industry is president of the council. The governing body consists of 25 members who are elected from among the council members. It lays down policies and guides the NPC secretariat in implementing its programmes. The chairman of the governing body and the director-general are nominated by the Government of India.

The council's policies and programmes are implemented through a network with headquarters in New Delhi and 16 regional offices established in most of the states. In addition, there are 49 local productivity councils to promote local initiative and talent in making the productivity drive a mass movement. The headquarters and the regional offices are manned by about 250 consultants in disciplines such as management services, industrial engineering, energy management, plant maintenance, pollution control, production engineering, behavioural science, marketing management, financial management and agricultural productivity.

Starting at the unit and the shop-floor level, the NPC moved into sectoral areas, adopting a multidisciplinary approach for a broad-based productivity drive at macro, sub-macro, and micro levels. In 1962-63 it pioneered its consultancy services to demonstrate the worth and validity of productivity techniques. Around the same time, the NPC was asked to set up a fuel efficiency service which, since then, has become a popular national service. Faced with diverse challenges, the NPC enhanced its capacity by developing trainers and consultants to provide services in management areas, plant engineering and production engineering. To meet the high standards required of its consultants, it started a two-year post-graduate training course in industrial engineering, which is the first course of its kind recognised in the country. Similar institutional training was extended to areas of fuel efficiency, plant engineering, behavioural science and financial management.

The productivity drive during the 1960s and 1970s sought to stimulate, promote and provide services through training, consultancy, research, publications and audio-visual materials. As an extension of the services, productivity activities were expanded to cover non-production areas such as health services and government.

In the 1980s the management of technology has become the focus of attention. Experience shows that technology unleashes tremendous forces; it creates employment opportunities in the value added and tertiary sectors and also in rural sectors of the economy.

In the process of productivity improvement it is necessary to ensure the participation of all concerned, and to create a climate conducive to the development and promotion of positive attitudes towards productivity. The intensive drive for higher productivity in India had to be backed up by infrastructure and institutional support, and the extension of productivity services at the macro, sectoral, enterprise and shop-floor levels.

At the macro level the most important activities in the productivity drive are the:

— impetus to productivity given by a parliamentary committee;

— integration of productivity in national planning by the planning commission;

— establishment of state-level productivity boards;

— mass productivity campaigns through television, radio, films, press, posters, publications, competitions, conferences and exhibitions.

Among the important sectoral activities are the establishment of industry productivity boards; productivity improvement studies in key sectors (power, coal, steel, paper and cement); recognition of achievement through productivity awards; productivity activities for small-scale and village industries through the promotion of export-oriented craft technology, quality improvement, marketing and financial assistance.

At the enterprise level the major activities are the creation of productivity consciousness; the application of productivity techniques; the development of productivity personnel and the establishment of productivity cells; productivity agreements between labour and management are also encouraged.

At the shop-floor level the focus is on cost-effectiveness and quality upgrading; training of supervisors and workers; workers' participation in management; productivity incentive schemes (payment); productivity awards to individuals.

The main targets of the productivity movement at the enterprise and shop-floor levels are energy and materials conservation; effective maintenance; quality improvement; and harmonious labour-management relations.

Case three: Japan Productivity Centre [4]

The Japan Productivity Centre (JPC) was established in 1955. Its approach to productivity is based on three guiding principles:

— improved productivity will lead to increased employment opportunity and provide greater job security;

— the methods of productivity improvement adopted should be discussed and agreed between labour and management;
— the gains resulting from improved productivity should be fairly distributed between consumers, labour and management.

A quarter of a century has passed since the productivity movement began nation-wide. During this period the Japanese economy has developed steadily with fewer problems than most other countries. Japan's entry into a period of slow economic growth in recent years has forced the JPC to respond to new situations by setting up new and more relevant goals. In general, they aim to establish the following: a new order of effective competition; a change in the goals of enterprises; a system of worker participation leading to greater co-operation between labour and management; more efficient use of resources; active promotion of technological development; fair distribution of wealth and increased social welfare; the JPC also participates in an international attempt to establish a new world economic order.

The structure of the JPC is as follows:

● The policy-making body, i.e. the board of directors, is composed of representatives of business, labour and academic institutions. The Government is not a party to this body. The Japanese productivity movement is, therefore, voluntary and oriented to the private sector. The Government supports the movement as a part of its overall industrial policies and programmes.

● The Japan Productivity Centre has established many special committees and study groups to deal with emerging issues. The committees and groups submit their findings and recommendations to government, employers and workers to help them set their goals, policies and programmes. Issues dealt with in the past have included productivity, prices, wages, tax benefits and public welfare.

The JPC is endeavouring to achieve more productivity improvement through the following approaches:

● It vigorously continues productivity education programmes directed towards both labour and management. The programmes emphasise teaching the three basic principles of the movement rather than studying input/output ratios. The programme exposes senior managers as well as shop-floor workers to such issues as labour-management relations and consultation systems, profit sharing and others.

● The important characteristic of Japanese labour unions is that they are organised within the corporate framework. The effort to install in-house labour-management consultation enables the JPC to say that 100 per cent of large corporations and 40-50 per cent of small businesses now use the system.

● Other important activities that the JPC has developed are:
    — sending study groups to the United States and Europe. Initially the groups consisted primarily of senior managers, but gradually middle

managers and professionals have been included. This project has enabled Japan's managers to become aware of the need to apply scientific management techniques. The JPC has published reports covering their findings and has sponsored meetings and seminars in order to assure the wide dissemination of information throughout Japan;

— management development programmes and consultation services.

The pursuit of productivity improvement is a basic factor in Japan's economic growth.

Case four: The Productivity Centre of the Federal Republic of Germany [5]

The Rationalisierungs Kuratorium der deutschen Wirtschaft (RKW) was originally established by large firms for the benefit of small firms. The purpose of the RKW is to serve the recovery and strengthening of the economy by furthering efforts towards rationalisation, and to promote technical, economic and social development. More specifically, its task is to apply relevant research results in management practice and to support all governmental and administrative bodies in the field of raising productivity.

The distinctive feature of the RKW is the active use of some 1,700 freelance consultants in RKW projects, in about 4,000 consultancy commissions a year. The main activities are training and individual consultancy services, publications and dissemination of information on productivity issues. The RKW has more than 7,000 members from industry, trade unions and government and co-operates with productivity centres and management institutions in more than 100 countries.

The individual consultancy services provided through the RKW regional groups offer an effective means of dealing rapidly with campaign problems. The RKW has local branches which organise subsidised consultancy services for small and medium-sized enterprises. The importance of this service is reflected in the fact that in 1984 the RKW assisted companies employing a total of over 100,000 people.

The areas covered by consultancy services in 1984 were as follows: 22.6 per cent were concerned with general company management; 28.9 per cent with finance and accounting; 17.1 per cent with marketing; 11.5 per cent with technology and production; 11 per cent with office and administration; 4.7 per cent with materials management; and 4.2 per cent with personnel and labour issues.

While consultancy is no panacea, an outside consultant, particularly for small and medium-sized enterprises, can often identify idle productive resources more quickly than managers, who are frequently blind to local problems.

The general consultancy activities of the RKW normally include critical analysis of an entire enterprise in technical, commercial and organisational areas, identifying weak spots and openings for rationalisation, developing appropriate suggestions for improvement, and determining priorities in implementing proposals which are financially possible. The specialised consultancy activities concentrate on one crucial functional area of the enterprise such as investment, energy, export or branching out in a new area of business.

* * *

To summarise, the role of a national productivity centre in productivity promotion could be described as that of a catalyst. Its functions are:

● To be an important part of the national mechanism for productivity promotion. This institutional mechanism consists of industrial, economic, and labour ministries and departments, governmental and independent research institutions, and associations dealing with the promotion of economic efficiency, professional associations and the educational and training system.

● To suggest a policy for productivity promotion at all economic levels.

● To help sectors and enterprises in the practical implementation of new forms and methods of production, organisation and management.

● To implement specific productivity improvement programmes and campaigns.

● To train representatives of government, labour and management in productivity promotion and relevant knowledge and skills.

● To serve as a methodology centre for the country, assisting regional, sectoral and local productivity institutions and centres in their respective activities, training their staff and implementing joint programmes.

● To undertake necessary research in productivity improvement and measurement, new forms of work organisation and management methods and techniques.

● To popularise the productivity culture, working closely with the mass media and educational systems.

Productivity campaigns

General awareness of the significance of productivity improvement in social and economic development plays an important role in creating a productivity culture in all strata of society. There should be some national institution, a centre or a ministry, responsible for the important task of organising nation-wide productivity education. Such education needs to be given continuously and systematically, but periodic intensive campaigns are also useful.

In some countries this type of education is undertaken by national productivity centres; in others by government departments or ministries. Sometimes it is given by employers' or workers' associations.

In Iceland the National Technological Institute has taken over this task. As part of its productivity campaigns it has organised general productivity programmes in all schools. Pupils are invited to participate in sessions and discussions led by representatives from industry.

Every programme is accompanied by discussions and information on such subjects as: why people work; how to make plans and carry out policy; measuring and improving work methods; improving productivity and cost control; conflict and co-operation; the art of leadership; training workers; avoiding grievances.

Such programmes are very useful for young people because they indicate their future adult responsibilities and expected attitudes. They give a better understanding of economics and of personal responsibility for developing new values relevant to a high productivity culture.

In 1985 the Japan Productivity Centre, in celebration of the 30th anniversary of the productivity movement in Japan, organised a Young People's Productivity Symposium in Tokyo. More than 100 representatives, selected by industrial organisations as well as labour unions, participated in the three-day symposium aiming at new productivity and the humanisation of labour.

There are many examples of effective but uncoordinated individual actions intended to improve productivity consciousness at the national or sectoral level. The best results are normally achieved through running a nation-wide co-ordinated and purpose-oriented productivity campaign.

There appears to have been a change of direction in European countries from the late 1970s. "Productivity" has appeared on the national agenda again for many reasons. There was a significant national productivity campaign lasting one full year in Norway in 1982 (for which preparations went back to 1978-79); a national consortium effort ("Pro Swede") in Sweden, renewed industry-level campaigning in Finland and discussions about possible campaigns in Denmark.

It is interesting that many campaigns have been launched in crisis or semi-crisis situations. Thus the campaign in Ireland was initiated at the time of that country's entry into the British Free Trade Area which, it was thought, would mean the influx of cheap British industrial goods after three decades of highly protected industrial development. In the United States a campaign was launched when the decline in the national productivity growth rate was seen to be more structural than cyclical and it was felt that the whole nation should be made to know "the facts". The situation was the same in Norway, where the notion of the campaign arose from a prices and incomes freeze.

In the United Kingdom the campaign "happened" to coincide with a considerable increase in the National Productivity Council's grant in aid following the advent of a new government. In Cyprus the idea has been brought to the fore as the country has changed from an economic situation of unemployment to one of over-heating rates of inflation.

In other cases economic crisis has been less important and some campaigns have been politically inspired by governments giving considerable emphasis to the need for productivity improvement as part of an economic revival programme.

However, in all instances emphasis has been placed on the need for ideas to emerge from the major socio-economic groups. These include not only employers and employers' organisations, but also professional groups such as managers, engineers, supervisors and educators. Naturally the productivity centre, as the organising element in such a campaign, provides "seed" ideas. It services the discussions of the different groups and hence carries concepts from one group to another. In the United States most of the local promotional work on productivity improvement and quality of working life is performed by the American Institute of Industrial Engineers (AIIE), with local branches in all states. It runs local meetings concentrating on concrete issues such as benefits and how improvements can be made.

Governments usually fund the campaigns, though they rarely organise or administer them. However, the 1982 Norwegian programme specifically included the Government as an equal partner which ran its own public sector campaign. A few campaigns in south Asian countries have also been organised in this way.

The larger target groups in a productivity campaign vary considerably. They range from the general public, through schools, to individuals involved on the shop-floor. However, experience indicates that a broad appeal provides only a veneer of understanding which can soon be eroded and that action needs to be much deeper than the type of advertising or propaganda used in general media campaigns.

The type of media selected depends essentially on the target group. The vehicles used have ranged from country and folk music and special productivity songs, postage stamps (India, Japan, United States), to films, textbooks, classroom games, posters, booklets, stickers and badges (Philippines, Singapore). Some countries have also used specific manuals on implementing techniques and analysed performance, compared firms and awarded prizes.

Communication strategies in productivity improvement vary from region to region. In places such as Hong Kong, Japan, the Philippines, Singapore and other urban areas of Asia, productivity strategies emphasise technical and managerial skills and organisation development through productivity improvement circles. Co-ordination and extension activities are carried out through improved use of communication facilities. Information retrieval and delivery systems tailored to regional priorities are being set up. Other national productivity centres are focusing on human resource development by training entrepreneurs in small and medium-sized enterprises.

During its early years, the Japan Productivity Centre used radio, television, newspapers and audio-visual aids in promoting productivity consciousness. Its major public relations activity was the publication of *Productivity News*, a weekly newspaper which started in 1955. The news coverage consisted of items on the productivity movement, industrial relations, computerisation and in-service training.

In Africa similar attempts seem to have confirmed the advantages of applying new communication technology. In the Sudan, for instance, both radio and television offer functional adult education programmes aimed at increasing the income of the rural population through better productivity. For example, group discussions with specialists on the spot are organised in conjunction with regular television programmes for cotton farmers.

Other examples are the rural radio forum scheme, which originated in Canada, and which was tried in India in 1956 with village workers who had migrated to Bombay. It was later extended to the whole of India as an instrument of local and national development. The programme "Desarrollo cooperación por radio", aimed at farmers and fishermen in rural villages, was launched by the Ministry of Community Administration and Development in the Philippines and broadcast over 2,000 islands in the early 1970s.

The content of a campaign has to be visible and newsworthy. The Norwegian campaign consisted of publication of relevant national data with international comparisons, which could easily be used by different target groups. The campaign was launched by a national event which was repeated in some of the regions. As the campaign progressed it was necessary to be able to provide more direct services (lecturers and consultants) and to build up more data on what was taking place. This essentially took the form of demonstrations where the NPI (the Norwegian Productivity Institute) helped provide a consultant, and interested enterprises provided an accompanying committee to appraise developments in a demonstration enterprise. A more detailed description of the Norwegian campaign is given in the next section.

In Turkey a film was produced as well as a special issue of the National Productivity Centre's monthly journal, both of which were used for a seminar and television round-table. In New Zealand and the United States standard slide cassette material was prepared and made available at little or no cost. Linked with the national campaign, the Norwegian Employers' Confederation (NAF) produced a manual and supporting documents for its members.

Posters and stickers are commonly used, and in Singapore taxis were also encouraged to carry a productivity flag on their roofs during the productivity month of November 1982.

Five conclusions can be drawn from these cases:

- The customers/clients are the most important participants in the change process. Their needs are therefore the most important consideration in planning any communication strategy.
- A communication strategy must be directed at several levels — at opinion leaders or policy planners, group members, and the people. Communication should focus on mechanisms to encourage these various groups to interact.
- Social change occurs faster when communication is used both in improving technical know-how and in awakening interest.
- Mutual trust is often the result of dialogue and frequent exchange of information.
- Productivity improvement messages should focus on specific goals and should be constantly reinforced by all available channels.

Although there is a wide acceptance of its importance, most countries are not yet ready to invest as much in communications infrastructure as they would in other physical infrastructures.

Case study: The Norwegian productivity campaign [6]

Background

The immediate and direct origin of the campaign in Norway was concern about restoring the manufacturing industry's ability to compete in the international market. At the same time, it was understood that the impact of productivity reaches far beyond industry's labour unit cost. General economic development, taking costs and prices into consideration, is obviously important, but the importance of the creation of values must not be overlooked. It was therefore immediately realised that the productivity campaign should include all sectors of the economy, every type of production factor, and all levels of personnel.

Of crucial importance was the fact that from the very start the campaign had the full support and backing of the main institutions of Norwegian working life. The Government decided upon the campaign in the autumn of 1980; it was prepared during 1981 and officially launched in January 1982. The aims of the campaign were:

- To create a broad understanding of the impact of and the necessity for increased productivity in society.
- To encourage initiatives to increase productivity.
- To supply general information regarding productivity development and problems in Norway.

A central concept in the campaign was the notion of "total productivity". Productivity was seen as an interplay between various factors of production and a combination of technological, economic and organisational talents and insights. Productivity improvement may be achieved both by the improved effectiveness of each of the production factors, and by improved co-ordination between various elements of production.

It was also realised that most productivity improvements can be seen as series of small steps of "every day rationalisations"; they seldom take the form of giant technological breakthroughs or revolutions. It was also evident that productivity growth is usually the result of contributions from many people.

Organisation

In the autumn of 1980 an advisory committee was set up with representatives from: the Norwegian Employers' Confederation; the Federation of Norwegian Industries; the Norwegian Federation of Trade Unions; and the Norwegian Productivity Institute.

The Ministry of Industry was represented by the State Secretary, who also served as the chairman and had overall responsibility for the campaign. Other government ministries sent observers. In early 1981 representatives of the public sector were included on the advisory committee. The Norwegian Productivity Institute was to function as the executive secretariat.

The main task of the secretariat was to co-ordinate campaign planning and preparation and also to co-ordinate the practical implementation of all the activities throughout the campaign.

The productivity campaign was carried out in two steps. The first step was to shape the attitude of the general public and the second was concerned with information. This effort was oriented towards firms in the private sector, institutions and public administration units. Each step lasted for six months.

Productivity management

The formal organisation of the campaign committees was as follows:

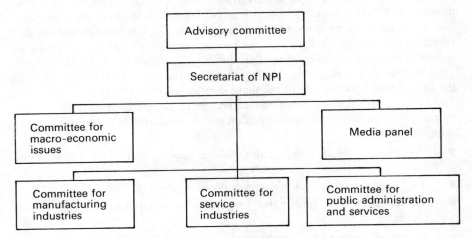

The media panel, consisting of public relations officers from the different organisations involved, was especially important during the first step of the campaign. Series of advertisements on five or six different themes were inserted in the professional and popular press.

Posters were printed, stickers, brochures, T-shirts and so on, were distributed. The role of the press in disseminating information on productivity matters was taken seriously from the very beginning of the campaign. Several seminars were arranged for journalists. Gallup International — Nordic Research was commissioned by the media panel to carry out opinion polls on productivity.

The committee for macro-economics was concerned with the:

— clarification of productivity concepts and measurement in different levels of society;

— analysis of productivity development in Norway, in the various sectors and industries; these analyses were to be compared with similar analyses in other countries.

The members of the committee were representatives of the organisations involved and the Government.

Activities

The committees for the different sectors (manufacturing industries, service industries and public administration and services) were to co-ordinate efforts in their respective sectors during the campaign.

They were to:

— clarify the concept of productivity as related to their sector;

— prepare practical material to be used for information and training;

— act as advisers in getting productivity work started locally;

—   take the initiative in other useful matters.

In order to achieve the desired decentralisation, local campaign advisory committees were set up throughout the country. For practical reasons the geographical area of the committees corresponded to the counties. There were two advisory committees in each county; one for the private sector and one for the public sector. These committees were usually closely connected with the local branch of the different organisations taking part in the campaign and/or the local chamber of commerce. Each of the committees had a secretariat with consultants paid out of local funds.

The local advisory committee consisted of the county governor; the chairman of the county council; the local federation of trade unions; the local employers' confederation; and the local federation of Norwegian industries.

In the first stage the local advisory committees took an active part in arranging seminars and other types of meeting to promote productivity. In the second part of the campaign the local advisory committees selected companies and public service units which were subsequently approved by the NPI secretariat to serve as case studies. The case studies were used as models of projects in different kinds of enterprise and local authority administration.

One of the purposes of the campaign was to disseminate information on practical productivity activities. Therefore, the experiences were described and discussed in local seminars and meetings.

Results

The results demonstrated a change in attitude during the campaign period. After the campaign it seemed easier to discuss problems related to productivity and to work out solutions without conflict arising between management and workers. Measured by the activity the campaign created and the results that were achieved, it was a successful undertaking.

In those cases where the campaign initiated continuous processes for systematic productivity improvements, the benefits will be felt for many years to come.

Nevertheless, there is a danger that an isolated effort like this campaign will create only temporary interest and activity, and that people will gradually return to their old and less productive habits.

But some of the improvements achieved by the campaign will indeed be permanent. A person who has *really* learned to do things in a smarter way does not simply forget that and return to the old way.

Case study: India Productivity Year – 1982 [3]

The year 1982 was declared by the Indian Prime Minister as the Year of Productivity. Co-ordinated efforts were directed at maximising the use of plant capacity in all sectors of the economy, and at achieving greater efficiency in the implementation of projects. This national campaign had to be organised at a high government level. The NPC participated in an advisory capacity.

Productivity management

After launching Productivity Year, the National Development Council, the Planning Commission and the Estimates Committee of Parliament examined the areas where the productivity drive should concentrate. Six major areas of national endeavour were identified: energy conservation; materials management; maintenance management; labour-management relations; pollution control; and development of small and very small enterprises, especially in rural areas.

Productivity efforts were intensified through the following activities:

The *industry- and enterprise-level programmes* covered studies for productivity improvements in vital industries with emphasis on energy conservation, plant maintenance and pollution control. They also promoted the training and motivation of supervisors and workers and organised productivity award schemes for vital industries.

Programmes for developing harmonious labour-management relations included surveys and regional seminars on workers' participation in management, and training of representatives of management, trade unions and workers to enable them to make their participatory role effective.

Productivity efforts at state level aimed at establishing closer liaison with state governments in their efforts to prepare and monitor production plans for capacity utilisation in industry, and for productivity improvements in the service sector, small-scale and village industries. The national Government also assisted state governments in setting up productivity boards and in organising state-level conferences on productivity.

Promotion efforts included essay and short story competitions, close liaison with mass communication media and publication of productivity literature, booklets, posters, etc., for wide circulation in English, Hindi and regional languages.

To support the national endeavour seven industry-wide productivity boards were set up. They were responsible for: equipment for the generation, transmission and distribution of power; industrial machinery; cement; machine tools; automobiles and ancillaries; paper, pulp and allied industries; leather and leather goods.

Productivity awards

To recognise good performance in industry, productivity awards were given for eight major industries.

The criteria for giving awards were capacity utilisation or value added; energy conservation; materials utilisation; maintenance of plant and equipment; manpower utilisation.

Workers and trade union activities

Being a tripartite organisation, the NPC must ensure the involvement of workers and trade unions in productivity. Seminars, conferences, workshops and training programmes are a continuous activity at the national and regional as well as enterprise levels. The aim of these activities during Productivity Year was to acquaint workers and trade unions with the concept, approach and techniques of productivity. This was in order to create a favourable climate for promoting productivity through better work ethics and discipline, to maintain sound industrial relations and to develop participatory skills.

Training activities were both general and technical. The general programmes aimed at orienting workers to the industrial environment: they dealt with such topics as the worker and productivity; productivity and trade unions; union-management relations; participatory management; quality circles; and office productivity.

The technical programmes were aimed at equipping workers with such job skills as efficient operation of boilers; energy conservation; maintenance; methods improvement; cost reduction; balance sheet reading; organisation and method.

Other programmes aimed at both macro- and long-range results. They included one-day productivity schools; publication of literature in regional languages; surveys of existing practice in workers' participation in management; productivity agreements; and productivity-linked bonus schemes.

Learning from experience

Activities initiated during the 1982 Productivity Year have improved the conservation of resources, working conditions, manpower development and job creation, and increased the involvement of workers and trade unions in the productivity movement.

Productivity efforts now recognise the importance of the "quality of life" as well as the importance of technical efficiency. Further, it is understood that the application of technology should be more relevant to national needs and requires the closer involvement of all concerned. Thus, training and education programmes are based on the following five critical principles:

- The development of people is more important than any other economic function.

- Machines can never replace human beings.

- With the constant development of technology trained manpower is essential.

- An expanding educated labour force, changing social values, collective bargaining and changing attitudes demand greater skills from managers.

- Changing financial problems call for new concepts of management in such areas as market research and the social responsibility of business.

Case study: Productivity campaigns in Singapore [7]

The Singapore National Productivity Board (NPB), together with workers' organisations, employers' organisations and other national institutions including the mass media, actively uses different educational approaches to promote a positive attitude to productivity. They organise a wide range of productivity improvement programmes, quality circles, productivity campaigns (yearly, monthly, weekly), at the national, sectoral and enterprise levels. Some good results have been achieved.

A recent survey (July 1985), for example, shows how work attitudes have changed.[8] The "productivity will" of Singapore workers increased — 52 per cent of them were making efforts to improve their work compared with 35 per cent in 1984; 91 per cent said that their fellow workers had done their work well, and 78 per cent found them constantly improving the quality of their work. Workers also recognised the importance of teamwork: 92 per cent had given help to their colleagues; 77 per cent had offered suggestions for work improvement. Team building, together with monetary rewards, was rated as the most effective way of encouraging workers to contribute ideas to productivity improvement.

The results of the survey were used to prepare for Productivity Month '85 and for presentations, articles and news stories by the media.

On 8 November 1985 the Prime Minister of Singapore launched Productivity Month '85. Its main objective was to raise awareness and to promote a productivity culture among workers, management and government. It aimed to help people recognise and accept that productivity is the key to higher incomes and standard of living and improved competitiveness on the international markets. Productivity Month '85 had seven highlights:

- Quality days were held five times during the month in different companies and locations.
- A seminar on management productivity was held by the NPB.
- An industrial relations seminar was conducted by the Japanese Chamber of Commerce and Industry.
- A national occupational safety and health convention and safety award presentation was organised by the NPB.
- A study mission was sent to Japan from the NPB.
- The 3Ps (Productivity Promotion through Participation) annual presentation by representatives of different companies was organised by the NPB.
- An international exhibition of the quality circle convention was organised by the NPB.

Productivity Month '85 included the most important issues for productivity improvement, inviting the participation of government, management, employers' and workers' organisations. The events were covered extensively by the mass media.

Generally, the productivity movement and campaigns in Singapore are examples of well-managed activities. They have avoided one of the negative aspects of productivity campaigns — the impression that the problem has to be or can be solved by a campaign and that after the campaign business can continue "as usual". Only systematic, on-going actions in productivity improvement change behaviour definitively.

Labour-management relations and the productivity movement

The nature of the relationship between management and workers has a powerful impact on the degree and nature of worker commitment. This commitment manifests itself in measurable factors such as quality and productivity, or in conflict and strikes, as the case may be.

Involvement in labour-management relations can also be a good opportunity for learning how to influence productivity culture and organisational efforts. It is not our purpose here to give advice on how to improve labour-management relations. However, it should be stressed that good labour-management relations are imperative for improved organisational values, norms and productivity culture.

A recent survey by the Japan Productivity Centre shows that an overwhelming majority of both labour and management representatives feel that labour is taking labour-management consultations more seriously than before (labour 82 per cent, management 80 per cent). Both have a positive approach towards labour-management consultations, although there is a strong feeling on the labour side that the manner of distribution of productivity gains is somewhat unfair. Again, traditional culture plays an important role in many countries. This is clearly shown in a comparison between American and Japanese labour-management relationships, control systems and personnel practices.

United States	*Japan*
Formal management-worker relationship. Employment commitment is dependent on economic conditions and performance. Workers oriented to occupation rather than organisation.	Paternalistic relationship with workers and their families, more employment security with reciprocal worker loyalty to the company.
Individual, formal performance standards and controls. Adviser management/worker relationship predominates.	Reliance on high group motivation and standards with social work controls. Joint management/worker problem-solving used as way of reinforcing common goals.
Worker selected primarily on the basis of job-related formal education and/or practical experience and skills for specific jobs with little or no employment security. Promotion and rewards primarily based on productivity as determined by management.	Workers selected directly from school based on academic achievement, corporate examinations, and extensive screening programme, including familial relationships and school ties, for lifetime. Promotion and compensation are a function of education, tenure, sex and family responsibility until age 55. Broad group evaluation criteria.

Labour-management relations should be considered not only as a tool for solving problems of wages or working conditions but also as an important learning institution which can change work attitudes, values and productivity culture if managed effectively. Participation in this experience is a good educational opportunity for both workers and managers.

It is crucial to secure workers' participation in productivity improvement. Productivity is not new to most trade unions, and their active involvement in productivity is vital since workers both contribute to and should benefit from productivity changes. Long ago the functions of trade unions came to be appreciated for their influence as a positive factor in social development and productivity movements. Given the economic state of affairs in many countries trade unions often recognise that it is only by being involved in increased productivity in all sectors that they can achieve an improved standard of living and increased employment opportunities. It is equally important that the basic rights of labour be guaranteed not only by employers, but by governments as well. Trade unions are starting to recognise that the principal factor for economic development is productivity improvement accompanied by technological innovation. At the same time government and employers have to recognise that the modern productivity movement is based on job security, human rights and consideration for people. Thus the productivity movement should depend on the increased strength of trade unions, the mutual understanding of all parties concerned and the democratisation of the economic, management and political institutions of any given country.

Trade unions can actively participate in productivity movements only when there is common ground on which labour and management can work together with mutual trust and co-operation. Management must create a climate in the enterprise which will enable trade unions and workers to contribute to productivity improvement. If labour-management relations are poor no formal productivity drive should be undertaken since it will have little chance of success. Trying to launch a productivity programme in such a context will probably create even more problems.

Productivity gains-sharing

Gains-sharing has already been discussed in previous chapters. However, it is useful to emphasise a few ideas which are important at the national level.

The national approach to gains-sharing needs to be flexible, equitable and simple to understand. A purely statistical approach should not be used since it is not easy to find a formula to calculate precisely the contribution to productivity growth made by every factor at the national level. The complexity of these issues is demonstrated by figure 8.2, which shows productivity gains accumulation and the distribution cycle. The figure shows that most of the factors and beneficiaries of productivity improvement cannot be differentiated numerically because of the many intangible benefits and contributions.

Experience has shown that only at the enterprise and, even more, at the individual and team levels is it safe to use numerical methods for calculating individual (team) contributions for implementing different incentive schemes. And even at this level there are still problems to be solved.

Figure 8.2. Productivity gains accumulation and the distribution cycle

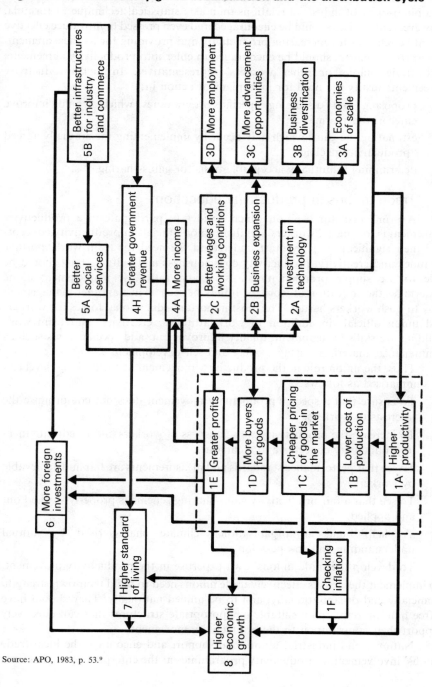

Source: APO, 1983, p. 53.[9]

At the national and sectoral levels, gains-sharing should be regarded more as a philosophy of industrial relations than as a statistical technique or formula. However, enterprises should be encouraged and even pressed to introduce effective incentive schemes for increasing productivity and providing for its measurement. Enterprise managers should be encouraged to enter into productivity agreements with trade unions or other workers' representatives. In fact, productivity agreements justify the need for joint plans of action in:

— proposing and discussing specific programmes which would improve enterprise performance;

— estimating the gains which may occur by implementing the mutually agreed "productivity package";

— determining a mutually acceptable basis for gains-sharing.

Trade unions in productivity education

A prime task for a union which decides to participate in a productivity movement is to educate workers and their union officials in productivity concepts and their significance. They must understand the need for team work, positive attitudes and creativity, productivity consciousness and culture; they should be able to use simple productivity statistics and ratios. If management alone undertakes the education of workers, it may be seen as just another management ploy to push workers harder. The most important educational topics for workers and union officials in addition to work attitudes, creativity, and team work building are skills development, quality improvement, and specific areas such as maintenance, materials wastage, safety and self-development.

Thus, the union role in the productivity movement at the national level can be summarised as follows:

● To ensure that a specific productivity movement does not compromise the interests of workers.

● To increase the productivity consciousness of workers and to educate them in productivity concepts and techniques.

● To see that performance standards and measurements are fair and achievable by workers.

● To see that a fair productivity gains-sharing scheme is properly worked out and applied.

● To help build an organisational climate characterised by mutual understanding and co-operation.

● To develop the trade unions' own expertise in the productivity movement.

To implement these tasks effectively trade unions need to build their own strength, financially and organisationally, and to be unified nationally. They should have a free hand in developing suitable or appropriate structures that can effectively support their contribution to the productivity movement.

National and industrial unions can support and encourage the local trade unions' involvement in productivity programmes at the enterprise level. Towards this, the national trade union centres and industrial unions could establish specialised departments to deal with productivity programmes.

Another role of national trade union bodies is to train the rank-and-file union leaders in enterprises. To meet all these needs it is worth considering the establishment of productivity service divisions to strengthen union representation in different government bodies, especially in legislation, planning and labour agencies.

A noteworthy example is the Japan National Trade Union Productivity Congress, established by the unions in co-operation with the JPC to deal exclusively with productivity. This institution has greatly helped Japanese workers recognise the importance of the productivity movement. The Japanese experiment also suggests that without the involvement of a formally established national trade union organisation, it will be very difficult to organise effective national productivity drives.

8.2 International co-operation and the productivity movement

In recent decades international activities in productivity improvement have greatly increased as a result of the following factors:
- Increased economic and technological co-operation between countries. This has resulted in the dissemination of modern management techniques and information, and therefore increased the need for common approaches to the evaluation and measurement of the effectiveness of the resources used.
- The increased need to make comparisons between different companies, sectors and countries for evaluation and policy-making purposes. This has resulted in the improvement of the statistical and data-processing bases, and their comparative unification.
- The increasing number of sectoral and national productivity institutions which organise their efforts on an international basis in order to exchange experience and information, measurement techniques, programmes, achievements and problems.
- The growing difference between developed and developing countries in economic and social development, and the scarcity of financial and material resources for direct transmission from the developed to the developing countries in the framework of international development programmes. International productivity improvement programmes have been recognised as an important factor in development, as they help to use all available resources effectively.
- Understanding by the United Nations and its specialised agencies of the importance of productivity improvement as an effective tool of international assistance to the developing countries. This has resulted in the setting up of institutional mechanisms for working out productivity improvement programmes and putting them into effect in some developing countries.

Productivity management

These factors have contributed to the emergence and strengthening of international mechanisms for productivity co-operation. There are now more than 30 internatonal organisations, federations and institutions, about 20 international governmental organisations and more than 40 regional organisations and institutes dealing directly or indirectly with productivity. The organisations concerned can be classified into five groups:

- The United Nations family: ILO, UNDP, UNESCO, UNIDO, which deal with different aspects of productivity promotion.
- Intergovernmental regional economic organisations of the European or Latin American Common Markets, OECD, CMEA (Council of Mutual Economic Assistance), etc.
- Regional organisations specifically dealing with productivity improvement and promotion among their member countries, such as the Asian Productivity Organisation (APO), the European Association of National Productivity Centres (EANPC) and the corresponding association for Latin American countries, which is called MECOPOR.
- International (or regional) professional associations dealing with management, engineering, work study, management development, etc.
- International and regional development banks and funds which finance country or regional projects dealing with economic and social development as well as productivity improvement.

These and other organisations undertake many activities in collecting, analysing and disseminating useful information on productivity and related problems among their members. They carry out research activities, organise meetings, courses, seminars, symposia and conferences and help governments in working out national productivity improvement policies and programmes. The organisations also finance and implement many programmes. Thus, they play the following important roles.

Leaders: By virtue of their intervention in economic and social development, they are able to look ahead and work out long-term strategies and policies. Most of these organisations recognise the human factor as a major force for development. Human development is therefore a priority for productivity and management organisations.

Catalysts: They promote co-operation between member countries and their effort to increase productivity strengthens national and regional ties. In this role organisations introduce new concepts and methods, undertake research on different dimensions and measures of productivity improvement, identify priorities in establishing objectives, share experience between countries and seek greater mutual co-operation.

Institution builders: They help countries to strengthen their professional capacity through human resource development programmes. They emphasise software development and productivity improvement at the macro-level, providing professional input to institutions in managerial and technological areas, building up technical expert services, undertaking surveys, study missions and research. They provide access to information and organise technology transfer through technical co-operation projects when necessary.

Clearing-houses: They organise information exchange between members all over the world and disseminate management and productivity concepts, knowledge and techniques. They report on the failure or success of different projects and experiences, and on technological and managerial innovations; they supply comparisons on productivity and give economic indices for different stages of development.

Human resource development agencies: They undertake major technical co-operation projects on education and training methods; they promote more productive employment of human resources, and the development of necessary skills and attitudes for productivity improvement; they train trainers and human resource development professionals.

Many other important roles could be identified in the promotion of knowledge, concepts, technology transfer and co-operation between member countries and institutions. To give a better insight into the role and practical activities of these organisations we would like to give a brief description of a few major international and regional organisations in the field of productivity improvement and co-operation. They are: ILO, EANPC, MECOPOR and APO.

The ILO role in productivity promotion

ILO conferences have repeatedly stressed the fact that living standards can be appreciably improved only by increasing productivity. The 1950 annual report expressed concern about productivity improvement and indicated a desire to expand ILO activity in this field. The next few years saw the launching of the management development and productivity programmes and ILO productivity missions were sent to several countries. Between 1950 and 1957 expert services were given to ten countries. The technique on which the initial teaching and practical work of the missions centred was work study.

The first phase of the ILO management development programme was devoted to the productivity programme; almost the whole emphasis was placed on raising productivity and improving efficiency in production or operation. The second phase (after 1960) emphasised training in general and functional management, expanding enterprises and increasing productive employment. Most projects included the establishment of national management development and productivity institutions.

The current ILO concept of productivity is reflected in a resolution adopted by the International Labour Conference in June 1984.[10] In its opening statement it says "... as a basic principle that production and productivity improvement must serve the well-being of the people". No longer does the term "productivity" bring to mind long shifts and exhausted assembly line workers. The basic objective of ILO programmes on productivity improvement is to assist member States to improve the quality of management both in the public and private sectors.

Since the early 1950s the ILO has assisted in strengthening national productivity management centres and related organisations in over 80 countries.

Productivity management

It has also introduced several thousand training and consulting programmes and assignments. With this large pool of experience and expertise, the ILO is today assisting governments, employers' and workers' organisations in their efforts to enhance productivity.

In Asia, for example, the ILO assisted in the productivity year programme in Singapore in 1981, and also in India in 1982 as discussed earlier. The ILO's traditionally strong ties with the productivity movement in India go back to the mid-1950s when the ILO participated in the establishment of the National Productivity Council of India as a tripartite organisation having equal representation of employers, labour and government.

All kinds of ILO programmes are directly or indirectly involved in productivity improvement through human resource development. For example, the ILO Vocational Training Programme, through its numerous technical co-operation activities, contributes to increasing productivity by assisting member States to strengthen their capacity to train workers. The ILO Workers' Education Programmes help strengthen trade union organisations, particularly in social and economic participation. They develop the ability of union representatives to participate in decision-making at all levels. ILO activities on wages and incomes are concerned with sharing the benefits of productivity through the growth of real wages and consultation.

A key contribution of the ILO to productivity comes from its management development programmes which assist national productivity centres and management institutes to develop research, policy advisory and training services. The national centres in turn help governments in decision-making; they also help local enterprises to apply total approaches to productivity, including the effective use of all resources.

The ILO programmes of technical co-operation for productivity enhancement offer the following services:

- Surveys covering the entire process of productivity measurement, improvement and gains-sharing at all economic levels. Training needs are identified, and training strategies are recommended to meet them.

- Management training in productivity improvement processes. Study, design and implementation of systems, procedures and techniques for productivity measurement, improvement and gains-sharing at any level from national campaigns to quality circles.

- Training in productivity management in critical economic sectors, particularly public institutions and enterprises; utilities, transport, construction and other enterprises concerned with the infrastructure; small enterprises; and rural development organisations.

- Surveys, planning and implementation of projects for the establishment or strengthening of training institutions.

To each technical co-operation project the ILO contributes its experience and expertise. This covers project planning and development, implementation and

270

evaluation; training policy, organisation and method, execution and evaluation; and institutional framework-building and networking.

The selection, recruitment and supervision of highly qualified international and local experts and consultants for the execution of the project is also an important part of ILO assistance. The planning and implementation of relevant international fellowship training programmes are frequently an integral part of the overall project design.

The ILO also plays a major role in international funding arrangements.

The ILO has an exceptionally well-developed body of knowledge and know-how in developing and implementing training methodology that incorporates the latest significant developments. Through a wide range of projects in developing countries, it has created a rich portfolio of management development approaches and techniques for adaptation in individual projects. Among them are action planning, notably planning for improved performance (PIP); campaign-type action, such as the training-through-consultancy programme; performance clinics, inter-firm productivity comparison; modular packaging, particularly modular programmes for supervisory development; and other self-development techniques such as action learning.

A survey conducted in 1980 indicated that national management and productivity centres continue to attach the highest priority to consulting and training techniques for productivity improvement. The management development programme has maintained close collaboration with regional organisations concerned with productivity promotion, such as EANPC, MECOPOR and APO.

The ILO is also trying to improve the diagnostic capacity of training institutions and their ability to innovate and to respond to innovation. It is necessary to achieve a closer link between training and productivity. For example, analysis of staff training needs is encouraged in order to improve the productivity of investment projects. Blending of new and traditional technologies is one way to increase productivity while minimising the adverse effects of technological change. The ILO intends to continue studies on the effect of the application of science and technology and aims to develop training programmes based on those studies (micro-electronics, office automation, etc.).

Important future themes of ILO management development programmes in the field of productivity improvement are:

- measuring productivity — this is an area of great concern to employers' and workers' organisations in view of its obvious link to wages and wage policies, cost-of-living indices and productivity gains-sharing; besides, productivity indices are among the most important management tools for monitoring production processes;
- strengthening national institutional mechanisms for productivity improvement and their role in training, research and productivity promotion down to the enterprise and shop-floor levels;
- improving public awareness at all levels of management and society; productivity is not only an economic or technical problem, but also an individual's state of mind;

— developing an international network of organisations, researchers and consultants, and promoting co-operation between them at the international and national levels.

The European Association of National Productivity Centres

An example of a regional institution is the European Association of National Productivity Centres (EANPC), which was founded as an independent non-governmental organisation in 1966, with membership open to all the European national productivity centres. Membership at present includes 19 national productivity centres. One of the main objectives of the association is to facilitate and increase exchange of information and experience, and to encourage co-operation between participating bodies, with special reference to scientific research. Organising conferences is an important EANPC activity.

The most important programmes of the EANPC focus on such areas as national policy and practice; quality of working life; job design; new technologies; developing and implementing industrial policies; productivity measurement; corporate early warning systems; and productivity and the organisation of working time.

Recently, EANPC policies have concentrated on productivity in services; corporate productivity; aids to smaller companies; productivity and competitivity; and productivity and employment.

The main forms of activity used by the EANPC are the publication and adaptation of existing knowledge for use by specific target groups; productivity campaigns; round-tables for staff of centres and similar bodies in charge of government-sponsored consultancy services; education and training; and meetings, symposia, workshops.

The EANPC works in close co-operation with OECD, the EEC, the ILO, with national productivity and management centres, and with a few professional associations, such as the European Foundation for Management Development and the European Centre for Work and Society.

"MECOPOR" — Latin America

"MECOPOR" is an organisation for the co-ordination of horizontal technical co-operation between productivity agencies in the Latin American and the Caribbean region. It was established only in 1984, in consultation with the member countries of the co-ordinating committee, the Organisation of American States and the ILO. It is the newest regional organisation dealing with productivity.

The main objectives of the MECOPOR are to co-ordinate technical co-operation activities between the productivity agencies and related institutions in the countries of the region.

The activities of the MECOPOR aim to:

— contribute to the development and strengthening of the productivity agencies and institutions in the region through a broad programme of technical co-operation supported by the international organisations that act in the field of productivity;

— facilitate and maximise communication among the regional productivity agencies and related institutions;

— make use of and give a multiplier effect to the resources available within the region.

It is still too early to reach any definite conclusions about the practical activites of the MECOPOR. What is important is the fact that creating the MECOPOR in the Latin America and Caribbean region can be considered an important step towards the regional integration of the activities of national productivity centres and organisations, similar to the EANPC and the APO.

The Asian Productivity Organisation

The Asian Productivity Organisation (APO) does a great deal to improve productivity in Asian countries by stressing research, methodology development and training. National productivity organisations in the APO member countries act as implementing agencies for APO projects and participate in the APO's multi-country projects. The APO programme thus reflects the long-term and short-term plans of its members.

Three guiding principles adopted by representatives from government, labour and management during the first APO conference are that:

● In the long run, improvement in productivity will increase employment. However, before the effects of improved productivity become apparent, governments and the people must co-operate to provide interim measures against unemployment, such as the transfer of surplus workers to areas deficient in manpower.

● Labour and management must co-operate in discussing, studying and deliberating measures to combat unemployment.

● The fruits of improved productivity must be distributed fairly among the contributors.

At present, 15 countries are official members of the APO. Each of these countries has a national productivity centre or institute. The APO promotes mutual co-operation through programmes which exchange and transfer conceptual, managerial and technological experience. Through symposia, seminars, study missions, fellowships, technical services, publications and other information services it enhances productivity consciousness and expertise.

The APO's programme of activities is divided into four categories: *macro-level projects*, *industry*, *agriculture* and *information*. Its annual programme includes projects concerned with productivity measurement, industrial relations, project feasibility and appraisal, and agro-industry and energy management.

Basic projects emphasise management and technical consulting and training activities. These projects aim at helping member countries build up a team of competent management trainers and consultants as a multiplier factor in disseminating productivity knowledge and techniques. There are two main types of training course: for management trainers and consultants, and for industrial or production engineers. Both types of course are designed to develop self-reliance in the participants.

Current information projects aim at raising productivity consciousness, the dissemination of productivity knowledge, and the support of industrial and agricultural projects by means of training aids and information-exchange among member countries.

The APO also plays an important role as a technology transfer agent, mainly through its training programmes for industrial technological development. Its training programmes for the development of small business managers and consultants, its study missions, its "technical expert" services and its series of publications in this field have all been helpful in developing a corps of "transfer agents" in the member countries.

Its impact may be seen in the advances made by the Asian productivity organisations. For example, the Hong Kong productivity centre and the national productivity organisations in India, Japan, the Philippines and Singapore have demonstrated the results of effective popularisation of productivity and its implications in their own activities.

The APO uses all the available media including seminars, conferences, training courses, study missions, publications and newsletters, consultancy and video packages.

Strong links have developed during the past decade between the APO and the ILO, the EANPC and other regional and international organisations dealing with productivity improvement and developmental issues.

---

[1] Samuel Paul: *Strategic management of development programmes* (Geneva, ILO, 1984), pp. 93-94.

[2] Arthur Smith: "The Canadian labour market and productivity centre", in *Europe Productivity Ideas* (Brussels, EANPC), Oct. 1985, pp. 9-10.

[3] A. N. Saxena: *Productivity improvements in developing countries*, Role of productivity and management institutions (Indian experience — A case) (New Delhi, National Productivity Council), n.d., Ch. 2.

[4] Akira Suzuki: "JPC's prime achievements", in *Europe Productivity Ideas* (Brussels, EANPC), Jan. 1984, p. 2.

[5] Hans Büttner: "RKW", ibid., pp. 2-3.

[6] Bjorn Herse/ILO: *Background, organisation, implementation and assessment of the Norwegian productivity campaign* (Nicosia, Cyprus Productivity Centre, 1986), pp. 2-7.

[7] *Singapore Productivity News* (National Productivity Board, Singapore), Dec. 1985, pp. 1-8.

[8] *Singapore Productivity News, Productivity Month Supplement* (National Productivity Board, Singapore), Nov. 1985, pp. 1-5.

[9] APO: *Involvement of trade unions in productivity*, Symposium report (Tokyo, Asian Productivity Organisation, 1983), p. 53.

[10] ILO: *Record of Proceedings*, International Labour Conference, 70th Session, Geneva, 1984, Resolution VII, p. XLI.

BIBLIOGRAPHY

Abramson, R.; Halset, W. *Planning for improved enterprise performance*. Geneva, ILO, 1979. 178 pp.

Agar, W. H. "Manage brain skills to increase productivity", in *Personnel* (New York, AMACON), Aug. 1986, pp. 42-46.

Ahern, R. W. "Labour-management committees raise productivity in the USA", in *Industrial Participation* (London), Summer 1983, pp. 16-24.

Alexander, K. O. "Promise and perils of worker participation in management", in *American Journal of Economics and Sociology* (New York), Apr. 1984, pp. 197-204.

Alvarez, D.; Cooper, B. "Productivity trends in manufacturing in the US and 11 other countries", in *Monthly Labor Review* (Washington, DC), Jan. 1984, pp. 52-58.

American Productivity Center. *Dimensions of productivity research*. Houston, Texas, 1980. Vol. II.

Asian Productivity Organisation. *Productivity and role of top management*. Tokyo, 1986. 94 pp.

—— . *Measuring productivity: Trends and comparisons from the first international productivity symposium*. First International Productivity Symposium, Tokyo, 1983. New York, Unipub, 1984. 290 pp.

Barnes, R. M. *Work sampling*. New York and London, John Wiley, 2nd ed., 1957.

Belcher, J. G. "Gainsharing: Designed for success", in *Productivity Digest* (Singapore), Nov. 1986, pp. 35-45.

Bittel, L. R. (ed.) *Encyclopaedia of professional management*. New York and London, McGraw-Hill, 1978. 1304 pp.

Bolte, K. A. "Intel's war for white-collar productivity", in *National Productivity Review* (New York), Winter 1983-84, pp. 46-53.

Bowey, A. M.; Thorpe, R.; Hellier, P. *Payment systems and productivity*. London, Macmillan, 1985. 316 pp.

Burggraf, S. P. "Demographic shifts and productivity", in *Economic Impact* (Washington, DC), No. 2, 1985, pp. 74-78.

Carhart, S. C. "Capitalising productivity", in *National Productivity Review* (New York), Autumn 1984, pp. 430-438.

Carroll, P. *How to chart data*. New York and London, McGraw-Hill, 1960.

Chinloy, P. *Labour quality change in Canada*. Discussion Paper No. 231. Ottawa, Economic Council of Canada, 1983. 121 pp.

Clark, J. J.; Clark, M. T. *Statistics primer for managers*. New York, Free Press, 1983. 258 pp.

Clark, P. K.; Haltmaier, J. T. "Labor productivity slowdown in the United States: Evidence from physical output measures", in *Review of Economics and Statistics* (Cambridge, Massachusetts), Aug. 1985, pp. 504-508.

Craig, C. E.; Harris, R. C. "Total productivity measurement at the firm level", in *Sloan Management Review* (Cambridge, Massachusetts), Spring 1973, pp. 13-28.

Craig, R. L. (ed.) *Training and development handbook. A guide to human resource development.* New York and London, McGraw-Hill, 1976.

Daly, A.; Hitchens, D. M. W. N.; Wagner, K. "Productivity, machinery and skills in a sample of British and German manufacturing plants", in *National Institute Economic Review* (London), Feb. 1985, pp. 48-61.

Dean, E.; Boisserain, H.; Thomas, J. "Productivity and labor costs trends in manufacturing, 12 countries", in *Monthly Labor Review* (Washington, DC), Mar. 1986, pp. 3-10.

Dogramaci, A. *Developments in econometric analyses of productivity: Measurement and modeling issues.* Boston, Kluwer Nijhoff, 1983. 172 pp.

Dogramaci, A.; Adam, N. R. (eds.). *Managerial issues in productivity analysis.* Boston, Kluwer Nijhoff, 1985. 245 pp.

Doran, P. K. "A total quality improvement programme", in *International Journal of Quality and Reliability Management* (United Kingdom), Vol. 2, No. 3, pp. 18-39.

Eilon, S.; Gold, B.; Soesan, J. *Applied productivity analysis for industry.* New York, Pergamon Press, 1976. 151 pp.

Fein, M. "Improving productivity by improved productivity sharing", in *Conference Board Record* (New York), July 1976.

Freemantle, D. *Superboss. The A-Z of managing people successfully.* Aldershot, United Kingdom, Gower, 1985. 275 pp.

Fritz, K. "Flexible working times", in *Office Management* (London), Jan. 1986, pp. 30-34.

Geber, B. "Quality circles. The second generation", in *Training* (New York), Dec. 1986, pp. 54-61.

Giersch, H.; Wolter, F. "Towards an explanation of the productivity slowdown: An acceleration-deceleration hypothesis", in *Economic Journal* (London), Mar. 1983, pp. 35-55.

Gmelch, W. H.; Miskin, V. D. *Productivity teams: Beyond quality circles.* New York, John Wiley and Sons, 1984. 244 pp.

Gorlin, H.; Schein, L. *Innovations in managing human resources.* Report No. 849. New York, Conference Board, 1984. 38 pp.

Grant, E. L. *Statistical quality control.* New York and London, McGraw-Hill, 4th ed., 1972.

Helliwell, J. F.; Sturm, P. H.; Salov, G. "International comparison of the sources of productivity slowdown 1973-1982", in *European Economic Review* (Amsterdam), June-July 1985, pp. 157-200.

Herzberg, F.; Mausner, B.; Syndeman, B. *The motivation to work.* New York, John Wiley and Sons, 2nd ed., 1959. 278 pp.

Herzberg, F. *Work and the nature of man.* New York, World Book Company, 1966. 342 pp.

Hutchins, D. *Quality circles handbook.* London, Pitman, 1985. 272 pp.

ILO . "Flexible working time in production", in *Social and Labour Bulletin* (Geneva), Mar. 1985, pp. 133-136.

—— . *Introduction to work study.* Geneva, 3rd ed., 1979. 441 pp.

—— . "Motivation and productivity rise with 6-hour day on full pay", in *Social and Labour Bulletin* (Geneva), Mar. 1985, pp. 118-119.

—— . "The human factor and higher productivity: Missing links in the austerity plan", ibid., Apr. 1986, p. 24.

—— . "Work study increases productivity", ibid., Dec. 1983, pp. 546-547.

Inagami, T. "QC circle activities and the suggestion system", in *Japan Labor Bulletin* (Tokyo), Jan. 1982, pp. 5-8.

Institute of Industrial Engineers. *Issues in white collar productivity*. Atlanta, Georgia, Industrial Engineering and Management Press, 1984. 265 pp.

Jaeger, A. M. "Organisational development and national culture: Where's the fit?", in *Academy of Management Review* (Seattle), Vol. II, No. 1, 1986, pp. 178-190.

Jonsson, B.; Lank, A. G. "Volvo: Production technology and quality of working life", in *Human Resource Management* (Ann Arbor, Michigan), Winter 1985, pp. 455-466.

Kanawaty, G. (ed.). *Managing and developing new forms of work organisation*. Geneva, ILO, 1981. 206 pp.

Katzell, R. A. et al. *Work, productivity and job satisfaction: An evaluation of policy-related research*. New York, Harcourt Brace Jovanovich, 1975. 432 pp.

Klodt, H. *Statistics on labour productivity in West Germany: A guide to sources and methods*. Kiel, ILO, 1985. 95 pp.

Kraus, J. *How US firms measure productivity*. New York, National Association of Accountants, 1984. 100 pp.

Lane, T. "Industrial efficiency and the West German worker", in *Industrial Relations Journal* (Nottingham, United Kingdom), Autumn 1984, pp. 75-87.

Lawlor, A. *Productivity improvement manual*. Aldershot, United Kingdom, Gower, 1985. 306 pp.

Lefton, R. E. "Performance appraisals", in *National Productivity Review* (New York), Winter 1985-86, pp. 54-64.

Levitan, S.; Werneke, D. "Worker participation and productivity change", in *Monthly Labor Review* (Washington, DC), Sep. 1984, pp. 28-33.

Lippitt, G. L.; Langseth, P.; Mossop, J. *Implementing organisational change*. San Francisco, Jossey-Bass, 1985. 185 pp.

Maki, D. R. "Trade unions and productivity: Conventional estimates", in *Relations industrielles* (Quebec), Vol. 38, No. 2, 1983, pp. 211-228.

Mark, J. A. "Problems encountered in measuring single- and multi-factor productivity", in *Monthly Labor Review* (Washington, DC), Dec. 1986, pp. 3-11.

Maynard, H. B. (ed.) *Industrial engineering handbook*. New York and London, McGraw-Hill, 3rd ed., 1971. 1532 pp.

McGuire, J. B.; Liro, J. R. "Flexible work schedules, work attitudes, and perceptions of productivity", in *Public Personnel Management* (Washington, DC), Spring 1986, pp. 65-73.

Medoff, J. L. "U.S. labor markets: Imbalance, wage growth, and productivity in the 1970s", in *Brookings Papers on Economic Activity* (Washington, DC), No. 1, 1983, pp. 87-128.

Miles, L. D. *Techniques of value analysis and engineering*. New York and London, McGraw-Hill, 2nd ed., 1972.

Morley, E. *Practitioner's guide to public sector productivity improvement*. New York, van Nostrand Reinhold, 1986. 299 pp.

Mundel, M. E. *Motion and time study: Principles and practice*. Englewood Cliffs, New Jersey, Prentice Hall, 4th ed., 1970.

——. *Improving productivity and effectiveness*. Englewood Cliffs, New Jersey, Prentice-Hall, 1983. 467 pp.

Nakazawa, M. "Measurement of labour productivity: The Japanese experience", in *Productivity* (New Delhi), July-Sep. 1985, pp. 145-148.

Nankivell, O. M. *Productivity statistics: Review of sources and uses in the United Kingdom*. Geneva, ILO, 1985. 83 pp.

Productivity management

Neef, A. "International trends in productivity unit labor costs in manufacturing", in *Monthly Labor Review* (Washington, DC), Dec. 1986, pp. 12-17.

OECD. *Productivity in industry: Prospects and policies.* Paris, 1986. 108 pp.

Ohkawa, K.; Takamatsu, N. *Capital formation, productivity and employment: Japan's historical experience and its possible relevance to LDCs.* Working Paper Series No. 26. Tokyo, International Development Centre of Japan, 1983. 36 pp.

Olson, V. *White collar waste: Gain the productivity edge.* Englewood Cliffs, New Jersey, Prentice-Hall, 1983. 234 pp.

Paul, Samuel. *Strategic management of development programmes.* Geneva, ILO, 1984. 137 pp.

Postner, H. H.; Wesa, L. *Canadian productivity growth: An alternative (input-output) analysis.* Ottawa, Economic Council of Canada, 1983. 96 pp.

Reuter, V. G. "What good are value analysis programs?", in *Productivity Digest* (Singapore), Nov. 1986, pp. 73-83.

"Revival of productivity", in *Business Week* (New York), Feb. 1984, pp. 46-51.

Robson, M. *Quality circles in action.* Aldershot, United Kingdom, Gower, 1984. 167 pp.

Sbytova, L. "Employment and raising the effectiveness of labor in the service sector", in *Problems of Economics* (New York), Jan. 1984, pp. 65-80.

Schuster, M. "Impact of union-management cooperation on productivity and employment", in *Industrial and Labor Relations Review* (Ithaca, New York), Apr. 1983, pp. 415-430.

Shetty, Y. K. "Quality, productivity, profit, performance: Learning from research and practice", in *Productivity Digest* (Singapore), Oct. 1986, pp. 39-49.

Sink, D. S. *Productivity management: Planning, measurement and evaluation, control and improvement.* New York, John Wiley and Sons, 1985. 518 pp.

—   . "Productivity measurement using creative scoreboards", in *Industrial Engineering* (New York), Jan. 1986, pp. 86-91.

Skinner, W. *Manufacturing. The formidable competitive weapon.* New York, John Wiley and Sons, 1985. 330 pp.

Slade, B. N. *Winning the productivity race.* Lexington, Massachusetts, Lexington Books/D. C. Heath and Company, 1985. 144 pp.

Smith, A. D.; Hitchens, W. N. "Comparative British and American productivity in retailing", in *National Institute Economic Review* (London), May 1983, pp. 45-60.

Smith, I. *The management of remuneration.* Aldershot, United Kingdom, Gower, 1983. 231 pp.

Stollery, K. R. *Productivity trends and their causes in the Canadian mining industry, 1957-79.* Discussion Paper No. 248. Ottawa, Economic Council of Canada, 1983. 86 pp.

Sudit, E. F. *Productivity based management.* Boston, Kluwer-Nijhoff, 1984. 158 pp.

Sullivan, T. "Trade unions and productivity: Theory and evidence", in *International Journal of Manpower* (Bradford, United Kingdom), Vol 5, No. 2, 1984, pp. 24-32.

—   . "Trade unions, management and productivity", in *Employee Relations* (Bradford, United Kingdom), Vol. 7, No. 2, 1985, pp. 8-11.

Szymanski, A. "Productivity growth and capitalist stagnation", in *Science and Society* (New York), Fall 1984, pp. 295-322.

Taguchi, G. *Introduction to quality engineering: Designing quality into products and process.* Tokyo, Asian Productivity Organisation, 1986. 191 pp.

Tausky, C.; Chelte, A. F. "Accountability and productivity: Some longitudinal data", in *Work and Occupations* (Albany, Ontario), May 1983, pp. 207-220.

Tracey, W. R. (ed.). *Human resources management and development handbook.* New York, AMACON, 1985. 1550 pp.

Vasquez, R. A. et al. *Productivity improvement circles: A manual.* Manila, Development Academy of the Philippines, 1983. 116 pp.

Vaught, B. C.; Walker, W. H. "Productivity through project teams", in *Industrial Management and Data Systems* (Bradford, United Kingdom), Jan.-Feb. 1986, pp. 22-27.

Westwick. C. A. *How to use management ratios.* Epping, Essex, Gower, 1973. 288 pp.

Woronoff, J. *Japan's wasted workers.* Totowa, New Jersey, Allaheld, Osmun and Company, 1983. 296 pp.

INDEX

Publications of the International Labour Office

Introduction
to work study

Third (revised) edition

This highly successful book, describing the basic techniques of work study as regularly practised in many parts of the world, has been widely recognised as the best available introduction to the subject. In this new revised edition, whilst the fundamental aims remain unchanged–to provide training in methods study and work measurement, the two main techniques of work study–, the opportunity has been taken to bring the contents up to date, to modify the book's purely introductory character whilst retaining the simplified approach to the explanation of complex problems, and thus to make it equally suitable for the work study practitioner and for the teacher and student.

To this end some chapters have been radically modified or completely rewritten and others have been added to take account of current advances in knowledge and to accommodate new ideas, whilst a final chapter on new forms of work organisation shows that work study can help to make work more human as well as to raise . productivity.

The copiously illustrated text is enriched with numerous examples of work study practice, a large number of which are based on the experience of ILO management development advisers engaged in work study in both developing and developed countries.

xiv + 441 pages   25 Swiss francs (hard cover only)   ISBN 92-2-101939-X

Available from booksellers, ILO offices in many countries or direct from ILO Publications, International Labour Office, CH-1211 Geneva 22, Switzerland.